CONTENTS

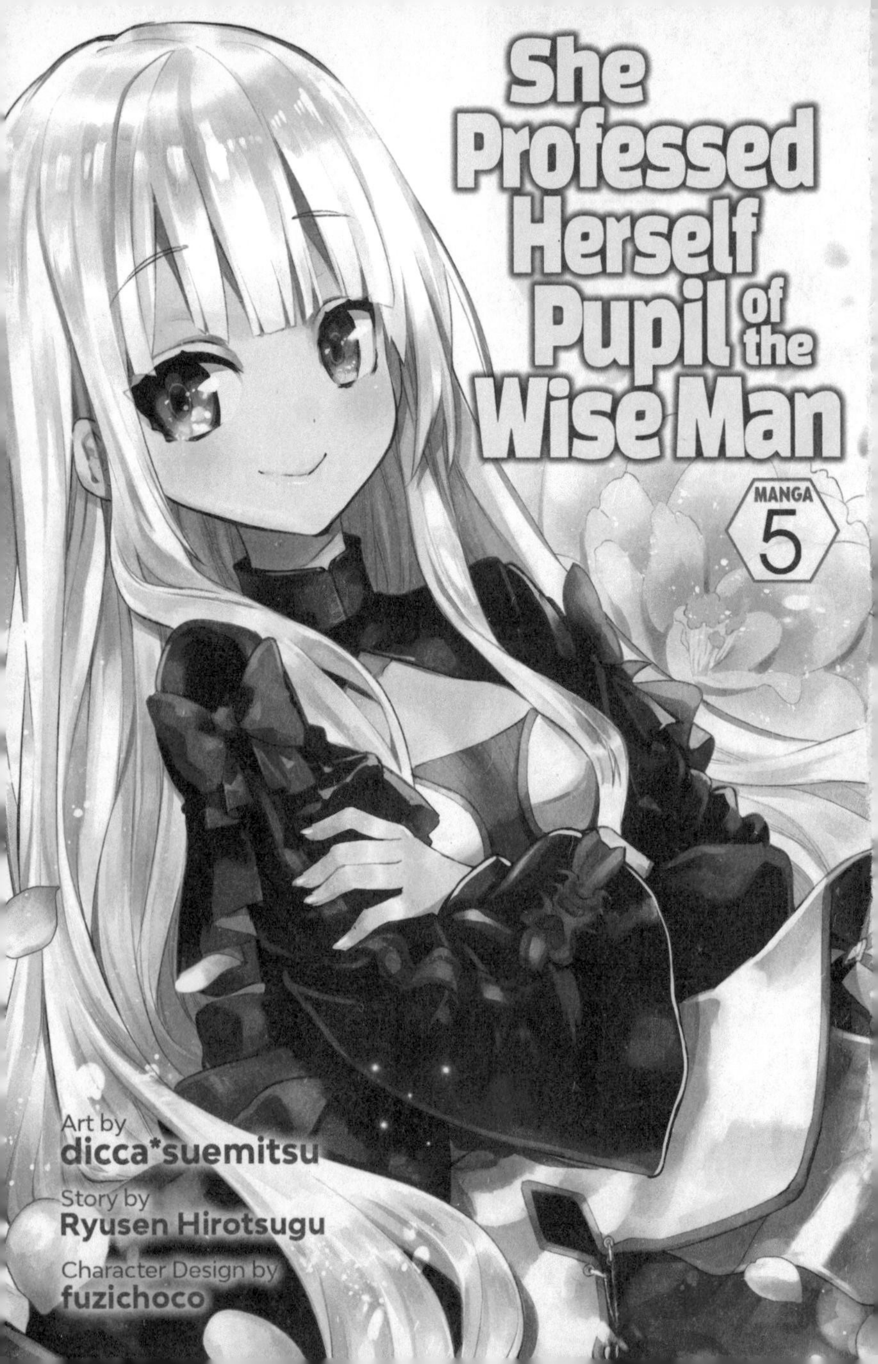
She Professed Herself Pupil of the Wise Man
MANGA
5
Art by
dicca*suemitsu
Story by
Ryusen Hirotsugu
Character Design by
fuzichoco

Summon 25: [Symposium Match]

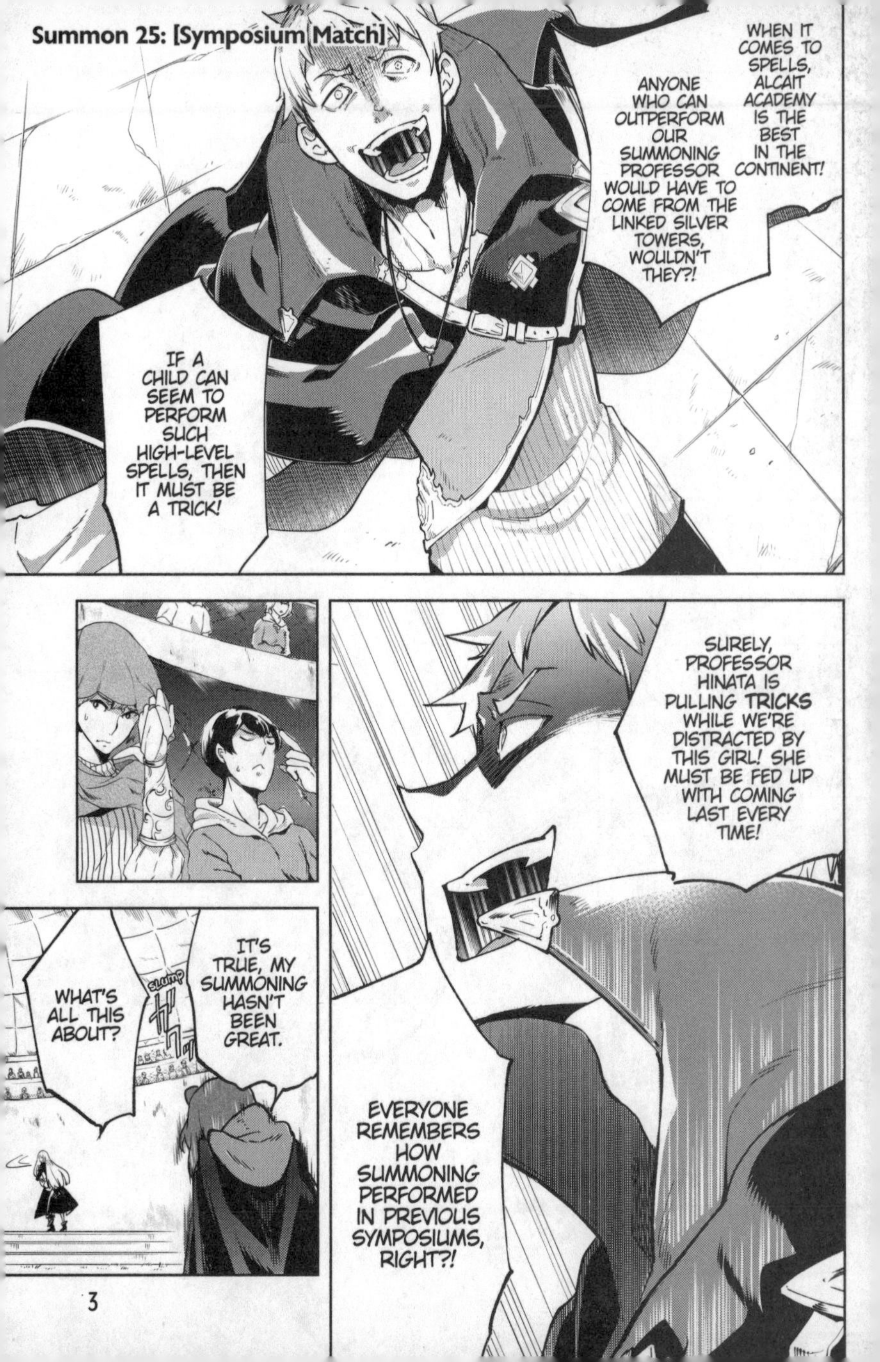

WHEN IT COMES TO SPELLS, ALCAIT ACADEMY IS THE BEST IN THE CONTINENT!
ANYONE WHO CAN OUTPERFORM OUR SUMMONING PROFESSOR WOULD HAVE TO COME FROM THE LINKED SILVER TOWERS, WOULDN'T THEY?!
IF A CHILD CAN SEEM TO PERFORM SUCH HIGH-LEVEL SPELLS, THEN IT MUST BE A TRICK!
SURELY, PROFESSOR HINATA IS PULLING TRICKS WHILE WE'RE DISTRACTED BY THIS GIRL! SHE MUST BE FED UP WITH COMING LAST EVERY TIME!
EVERYONE REMEMBERS HOW SUMMONING PERFORMED IN PREVIOUS SYMPOSIUMS, RIGHT?!
IT'S TRUE, MY SUMMONING HASN'T BEEN GREAT.
slump
WHAT'S ALL THIS ABOUT?

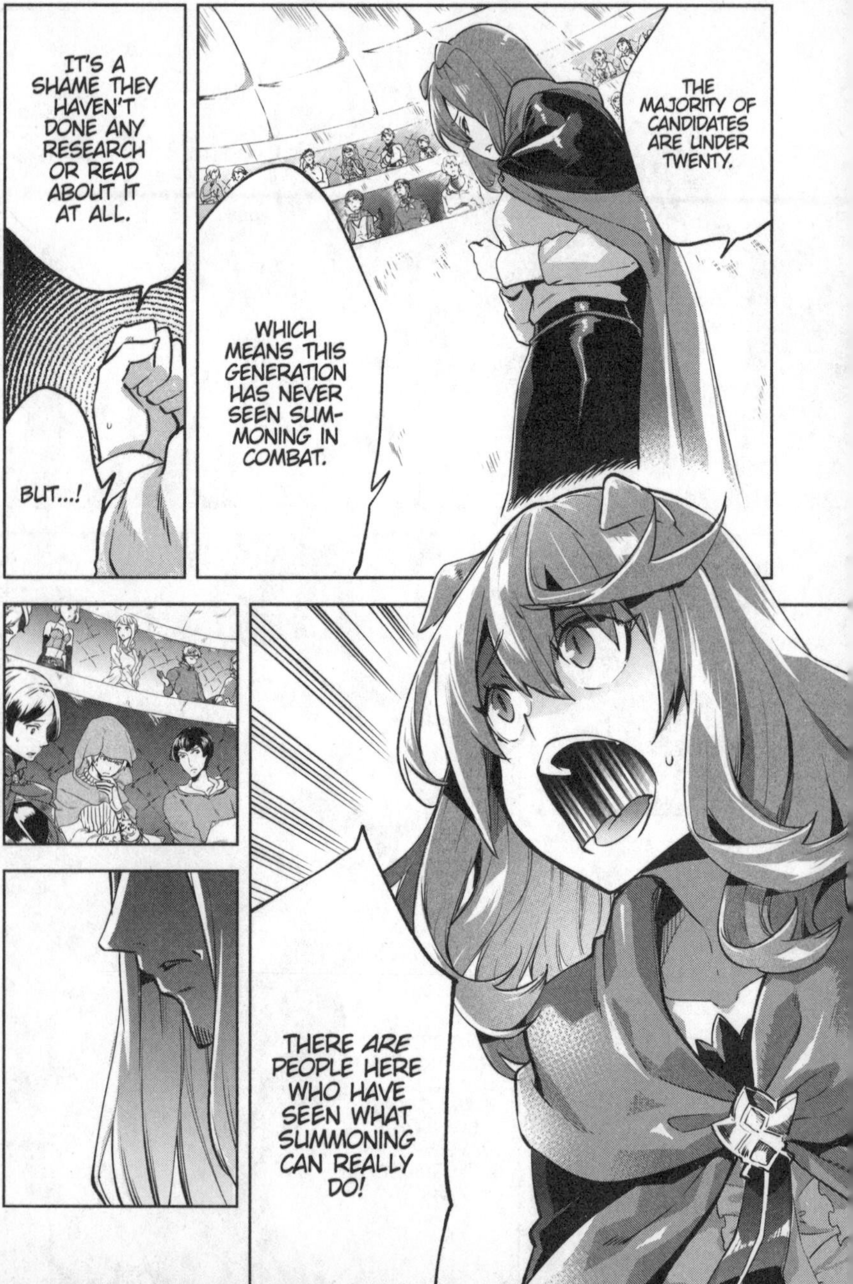
THE MAJORITY OF CANDIDATES ARE UNDER TWENTY.
WHICH MEANS THIS GENERATION HAS NEVER SEEN SUMMONING IN COMBAT.
IT'S A SHAME THEY HAVEN'T DONE ANY RESEARCH OR READ ABOUT IT AT ALL.
BUT...!
THERE *ARE* PEOPLE HERE WHO HAVE SEEN WHAT SUMMONING CAN REALLY DO!

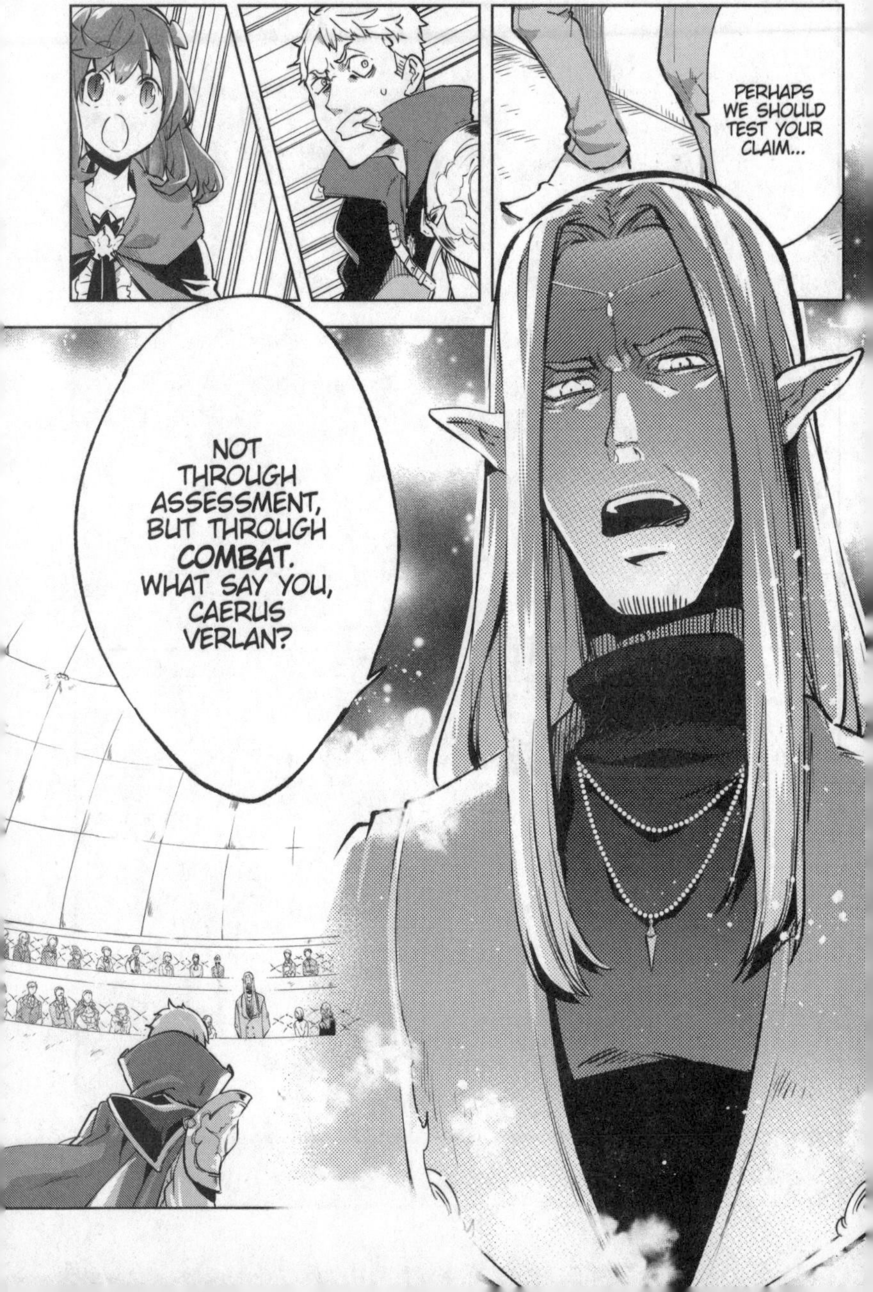
PERHAPS WE SHOULD TEST YOUR CLAIM...
NOT THROUGH ASSESSMENT, BUT THROUGH COMBAT. WHAT SAY YOU, CAERUS VERLAN?

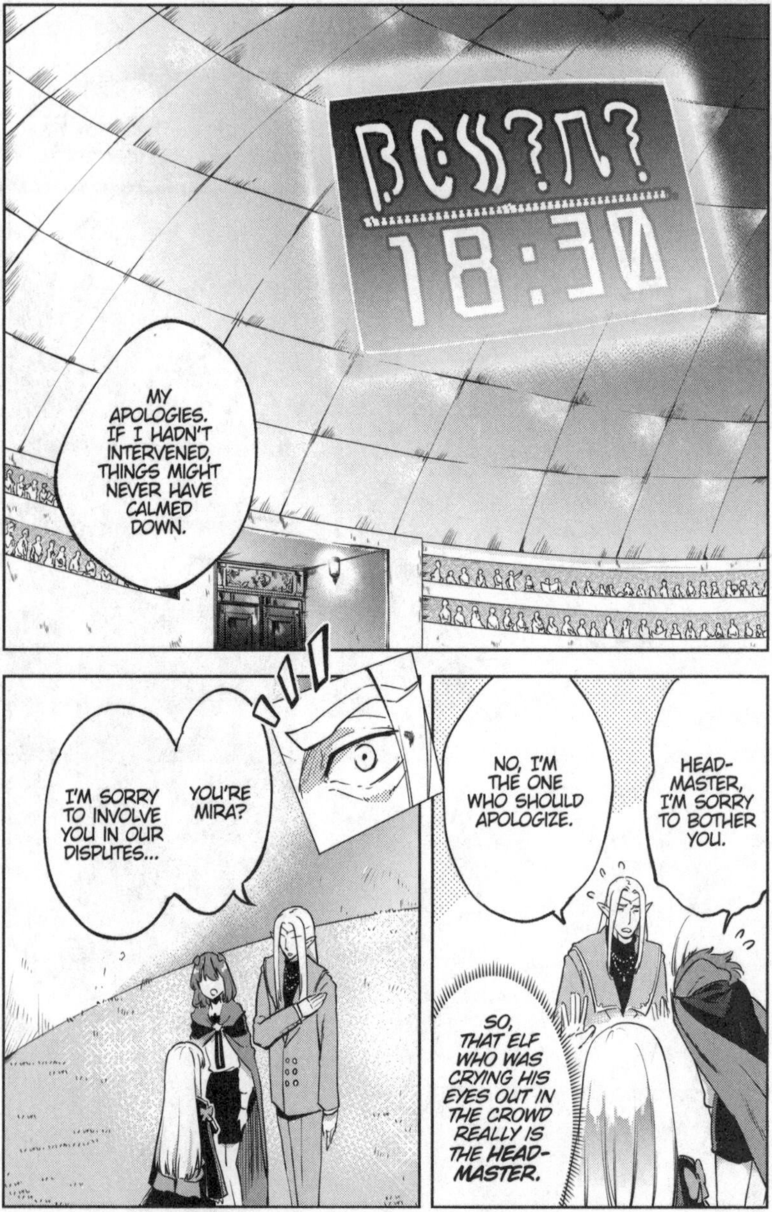
18:30
MY APOLOGIES. IF I HADN'T INTERVENED, THINGS MIGHT NEVER HAVE CALMED DOWN.
HEAD-MASTER, I'M SORRY TO BOTHER YOU.
NO, I'M THE ONE WHO SHOULD APOLOGIZE.
SO, THAT ELF WHO WAS CRYING HIS EYES OUT IN THE CROWD REALLY IS THE HEAD-MASTER.
YOU'RE MIRA?
I'M SORRY TO INVOLVE YOU IN OUR DISPUTES...

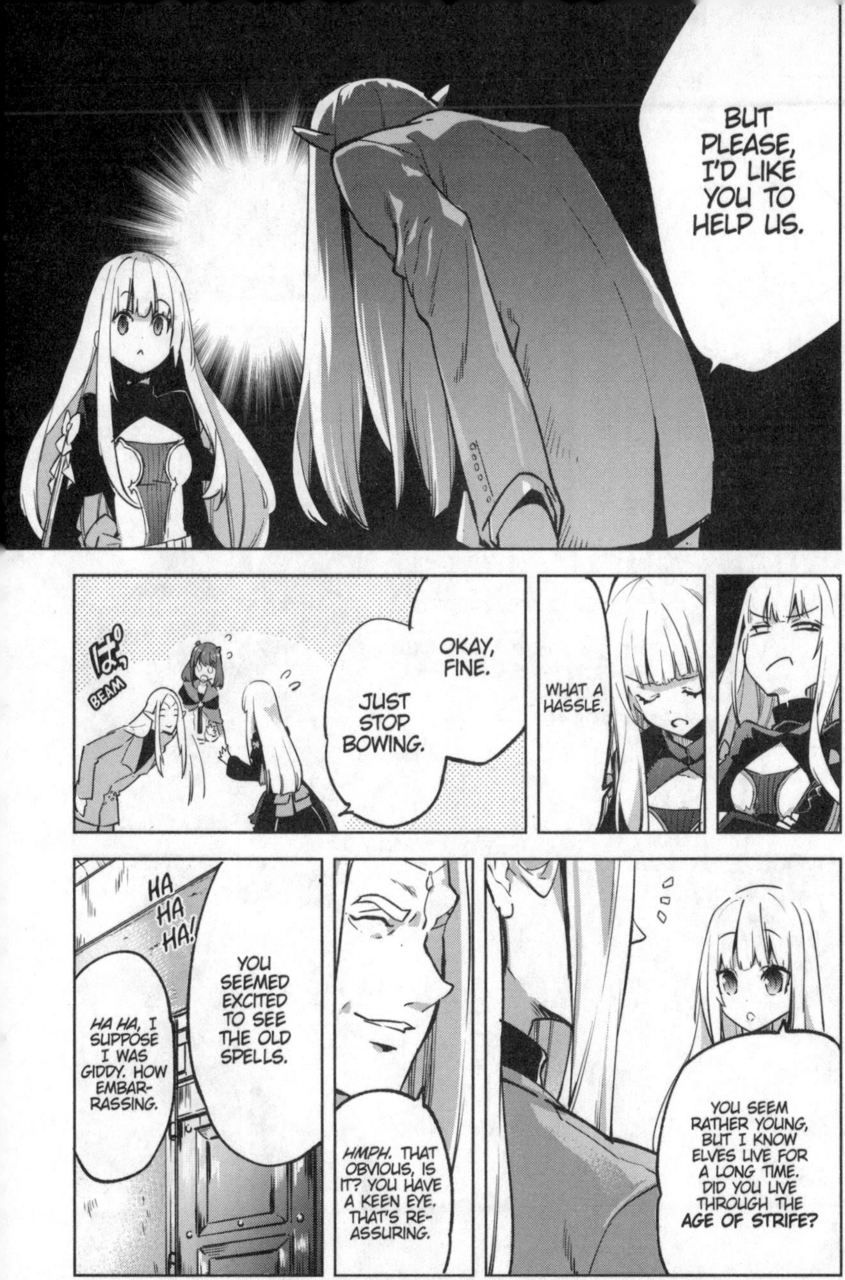
BUT PLEASE, I'D LIKE YOU TO HELP US.
WHAT A HASSLE.
OKAY, FINE.
JUST STOP BOWING.
ぱっ
BEAM
YOU SEEM RATHER YOUNG, BUT I KNOW ELVES LIVE FOR A LONG TIME. DID YOU LIVE THROUGH THE AGE OF STRIFE?
HMPH. THAT OBVIOUS, IS IT? YOU HAVE A KEEN EYE. THAT'S REASSURING.
HA HA HA!
YOU SEEMED EXCITED TO SEE THE OLD SPELLS.
HA HA, I SUPPOSE I WAS GIDDY. HOW EMBARRASSING.

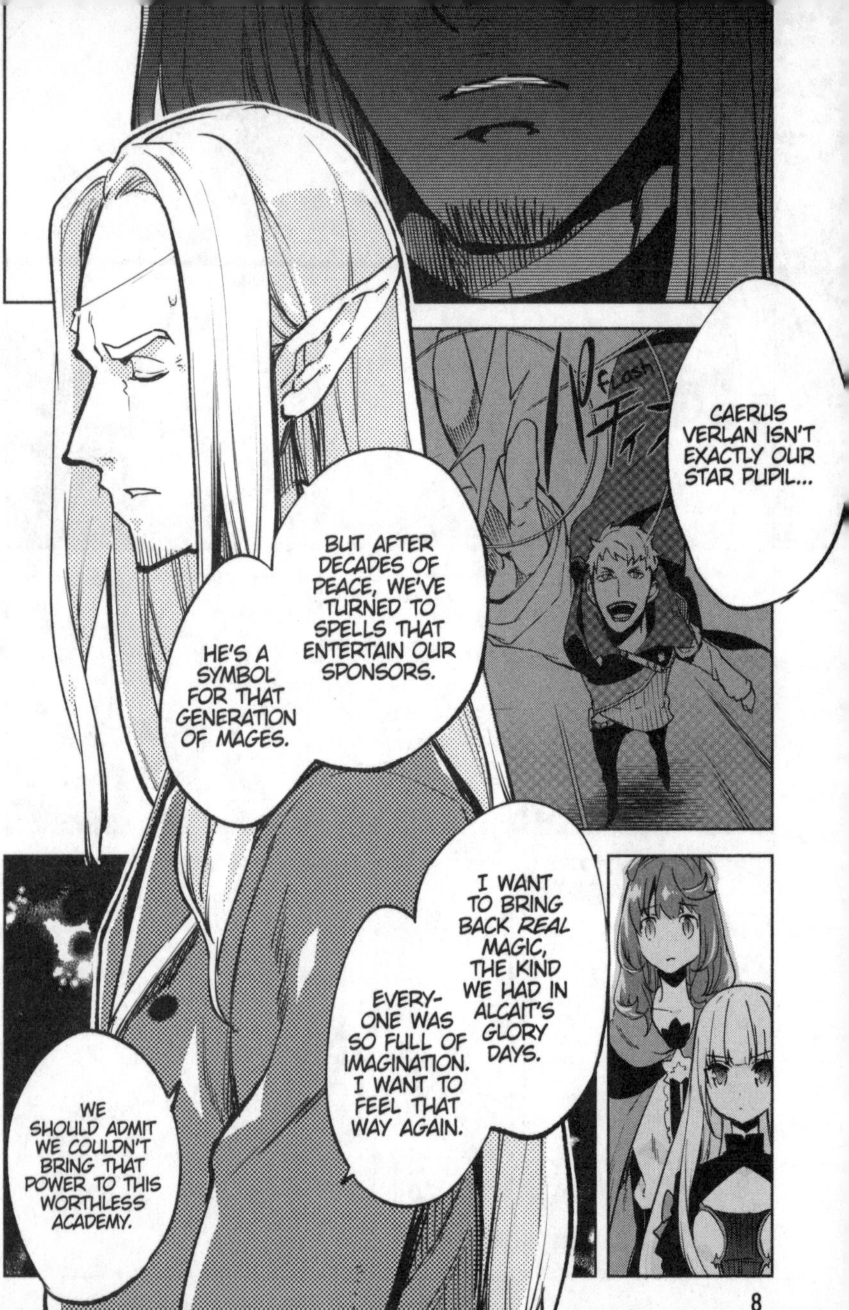
CAERUS VERLAN ISN'T EXACTLY OUR STAR PUPIL...
FLASH
BUT AFTER DECADES OF PEACE, WE'VE TURNED TO SPELLS THAT ENTERTAIN OUR SPONSORS.
HE'S A SYMBOL FOR THAT GENERATION OF MAGES.
I WANT TO BRING BACK *REAL* MAGIC, THE KIND WE HAD IN ALCAIT'S GLORY DAYS.
EVERY-ONE WAS SO FULL OF IMAGINATION. I WANT TO FEEL THAT WAY AGAIN.
WE SHOULD ADMIT WE COULDN'T BRING THAT POWER TO THIS WORTHLESS ACADEMY.

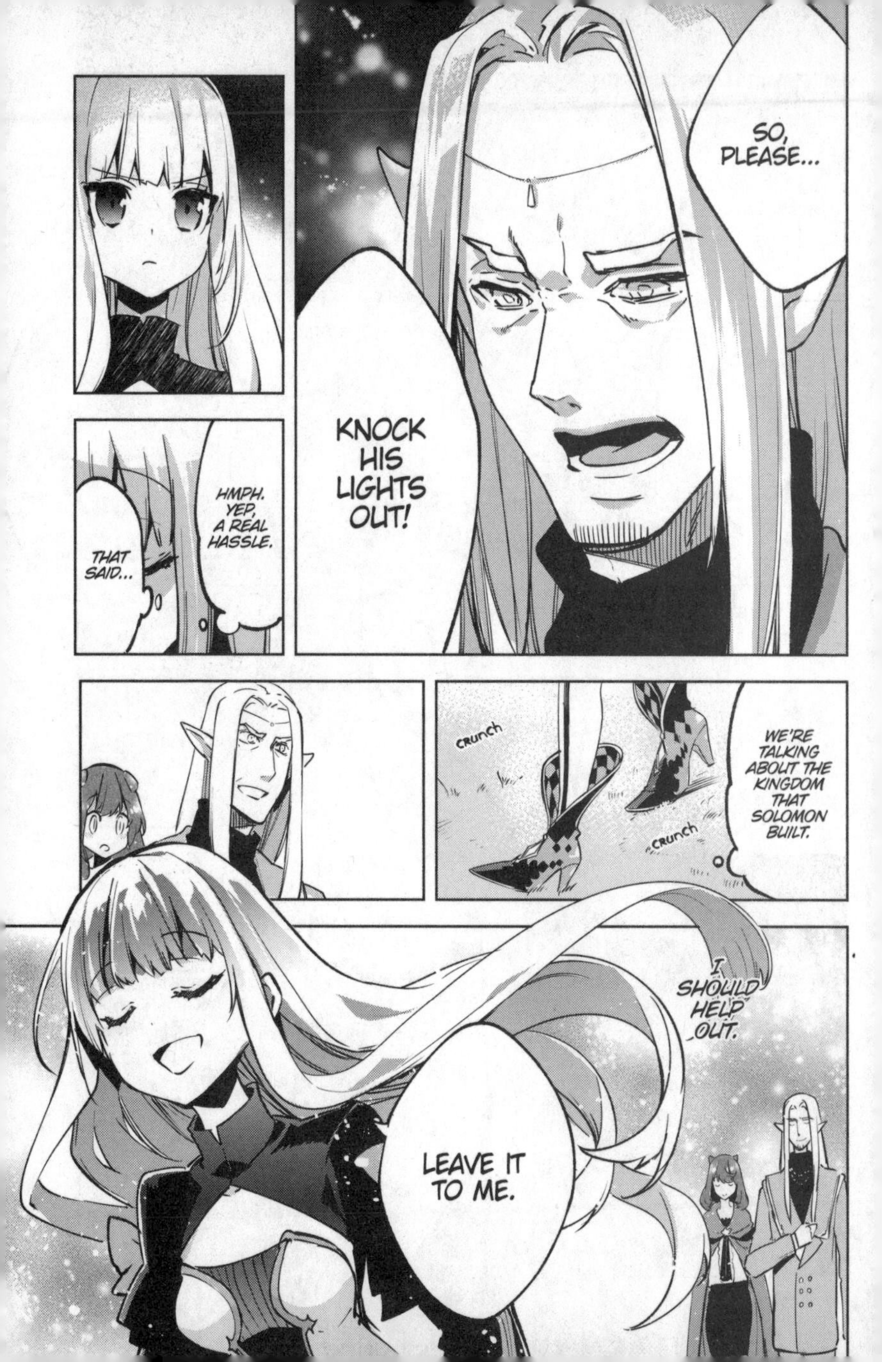
SO, PLEASE...
KNOCK HIS LIGHTS OUT!
HMPH. YEP, A REAL HASSLE.
THAT SAID...
WE'RE TALKING ABOUT THE KINGDOM THAT SOLOMON BUILT.
crunch
crunch
I SHOULD HELP OUT.
LEAVE IT TO ME.

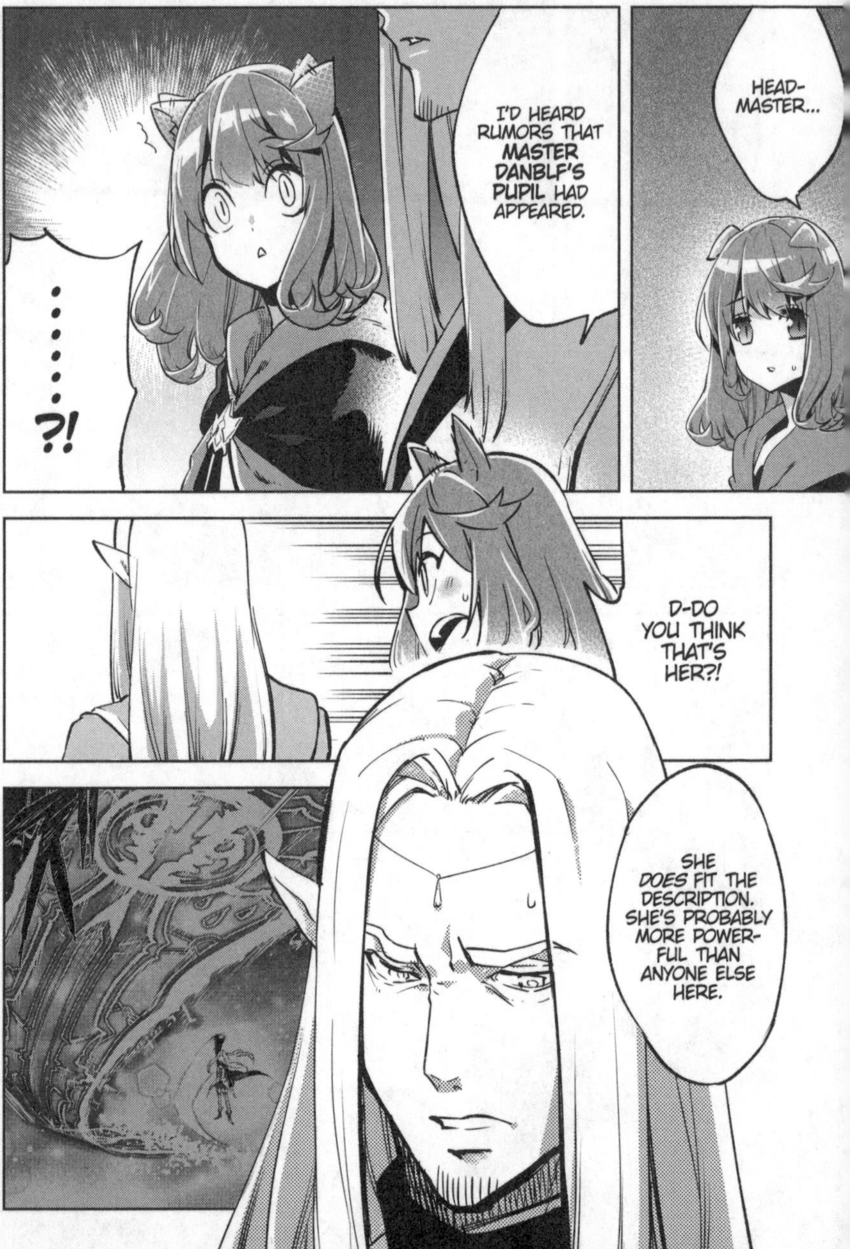
HEAD-MASTER...
I'D HEARD RUMORS THAT MASTER DANBLF'S PUPIL HAD APPEARED.
......?!
D-DO YOU THINK THAT'S HER?!
SHE DOES FIT THE DESCRIPTION. SHE'S PROBABLY MORE POWER-FUL THAN ANYONE ELSE HERE.

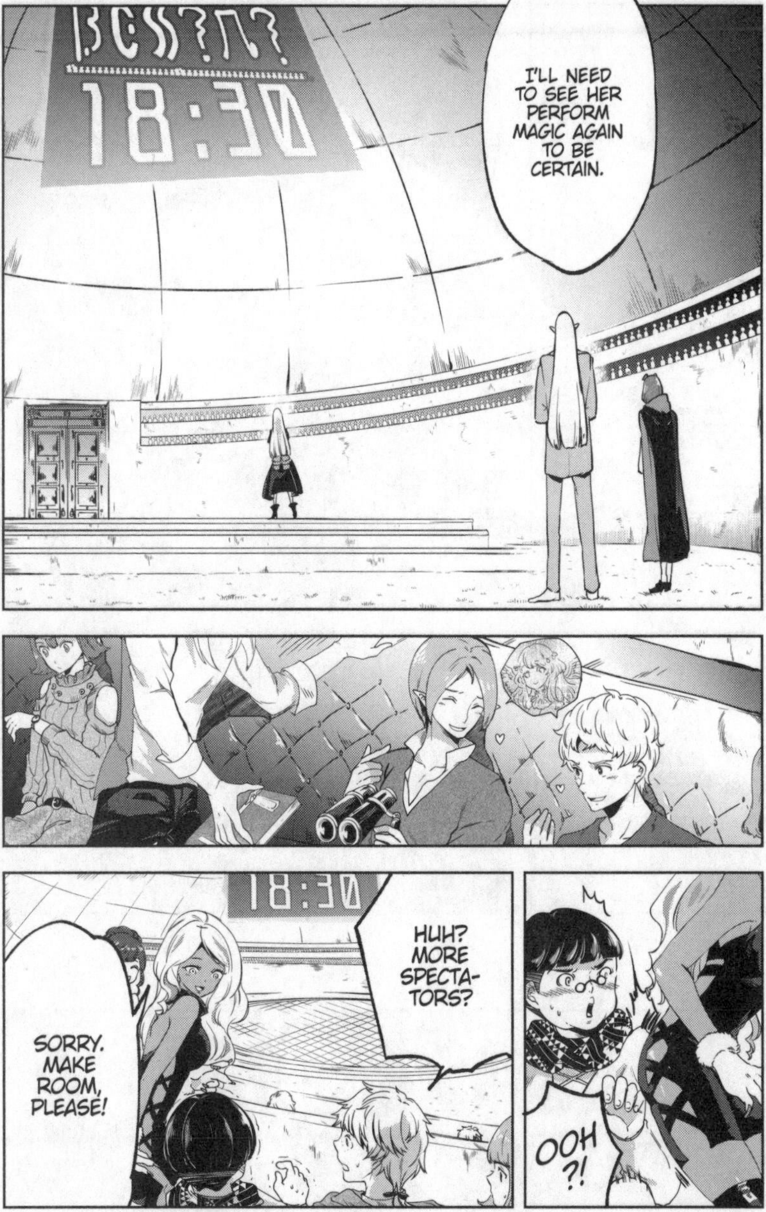
18:30
I'LL NEED TO SEE HER PERFORM MAGIC AGAIN TO BE CERTAIN.
OOH ?!
18:30
HUH? MORE SPECTATORS?
SORRY. MAKE ROOM, PLEASE!

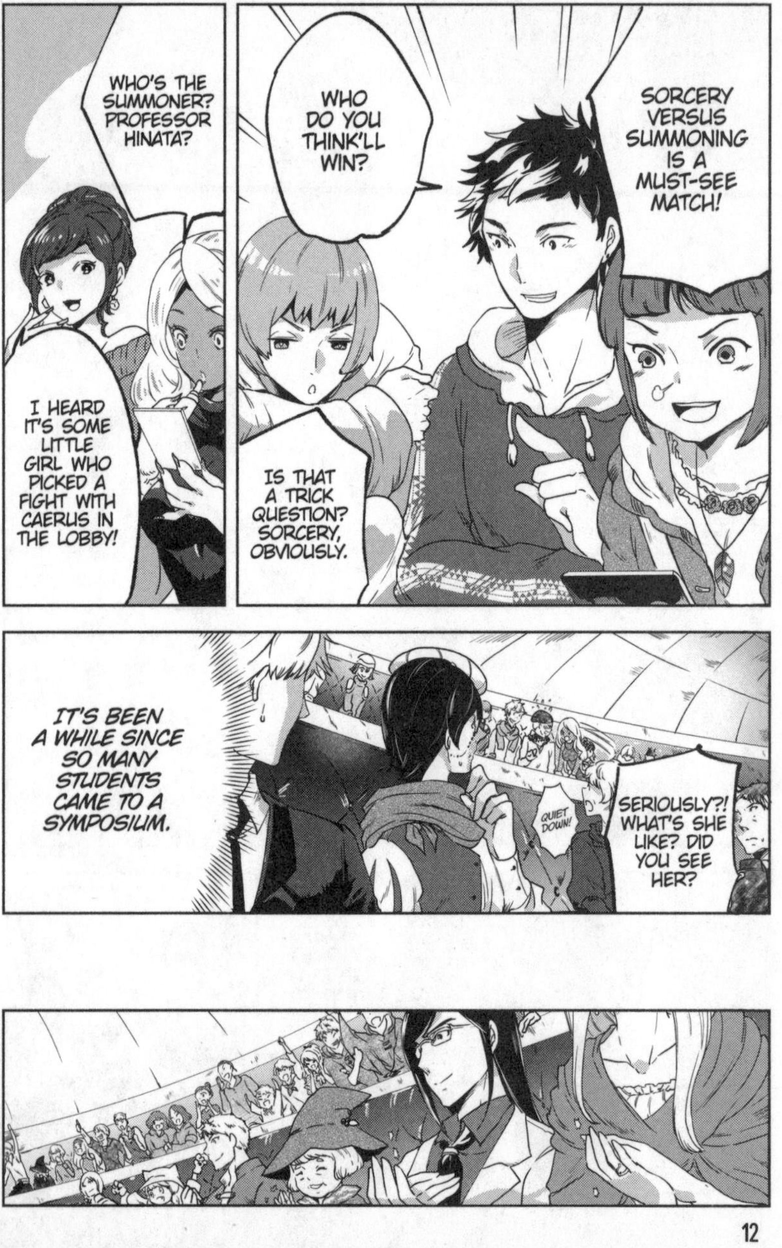
SORCERY VERSUS SUMMONING IS A MUST-SEE MATCH!
WHO DO YOU THINK'LL WIN?
IS THAT A TRICK QUESTION? SORCERY, OBVIOUSLY.
WHO'S THE SUMMONER? PROFESSOR HINATA?
I HEARD IT'S SOME LITTLE GIRL WHO PICKED A FIGHT WITH CAERUS IN THE LOBBY!
SERIOUSLY?! WHAT'S SHE LIKE? DID YOU SEE HER?
QUIET DOWN!
IT'S BEEN A WHILE SINCE SO MANY STUDENTS CAME TO A SYMPOSIUM.

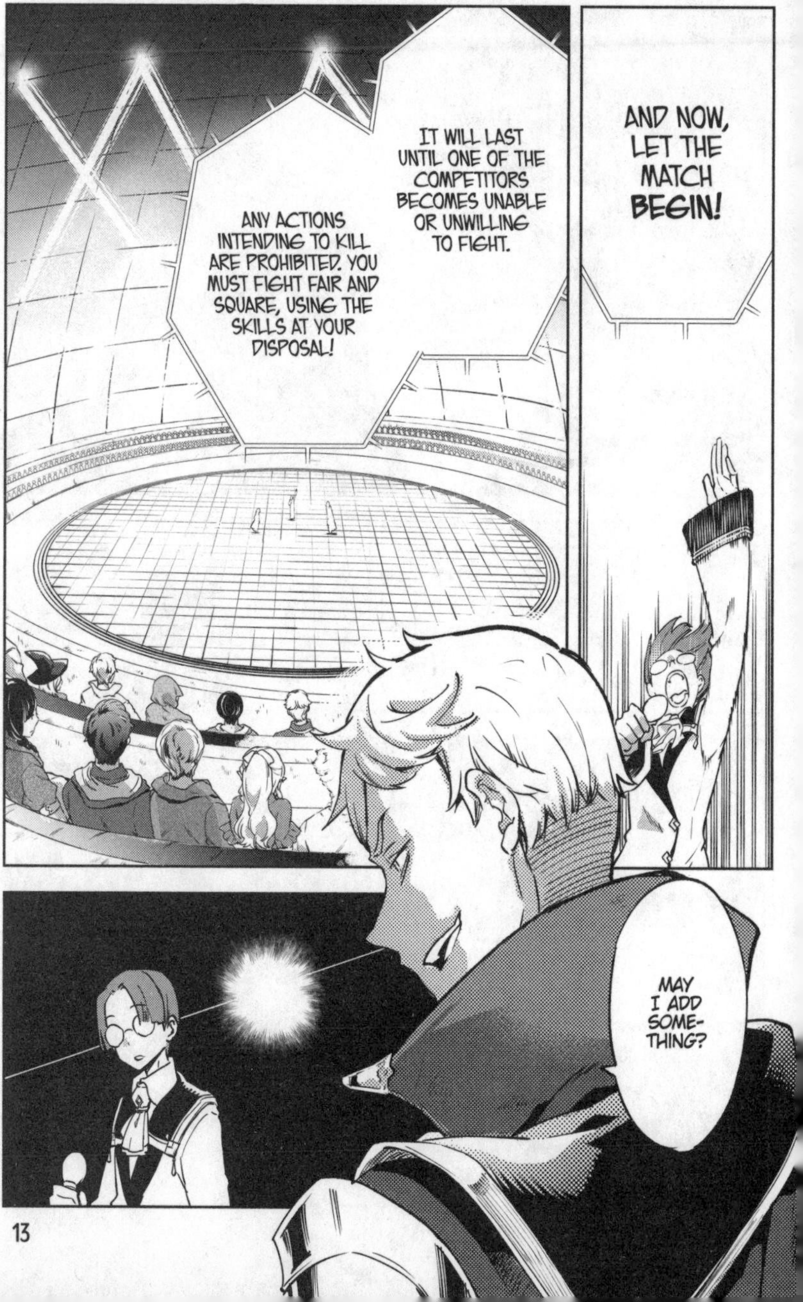
AND NOW, LET THE MATCH **BEGIN!**
IT WILL LAST UNTIL ONE OF THE COMPETITORS BECOMES UNABLE OR UNWILLING TO FIGHT.
ANY ACTIONS INTENDING TO KILL ARE PROHIBITED. YOU MUST FIGHT FAIR AND SQUARE, USING THE SKILLS AT YOUR DISPOSAL!
MAY I ADD SOME-THING?

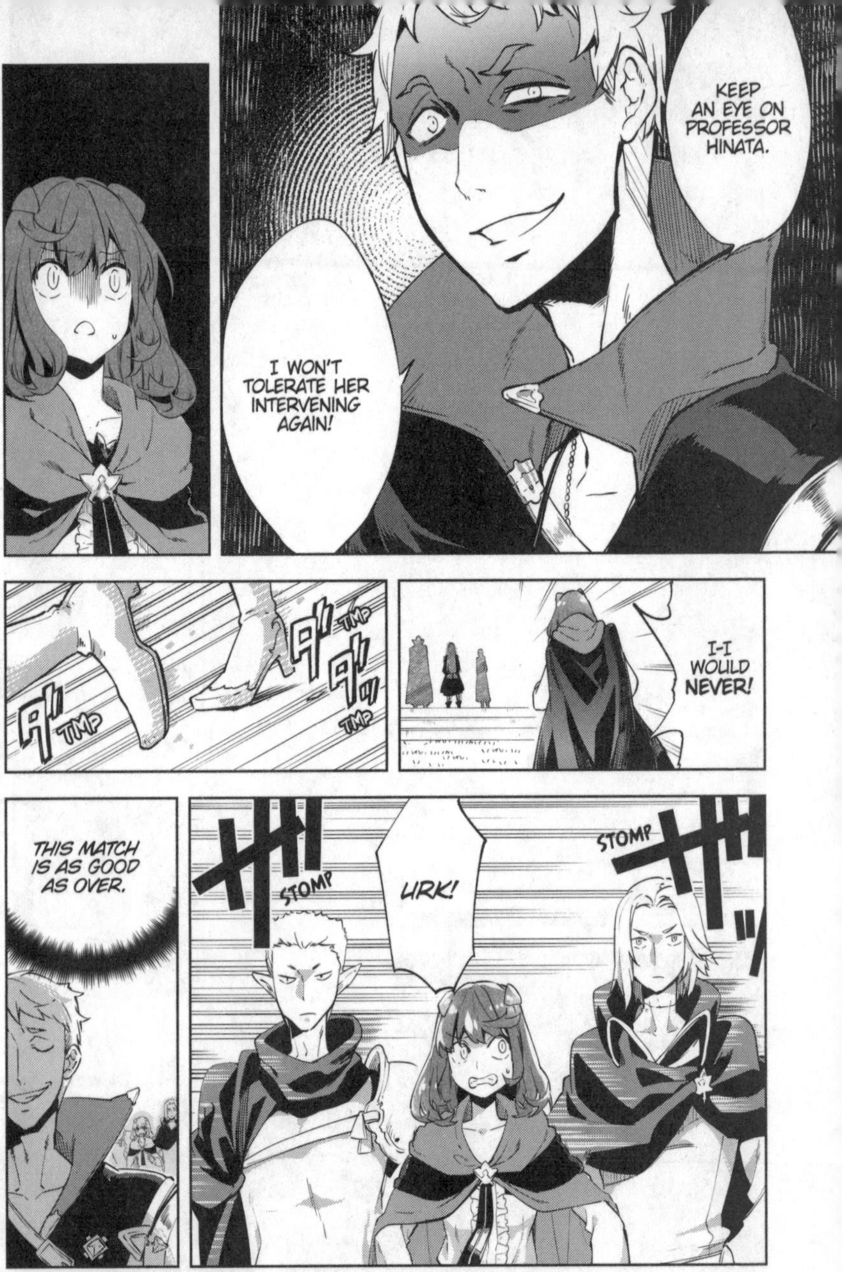
KEEP AN EYE ON PROFESSOR HINATA.
I WON'T TOLERATE HER INTERVENING AGAIN!
I-I WOULD NEVER!
ダッ
TMP
ダッ
TMP
ダッ
TMP
STOMP
URK!
STOMP
THIS MATCH IS AS GOOD AS OVER.

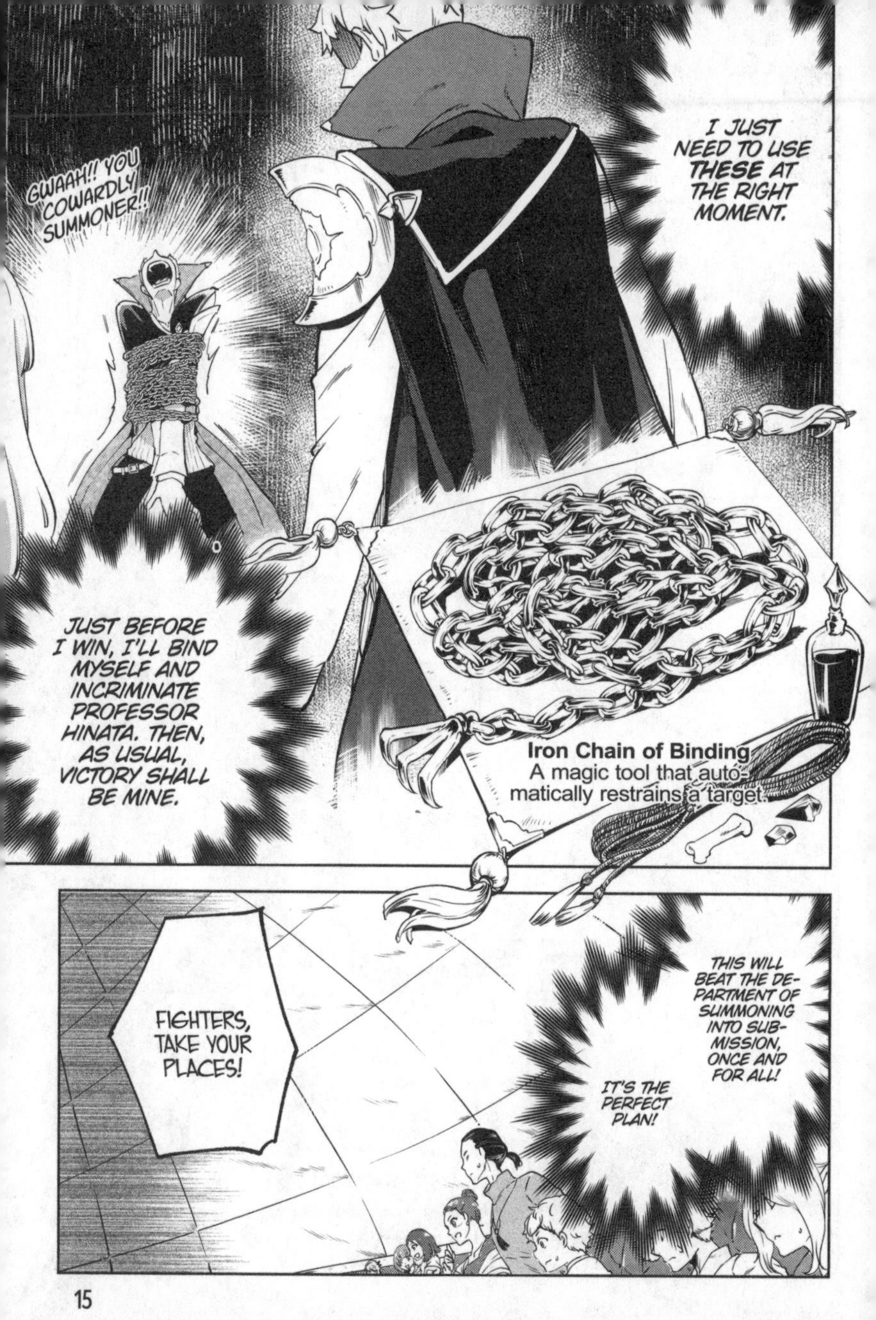
I JUST NEED TO USE THESE AT THE RIGHT MOMENT.
GWAAH!! YOU COWARDLY SUMMONER!!
JUST BEFORE I WIN, I'LL BIND MYSELF AND INCRIMINATE PROFESSOR HINATA. THEN, AS USUAL, VICTORY SHALL BE MINE.
Iron Chain of Binding
A magic tool that automatically restrains a target.
THIS WILL BEAT THE DEPARTMENT OF SUMMONING INTO SUBMISSION, ONCE AND FOR ALL!
IT'S THE PERFECT PLAN!
FIGHTERS, TAKE YOUR PLACES!

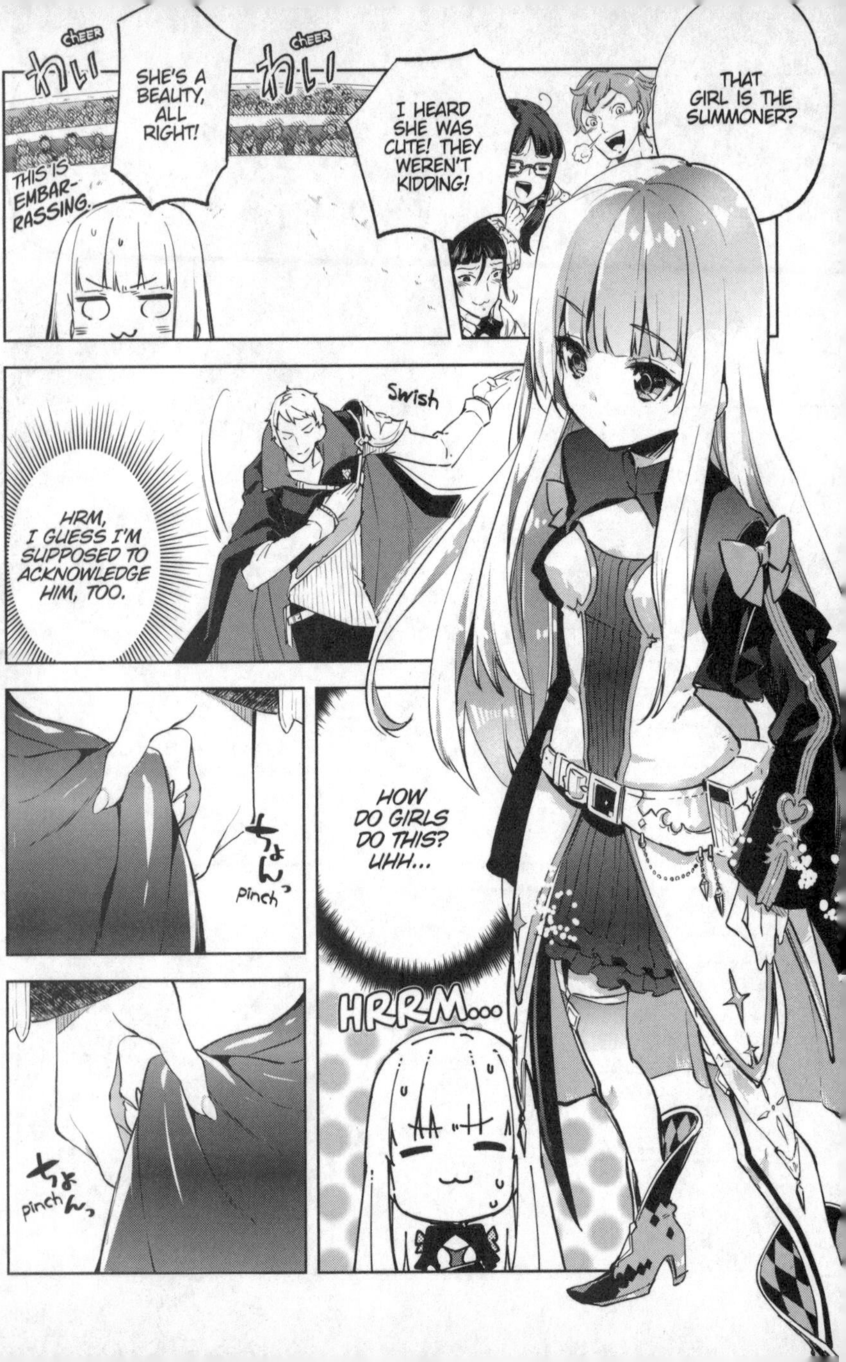
THAT GIRL IS THE SUMMONER?
I HEARD SHE WAS CUTE! THEY WEREN'T KIDDING!
わい
CHEER
SHE'S A BEAUTY, ALL RIGHT!
わい
CHEER
THIS IS EMBARRASSING.
Swish
HRM, I GUESS I'M SUPPOSED TO ACKNOWLEDGE HIM, TOO.
HOW DO GIRLS DO THIS? UHH...
ちょんっ
pinch
HRRM...
ちょんっ
pinch

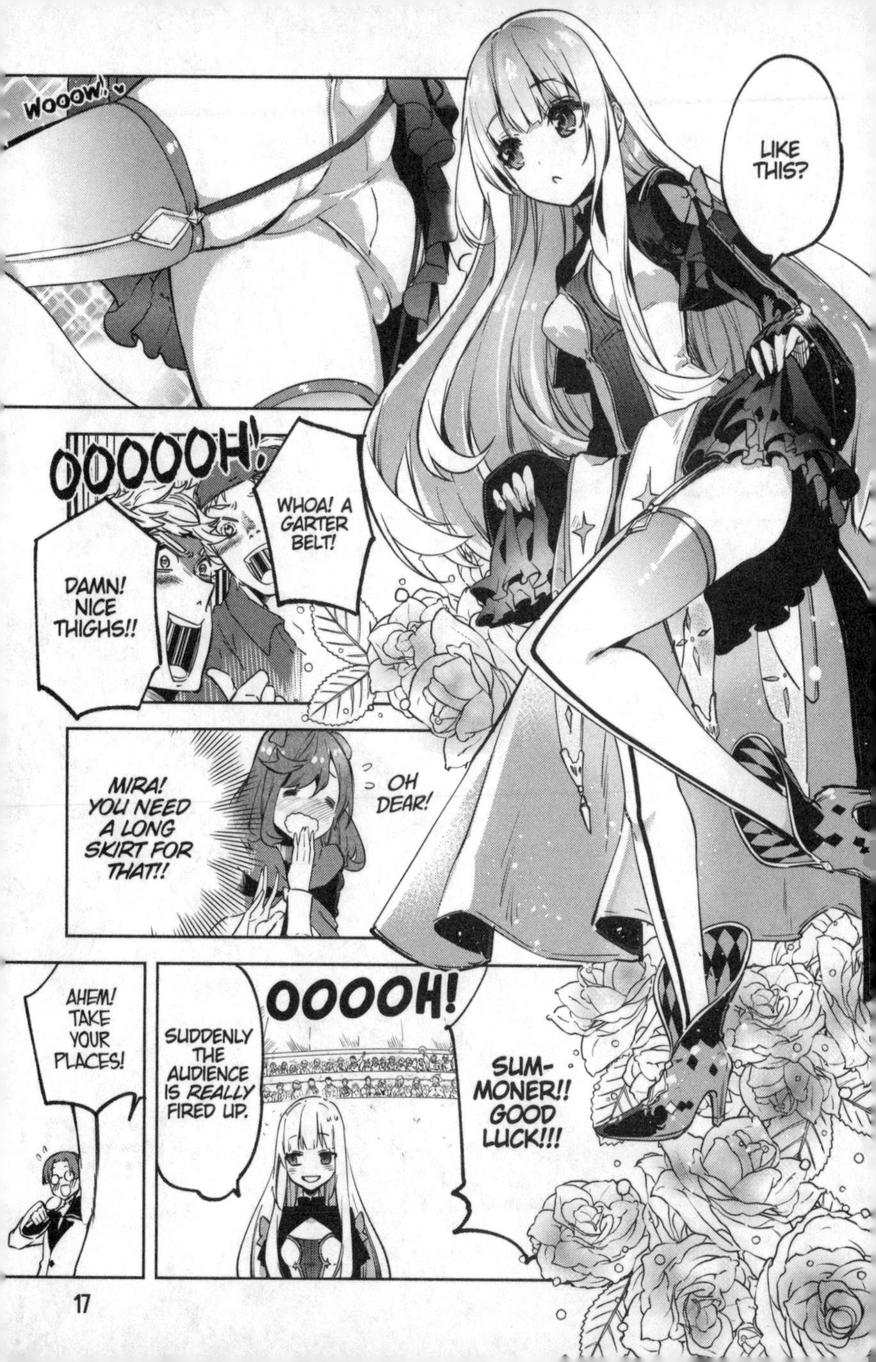
LIKE THIS?
WOOOW! ♥
OOOOOH!
WHOA! A GARTER BELT!
DAMN! NICE THIGHS!!
OH DEAR!
MIRA! YOU NEED A LONG SKIRT FOR THAT!!
SUM-MONER!! GOOD LUCK!!!
OOOOH!
SUDDENLY THE AUDIENCE IS *REALLY* FIRED UP.
AHEM! TAKE YOUR PLACES!

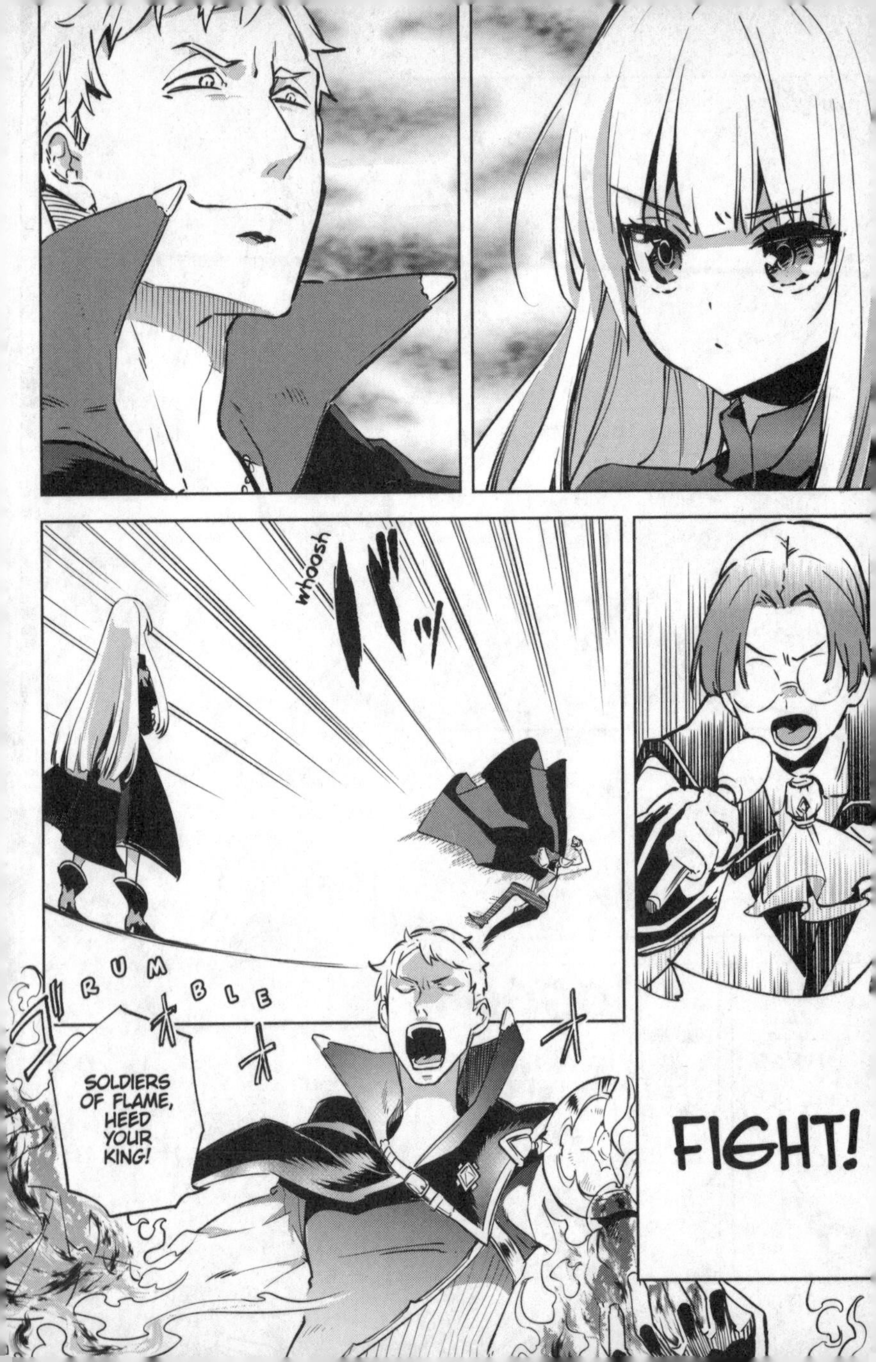
FIGHT!
whoosh
RUMBLE
SOLDIERS OF FLAME, HEED YOUR KING!

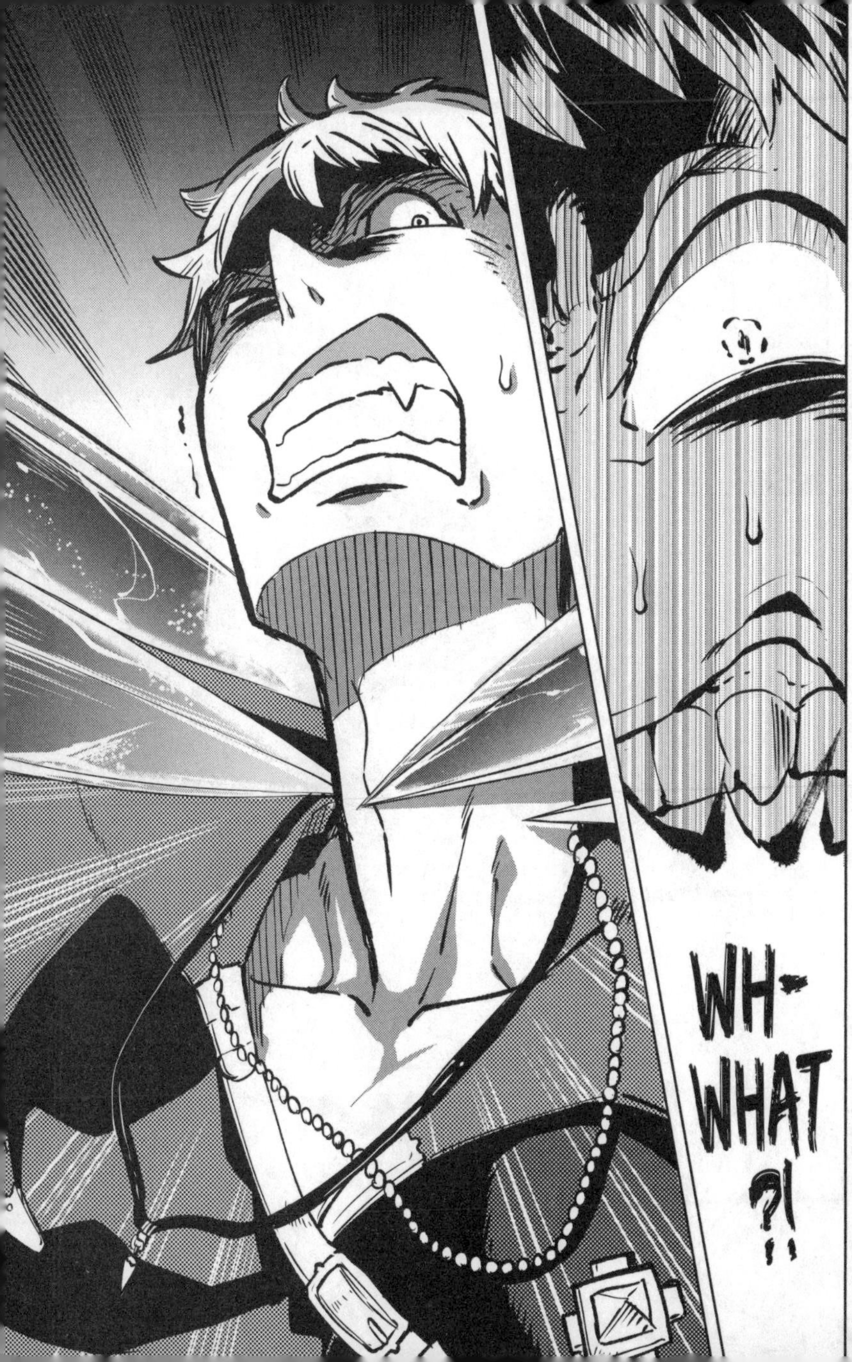
WH-WHAT?!

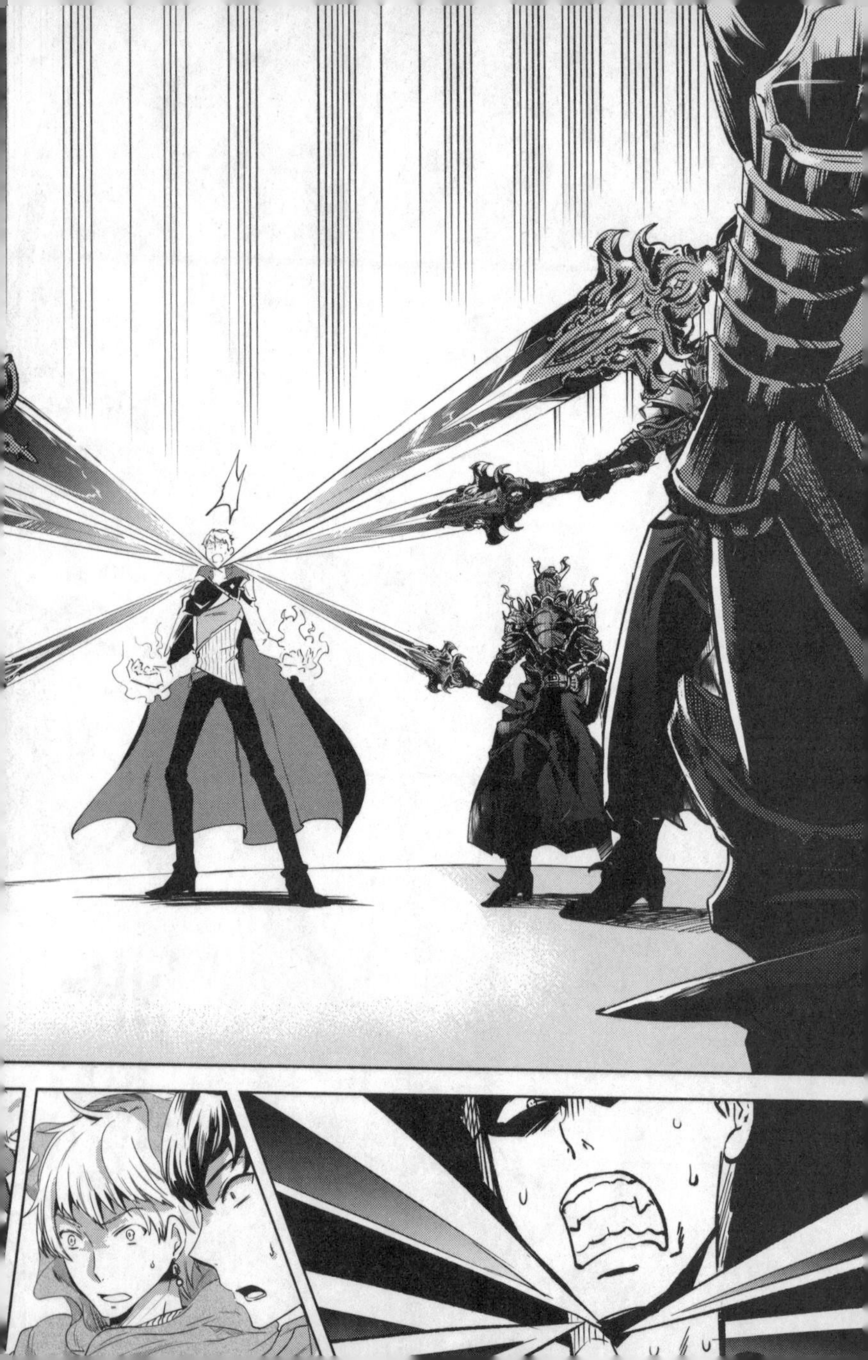

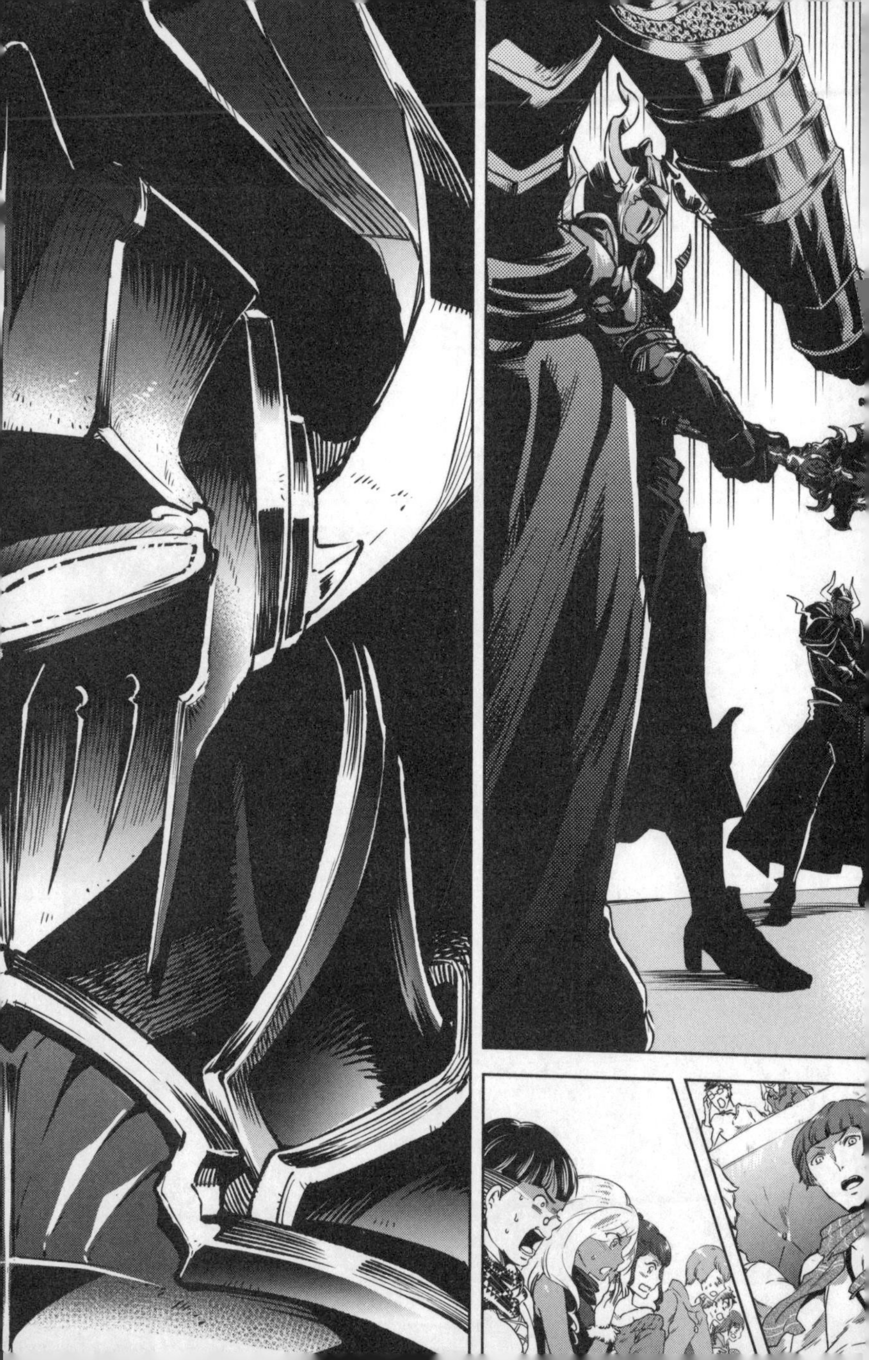

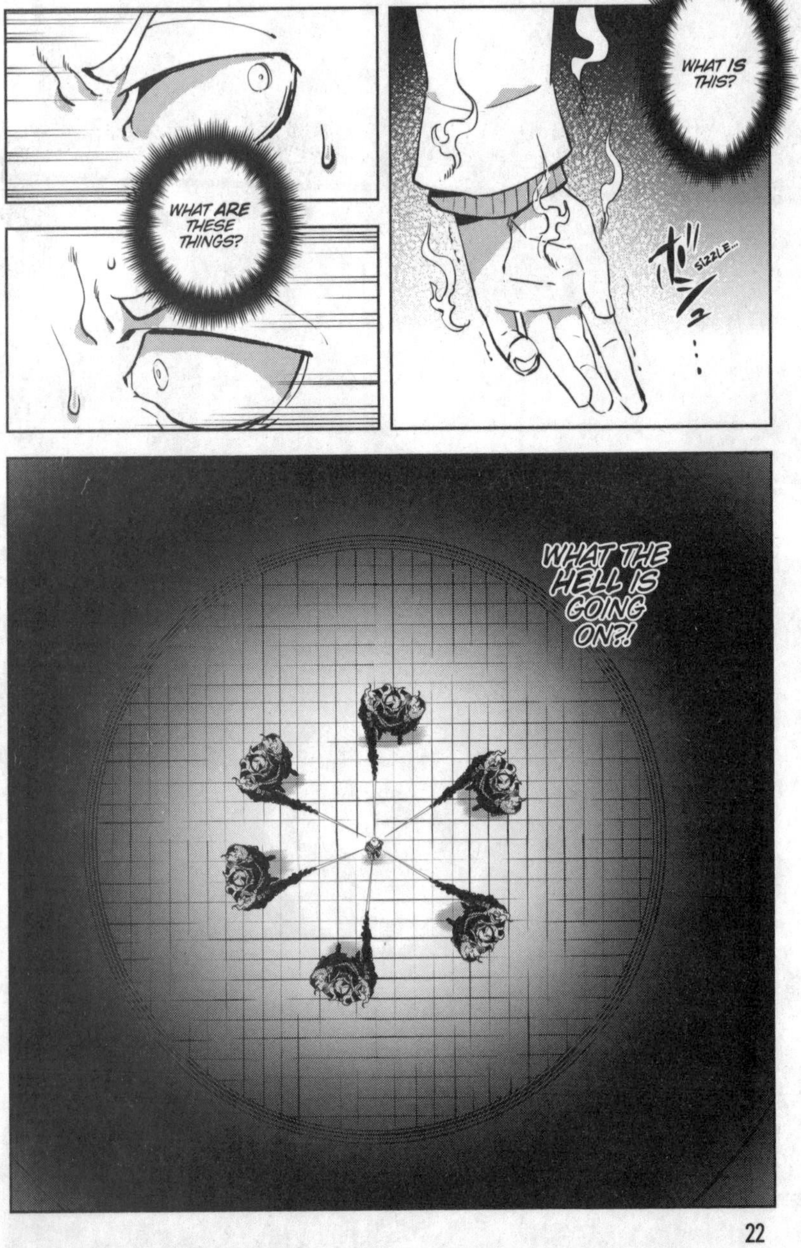
WHAT IS THIS?
SIZZLE...
WHAT ARE THESE THINGS?
WHAT THE HELL IS GOING ON?!

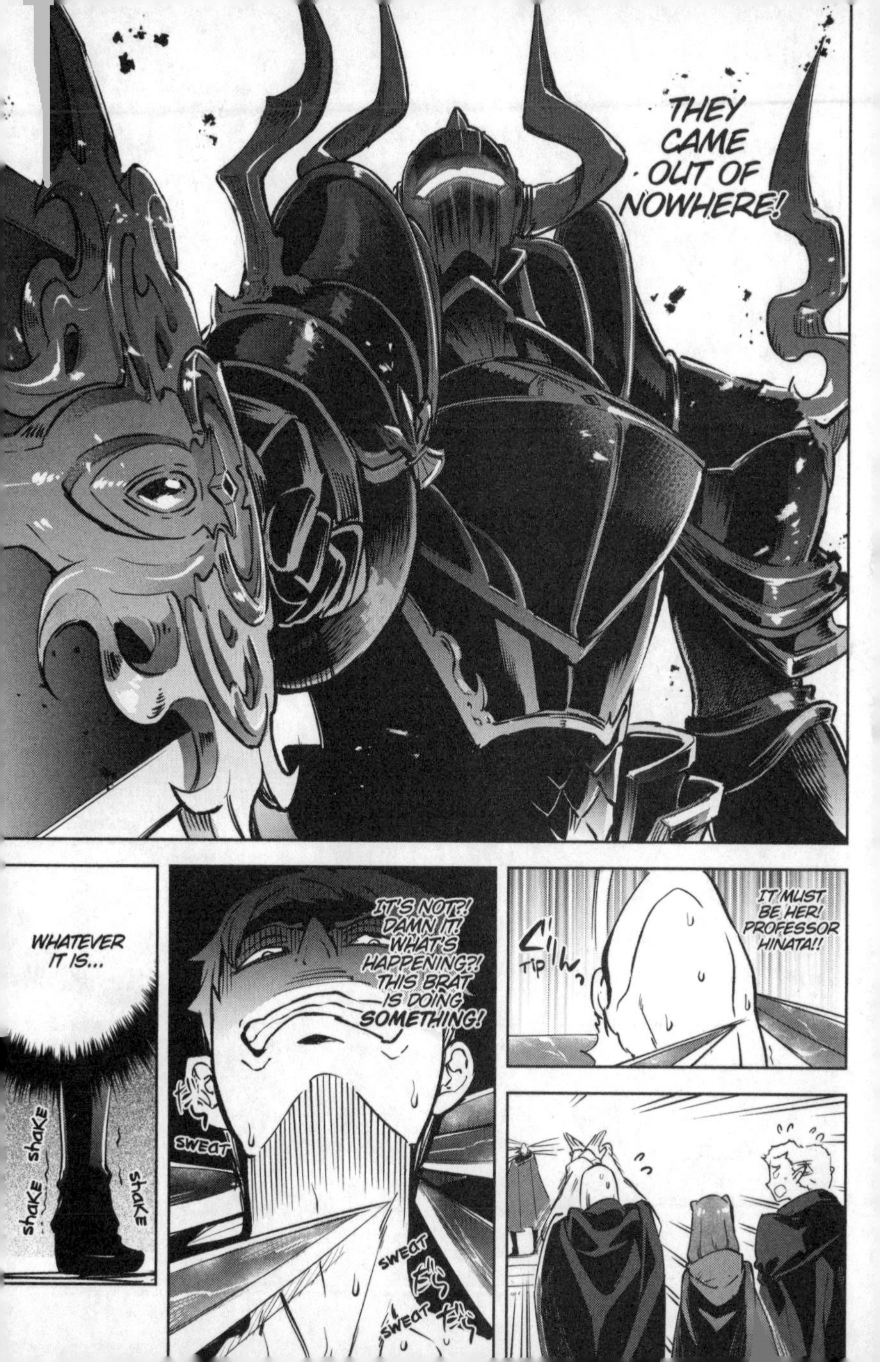
THEY CAME OUT OF NOWHERE!
IT MUST BE HER! PROFESSOR HINATA!!
TIP
IT'S NOT?! DAMN IT! WHAT'S HAPPENING?! THIS BRAT IS DOING SOMETHING!
SWEAT
SWEAT
SWEAT
WHATEVER IT IS...
shake
shake
shake

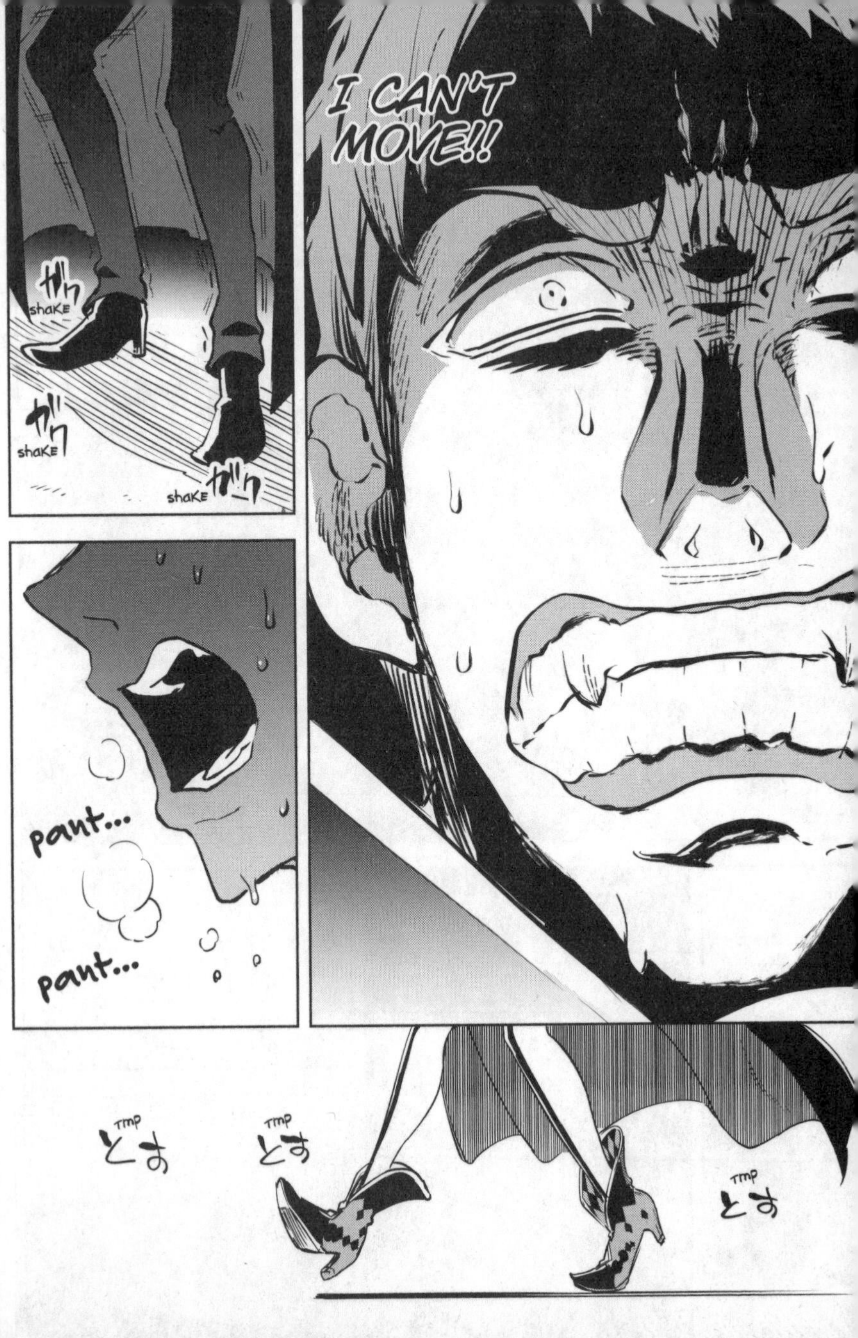
I CAN'T MOVE!!
ガク
shake
ガク
shake
ガク
shake
pant...
pant...
とす
tmp
とす
tmp
とす
tmp

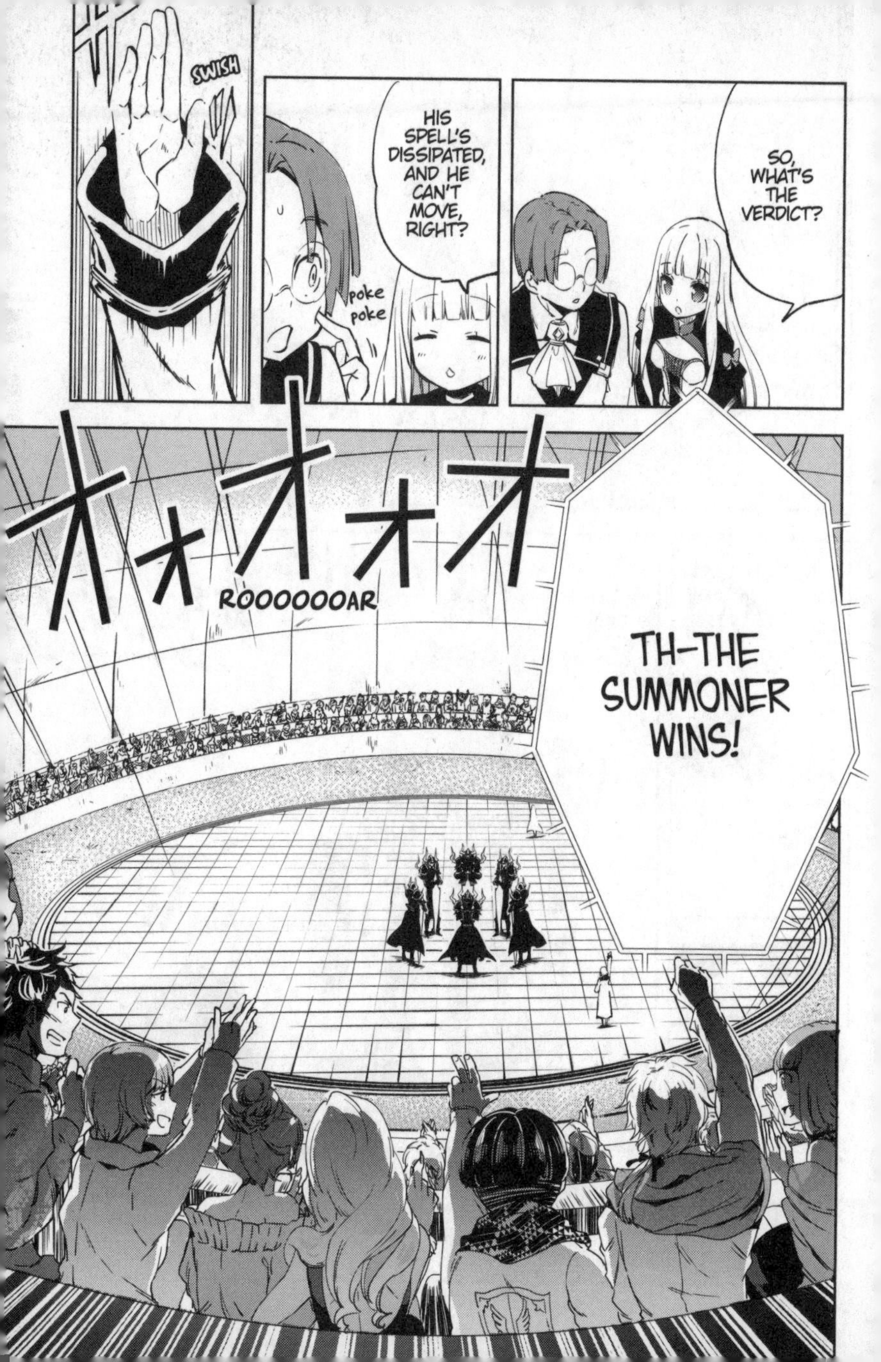
SO, WHAT'S THE VERDICT?
HIS SPELL'S DISSIPATED, AND HE CAN'T MOVE, RIGHT?
poke poke
SWISH
TH-THE SUMMONER WINS!
オォオォオ
ROOOOOOAR

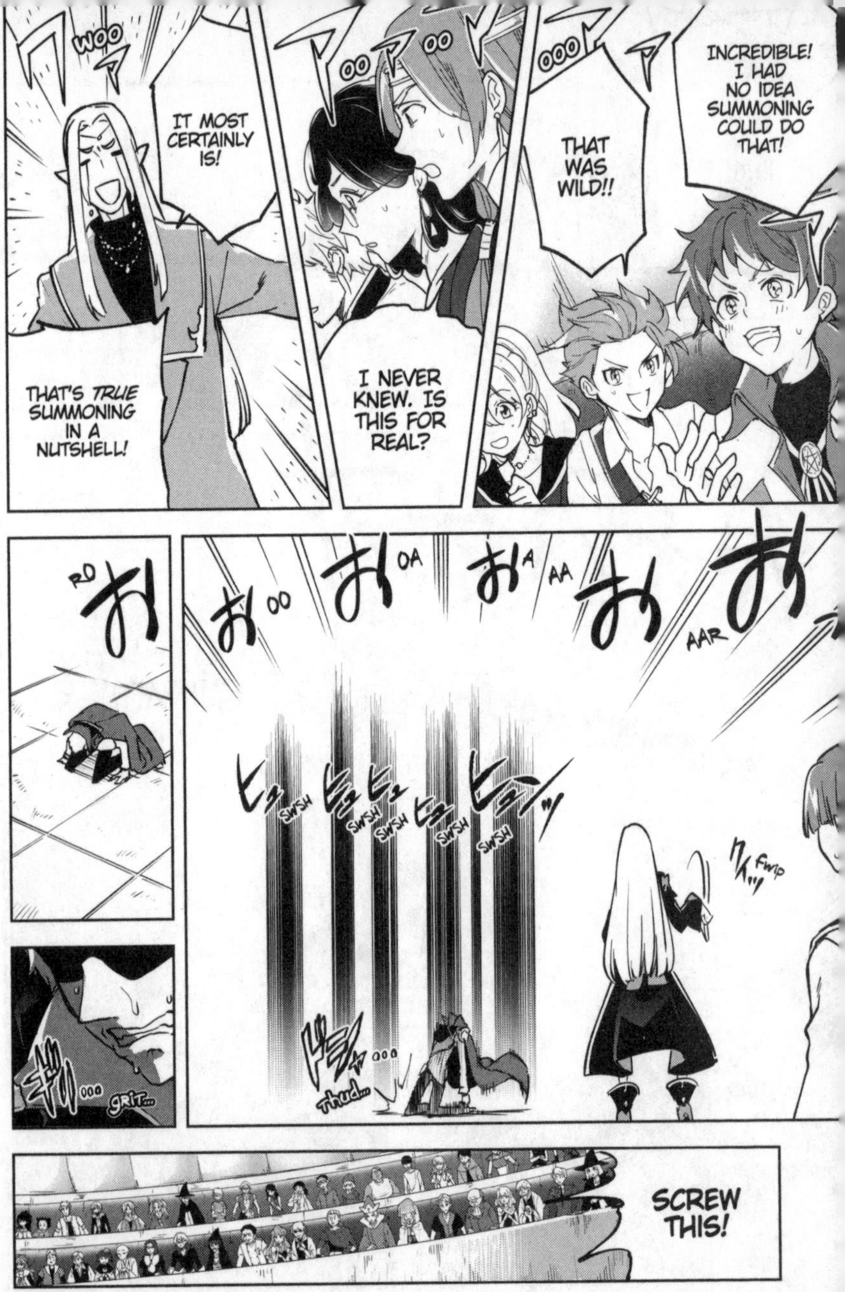
OOO
INCREDIBLE! I HAD NO IDEA SUMMONING COULD DO THAT!
THAT WAS WILD!!
OO
OO
I NEVER KNEW. IS THIS FOR REAL?
WOO
IT MOST CERTAINLY IS!
THAT'S TRUE SUMMONING IN A NUTSHELL!
AAR
AA
OA
OO
SWSH
SWSH
SWSH
SWSH
SWSH
fwip
thud...
RO
grit...
SCREW THIS!

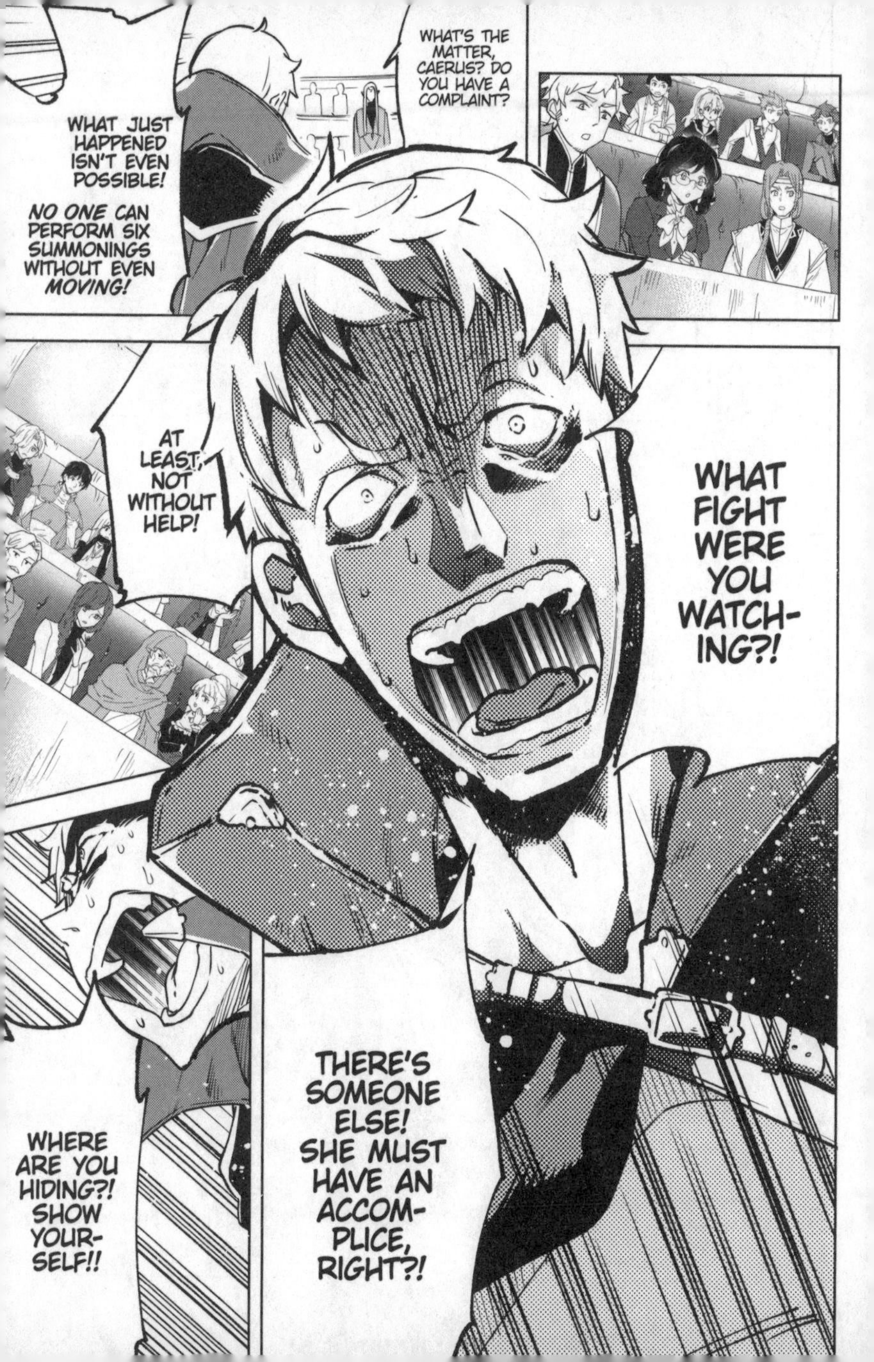
WHAT'S THE MATTER, CAERUS? DO YOU HAVE A COMPLAINT?
WHAT FIGHT WERE YOU WATCH-ING?!
WHAT JUST HAPPENED ISN'T EVEN POSSIBLE!
NO ONE CAN PERFORM SIX SUMMONINGS WITHOUT EVEN *MOVING!*
AT LEAST, NOT WITHOUT HELP!
THERE'S SOMEONE ELSE! SHE MUST HAVE AN ACCOM-PLICE, RIGHT?!
WHERE ARE YOU HIDING?! SHOW YOUR-SELF!!

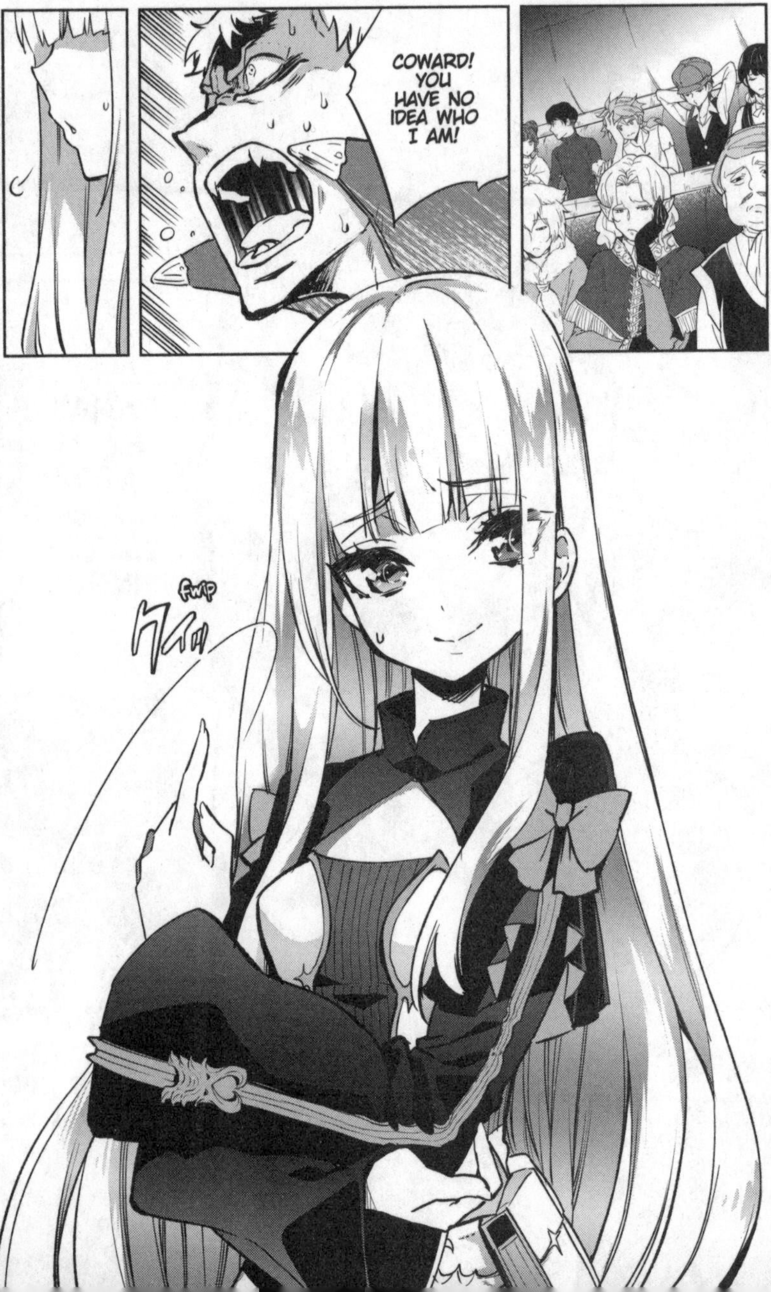
COWARD! YOU HAVE NO IDEA WHO I AM!
fwip

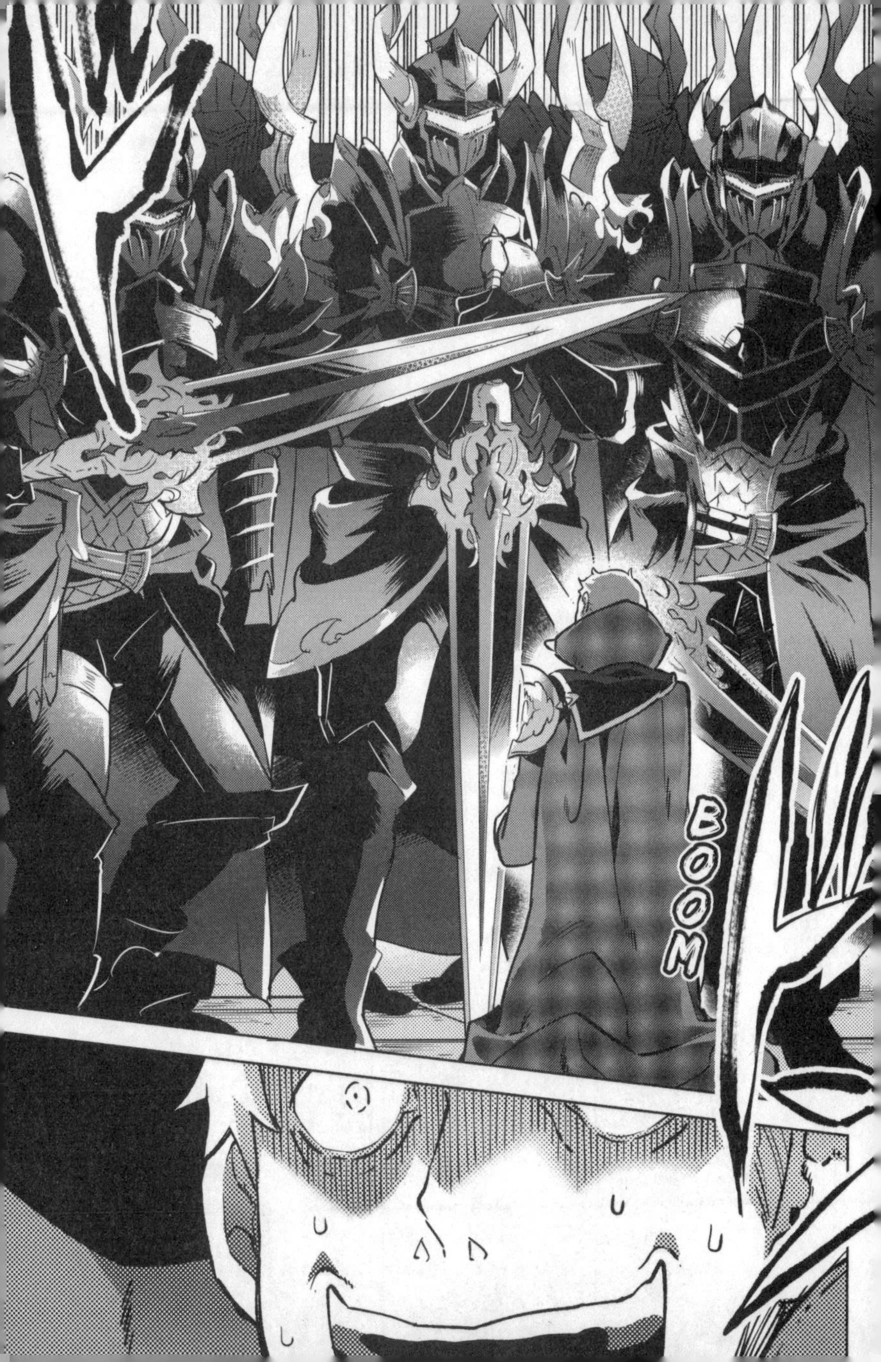
BOOM

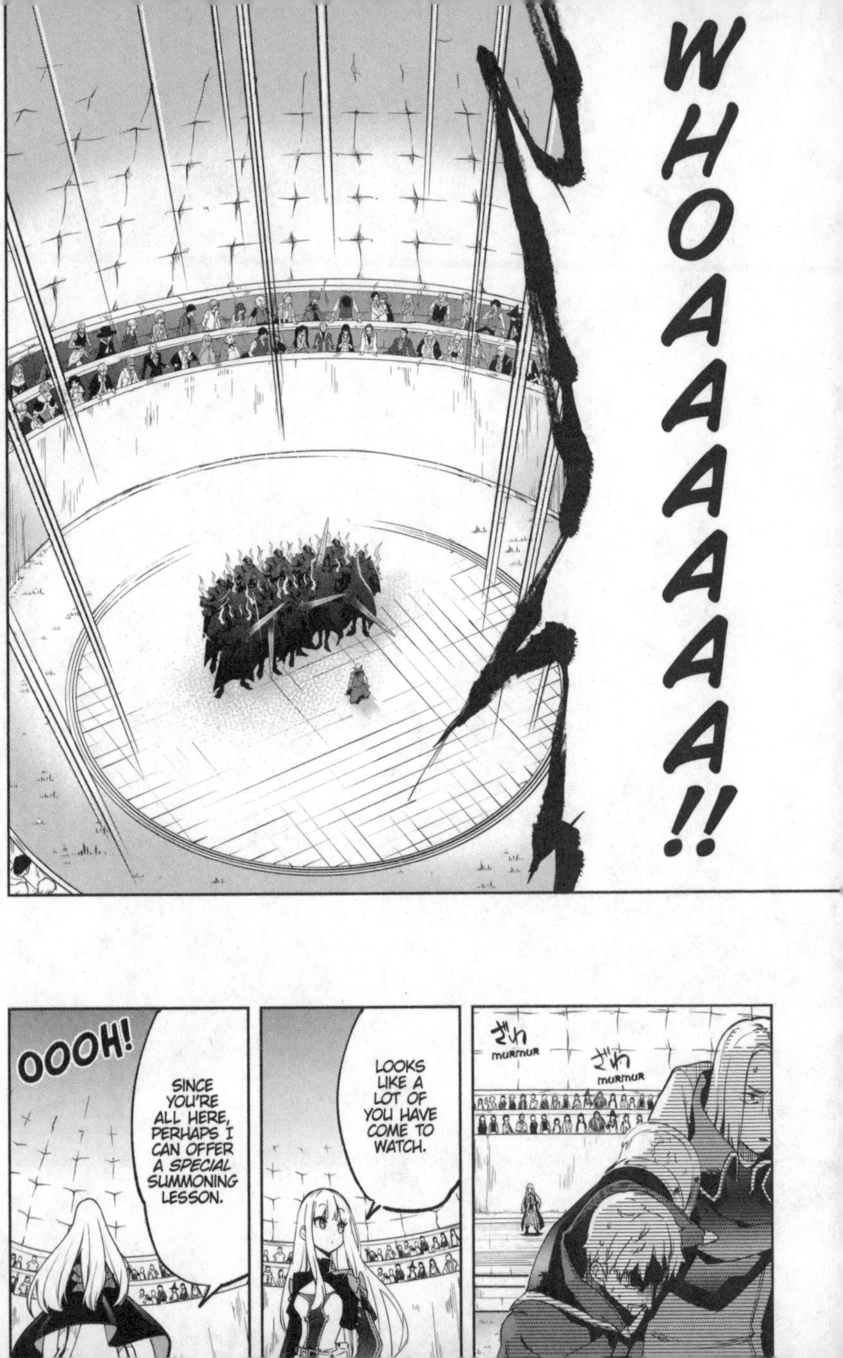
WHOAAAAAA!!
ざわ
murmur
ざわ
murmur
LOOKS LIKE A LOT OF YOU HAVE COME TO WATCH.
OOOH!
SINCE YOU'RE ALL HERE, PERHAPS I CAN OFFER A SPECIAL SUMMONING LESSON.

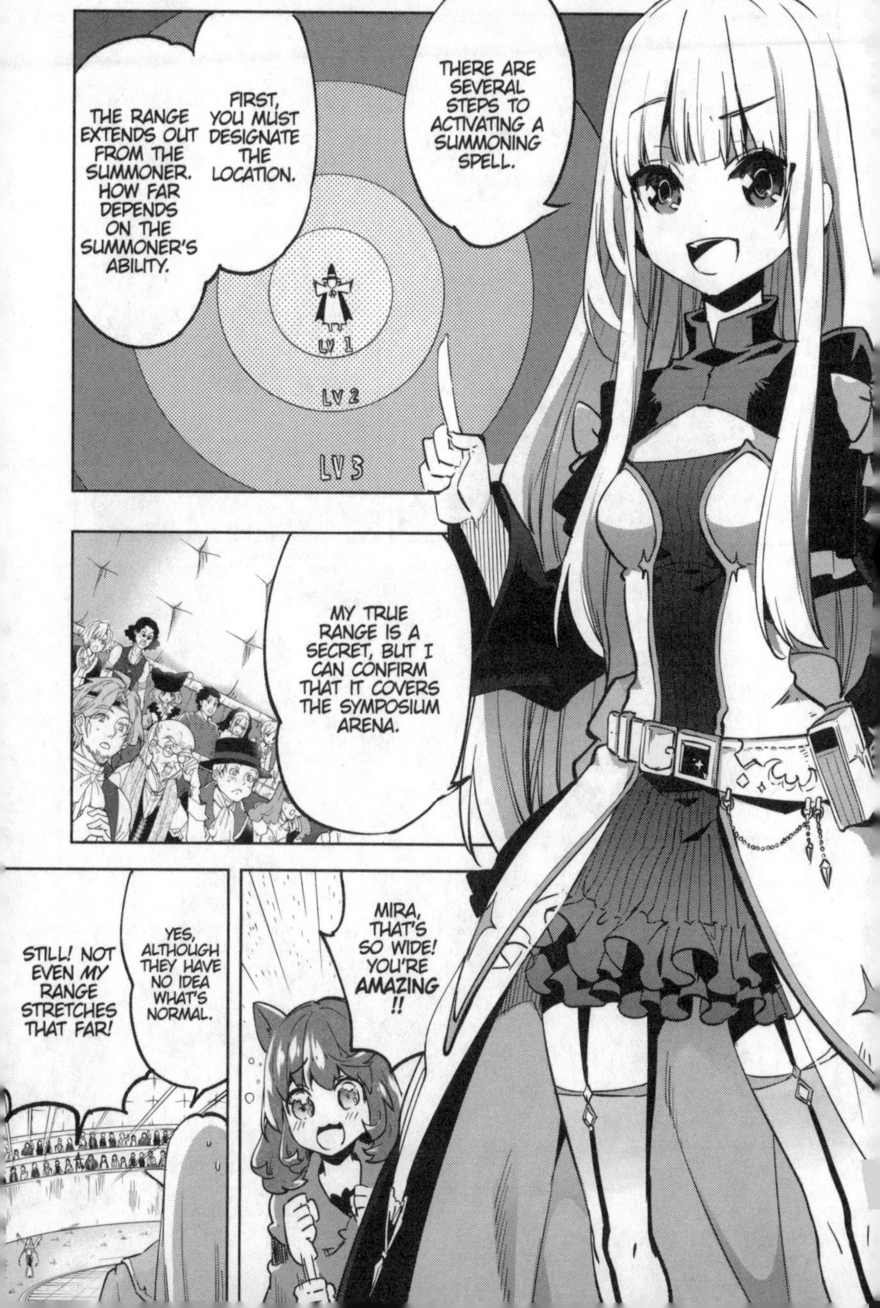
THERE ARE SEVERAL STEPS TO ACTIVATING A SUMMONING SPELL.
FIRST, YOU MUST DESIGNATE THE LOCATION.
THE RANGE EXTENDS OUT FROM THE SUMMONER. HOW FAR DEPENDS ON THE SUMMONER'S ABILITY.
LV 1
LV 2
LV 3
MY TRUE RANGE IS A SECRET, BUT I CAN CONFIRM THAT IT COVERS THE SYMPOSIUM ARENA.
MIRA, THAT'S SO WIDE! YOU'RE AMAZING !!
YES, ALTHOUGH THEY HAVE NO IDEA WHAT'S NORMAL.
STILL! NOT EVEN MY RANGE STRETCHES THAT FAR!

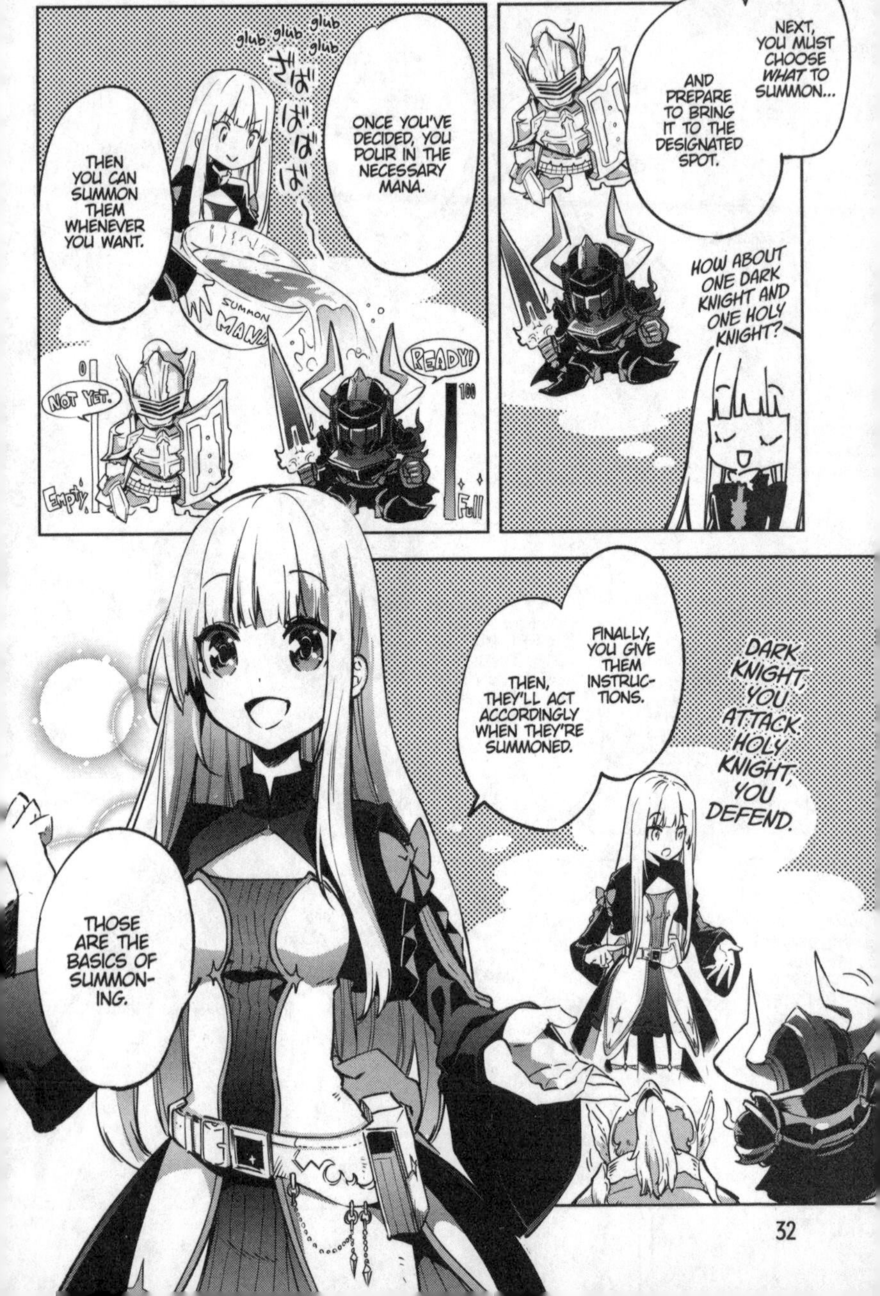
NEXT, YOU MUST CHOOSE *WHAT* TO SUMMON...
AND PREPARE TO BRING IT TO THE DESIGNATED SPOT.
HOW ABOUT ONE DARK KNIGHT AND ONE HOLY KNIGHT?
glub glub glub glub
ざばばばば
ONCE YOU'VE DECIDED, YOU POUR IN THE NECESSARY MANA.
THEN YOU CAN SUMMON THEM WHENEVER YOU WANT.
SUMMON MANA
READY!
100
Full
0
NOT YET.
Empty
FINALLY, YOU GIVE THEM INSTRUCTIONS.
THEN, THEY'LL ACT ACCORDINGLY WHEN THEY'RE SUMMONED.
DARK KNIGHT, YOU ATTACK. HOLY KNIGHT, YOU DEFEND.
THOSE ARE THE BASICS OF SUMMONING.

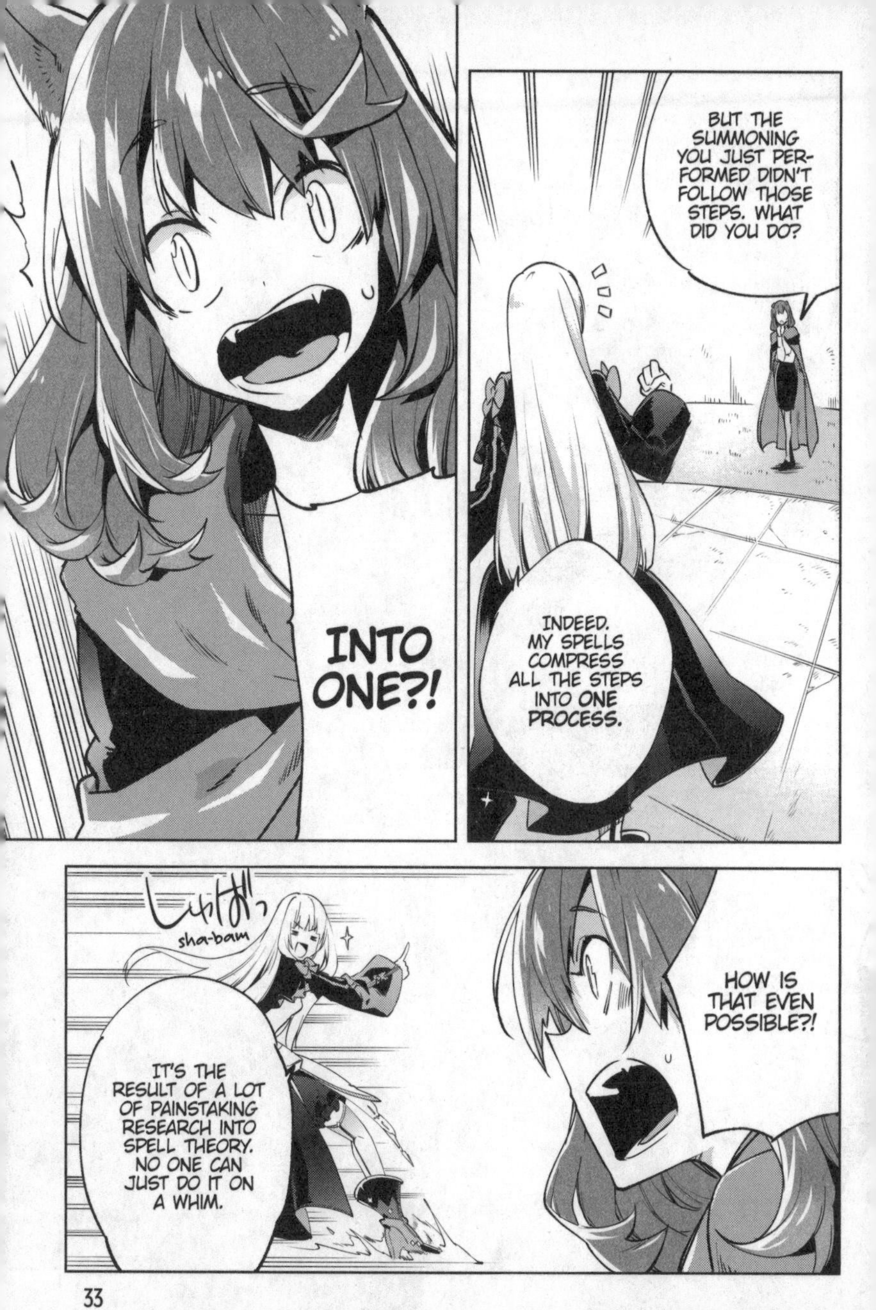
BUT THE SUMMONING YOU JUST PER-FORMED DIDN'T FOLLOW THOSE STEPS. WHAT DID YOU DO?
INDEED. MY SPELLS COMPRESS ALL THE STEPS INTO ONE PROCESS.
INTO ONE?!
HOW IS THAT EVEN POSSIBLE?!
sha-bam
IT'S THE RESULT OF A LOT OF PAINSTAKING RESEARCH INTO SPELL THEORY. NO ONE CAN JUST DO IT ON A WHIM.

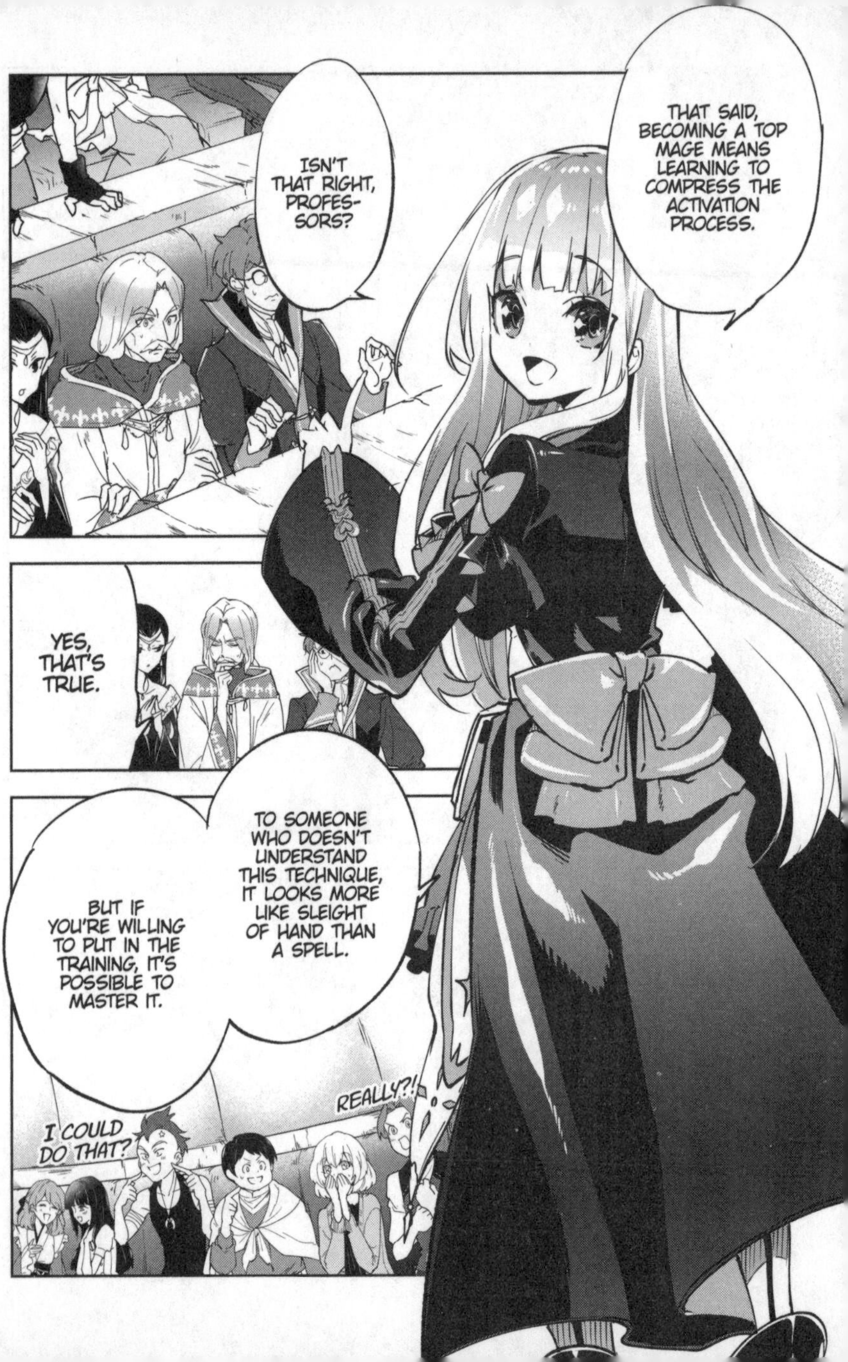
THAT SAID, BECOMING A TOP MAGE MEANS LEARNING TO COMPRESS THE ACTIVATION PROCESS.
ISN'T THAT RIGHT, PROFES-SORS?
YES, THAT'S TRUE.
TO SOMEONE WHO DOESN'T UNDERSTAND THIS TECHNIQUE, IT LOOKS MORE LIKE SLEIGHT OF HAND THAN A SPELL.
BUT IF YOU'RE WILLING TO PUT IN THE TRAINING, IT'S POSSIBLE TO MASTER IT.
REALLY?!
I COULD DO THAT?

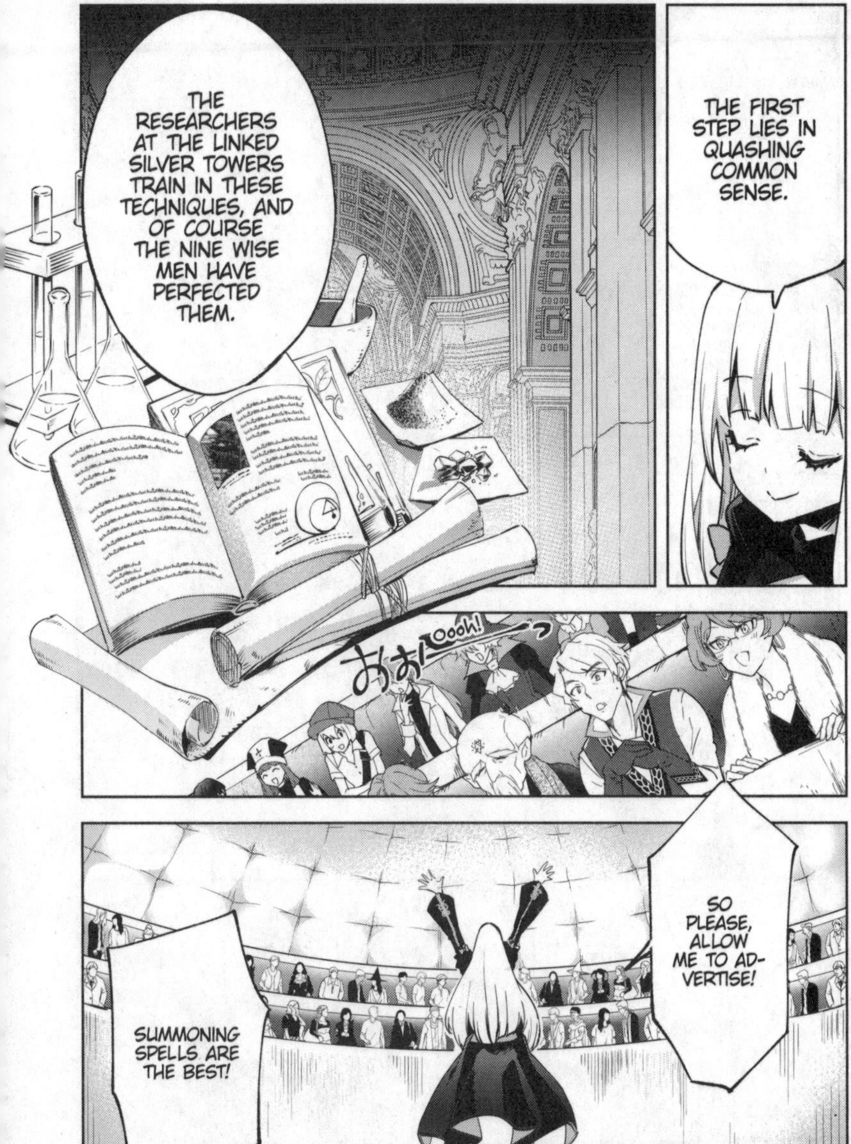
THE FIRST STEP LIES IN QUASHING COMMON SENSE.
THE RESEARCHERS AT THE LINKED SILVER TOWERS TRAIN IN THESE TECHNIQUES, AND OF COURSE THE NINE WISE MEN HAVE PERFECTED THEM.
おお! Oooh!
SO PLEASE, ALLOW ME TO AD-VERTISE!
SUMMONING SPELLS ARE THE BEST!

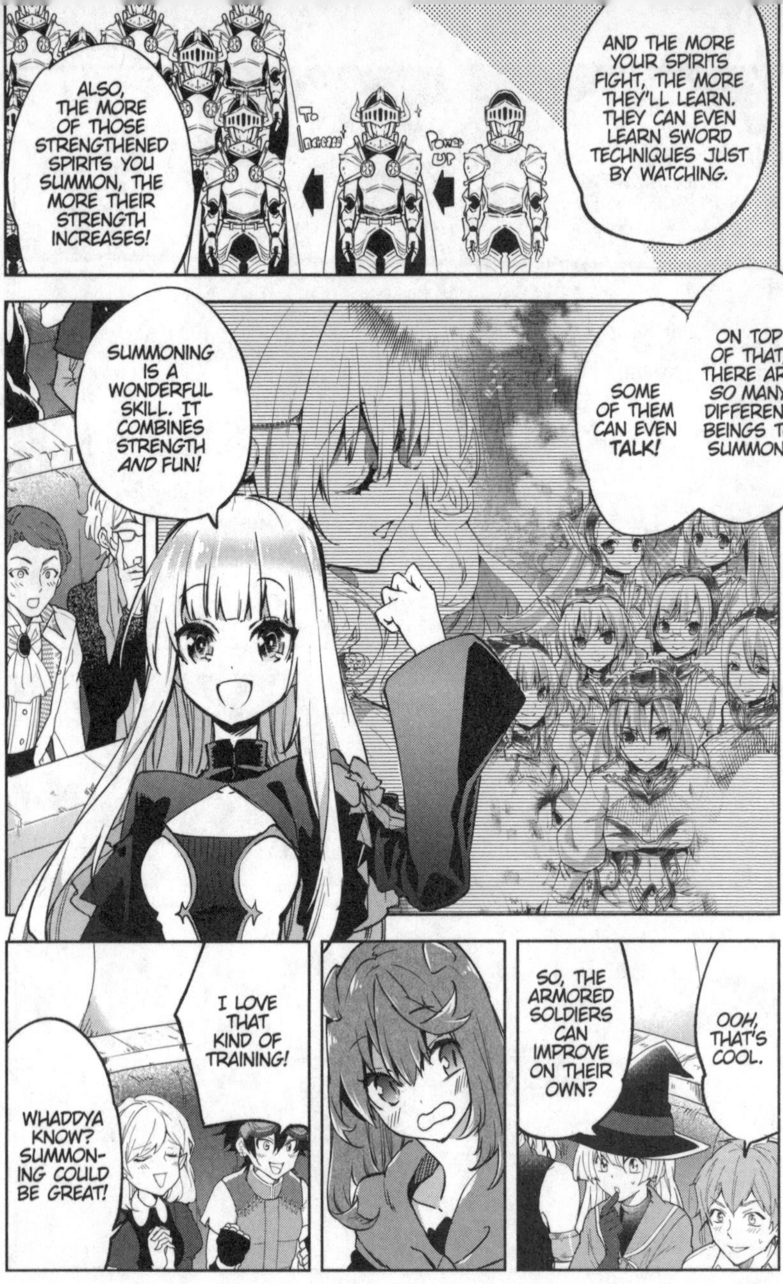
AND THE MORE YOUR SPIRITS FIGHT, THE MORE THEY'LL LEARN. THEY CAN EVEN LEARN SWORD TECHNIQUES JUST BY WATCHING.
Power Up
To Increase
ALSO, THE MORE OF THOSE STRENGTHENED SPIRITS YOU SUMMON, THE MORE THEIR STRENGTH INCREASES!
ON TOP OF THAT, THERE ARE SO MANY DIFFERENT BEINGS TO SUMMON!
SOME OF THEM CAN EVEN TALK!
SUMMONING IS A WONDERFUL SKILL. IT COMBINES STRENGTH AND FUN!
OOH, THAT'S COOL.
SO, THE ARMORED SOLDIERS CAN IMPROVE ON THEIR OWN?
I LOVE THAT KIND OF TRAINING!
WHADDYA KNOW? SUMMONING COULD BE GREAT!

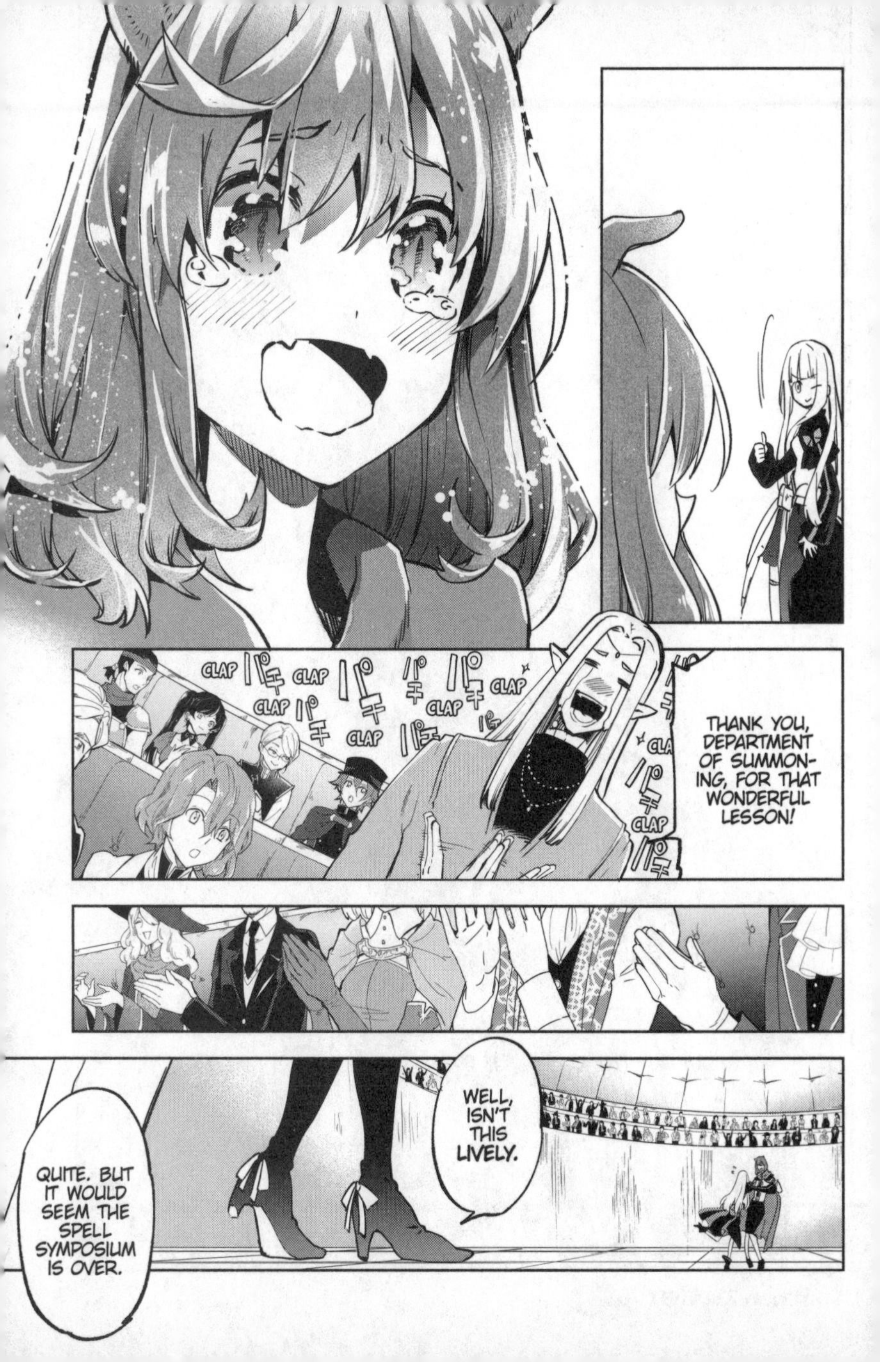
THANK YOU, DEPARTMENT OF SUMMONING, FOR THAT WONDERFUL LESSON!
CLAP パチ
CLAP パチ
CLAP パチ
WELL, ISN'T THIS LIVELY.
QUITE. BUT IT WOULD SEEM THE SPELL SYMPOSIUM IS OVER.

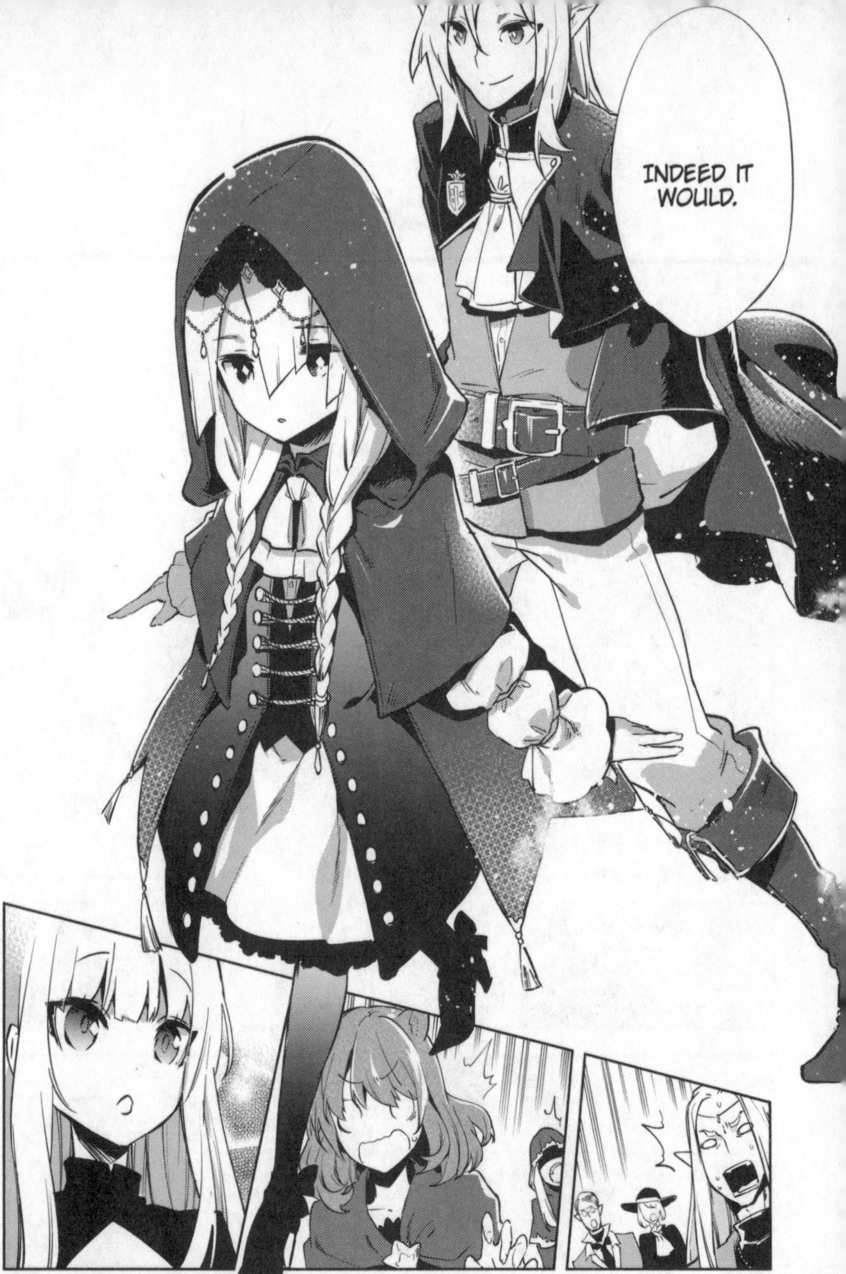
INDEED IT WOULD.

Summon 25: END

She
Professed
Herself
Pupil of the
Wise Man

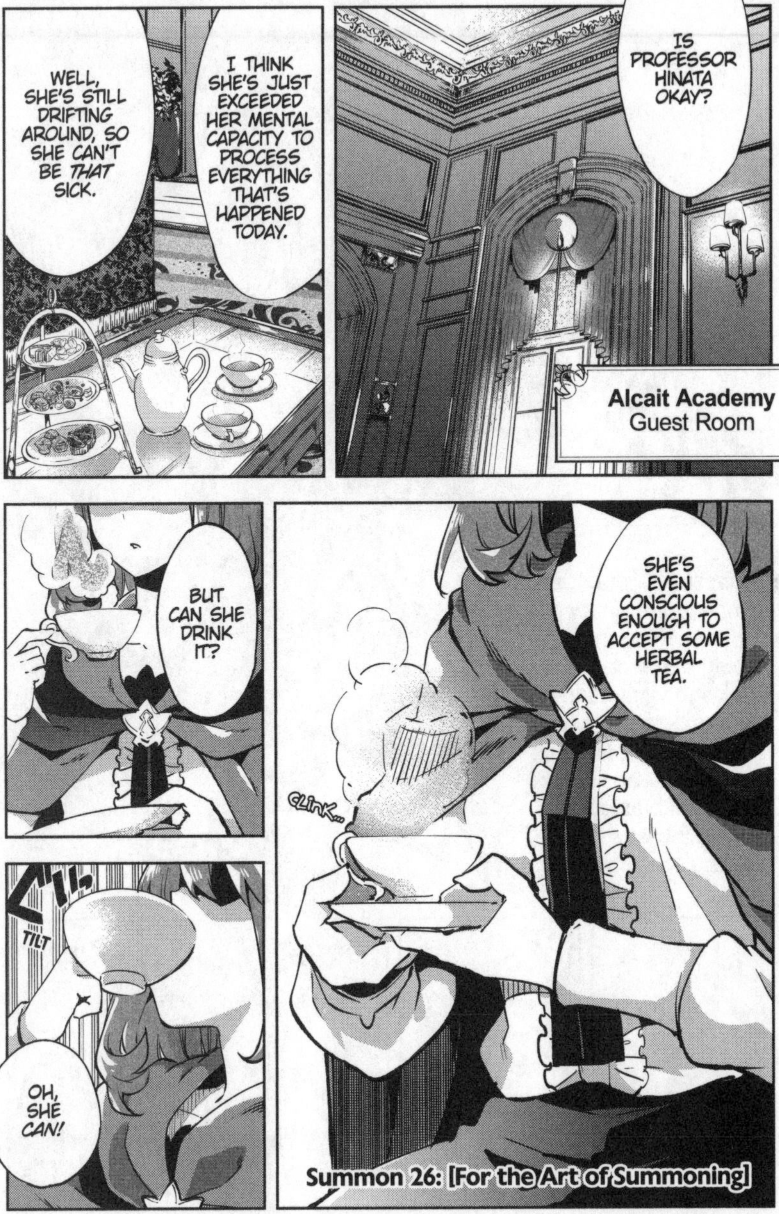
IS PROFESSOR HINATA OKAY?
Alcait Academy
Guest Room
I THINK SHE'S JUST EXCEEDED HER MENTAL CAPACITY TO PROCESS EVERYTHING THAT'S HAPPENED TODAY.
WELL, SHE'S STILL DRIFTING AROUND, SO SHE CAN'T BE *THAT* SICK.
SHE'S EVEN CONSCIOUS ENOUGH TO ACCEPT SOME HERBAL TEA.
CLINK...
Summon 26: [For the Art of Summoning]
BUT CAN SHE DRINK IT?
TILT
OH, SHE *CAN*!

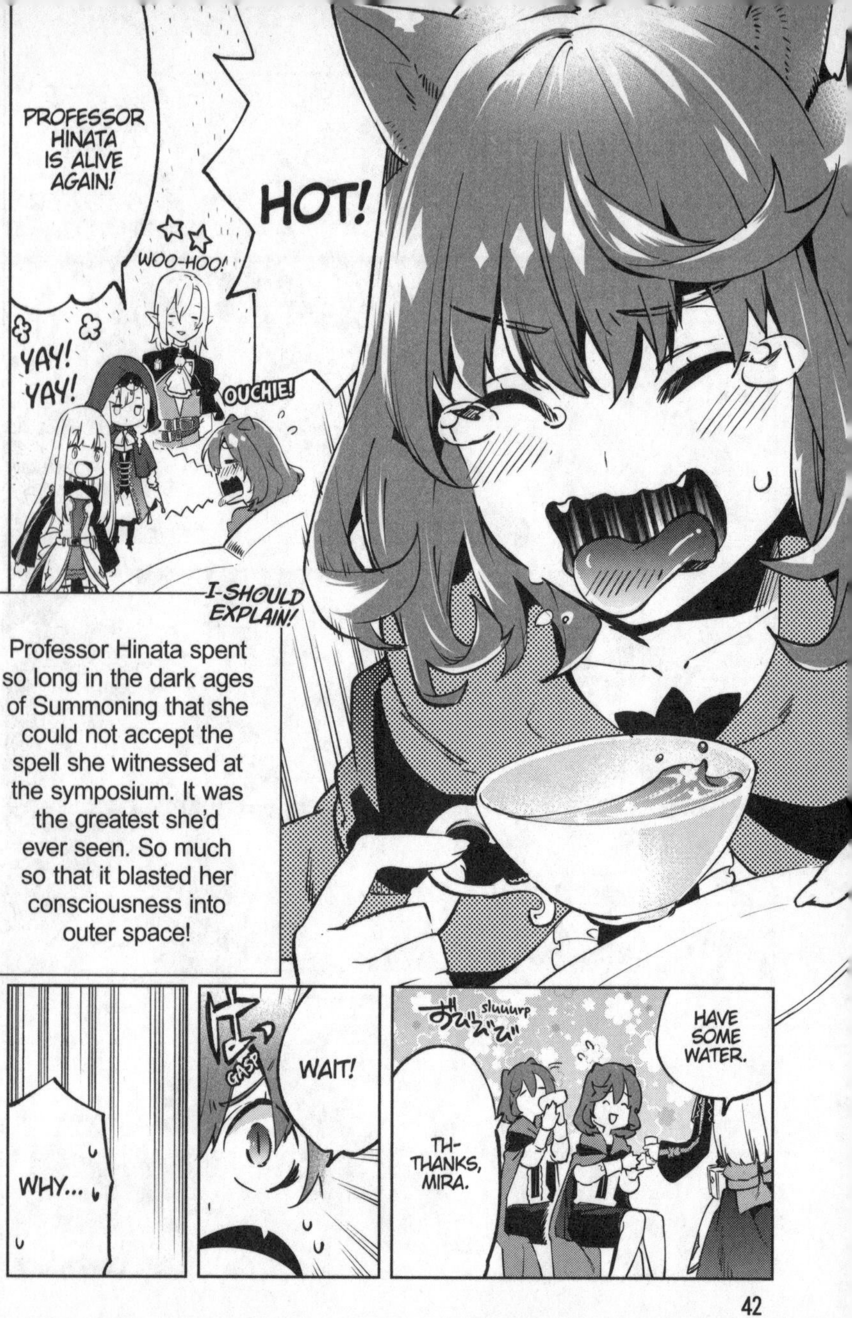

HOT!
PROFESSOR HINATA IS ALIVE AGAIN!
WOO-HOO!
YAY! YAY!
OUCHIE!
I-SHOULD EXPLAIN!
Professor Hinata spent so long in the dark ages of Summoning that she could not accept the spell she witnessed at the symposium. It was the greatest she'd ever seen. So much so that it blasted her consciousness into outer space!
HAVE SOME WATER.
sluuurp
TH-THANKS, MIRA.
GASP
WAIT!
WHY...

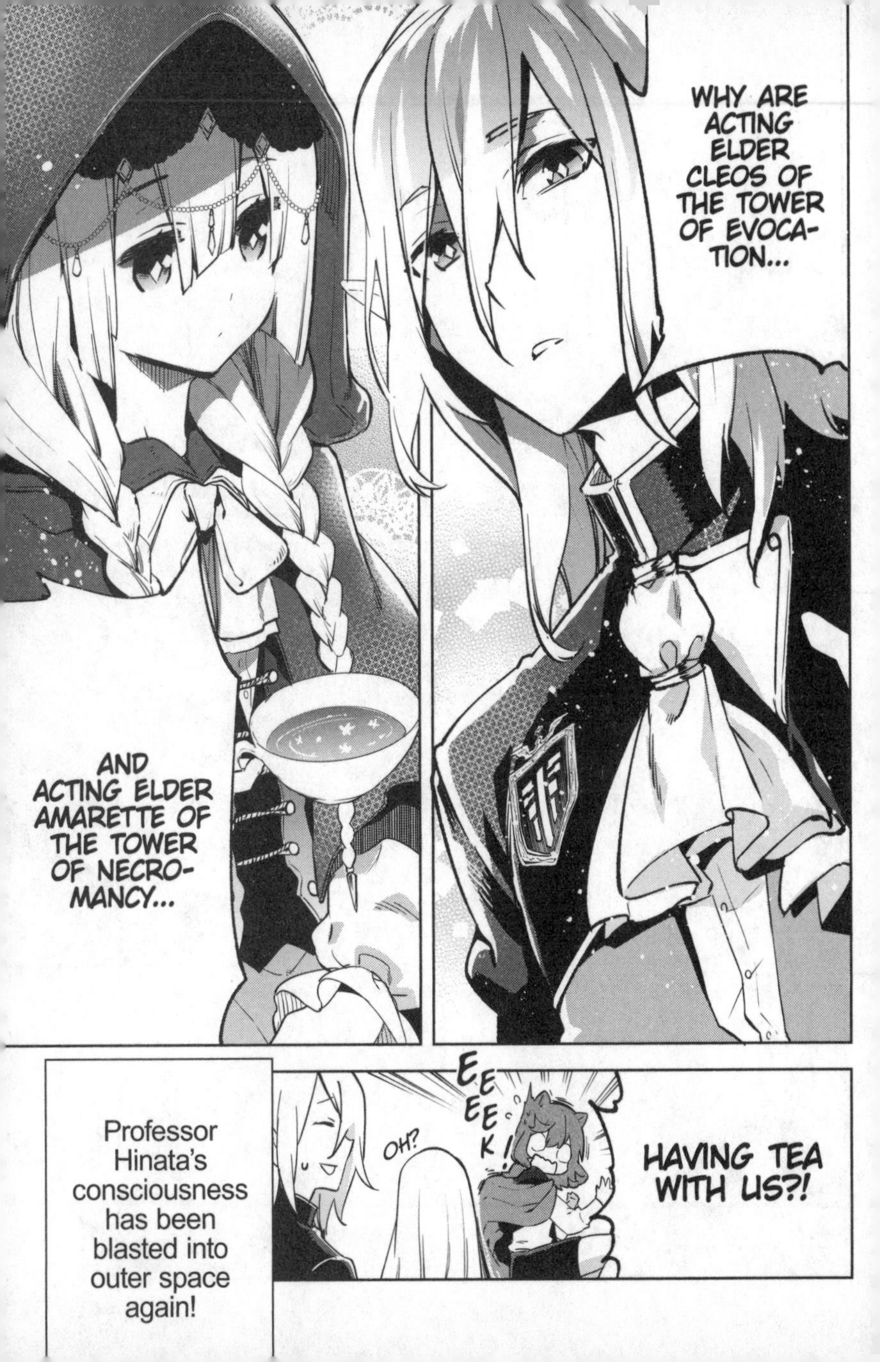
WHY ARE ACTING ELDER CLEOS OF THE TOWER OF EVOCA-TION...
AND ACTING ELDER AMARETTE OF THE TOWER OF NECRO-MANCY...
HAVING TEA WITH US?!
EEEEK!
OH?
Professor Hinata's consciousness has been blasted into outer space again!

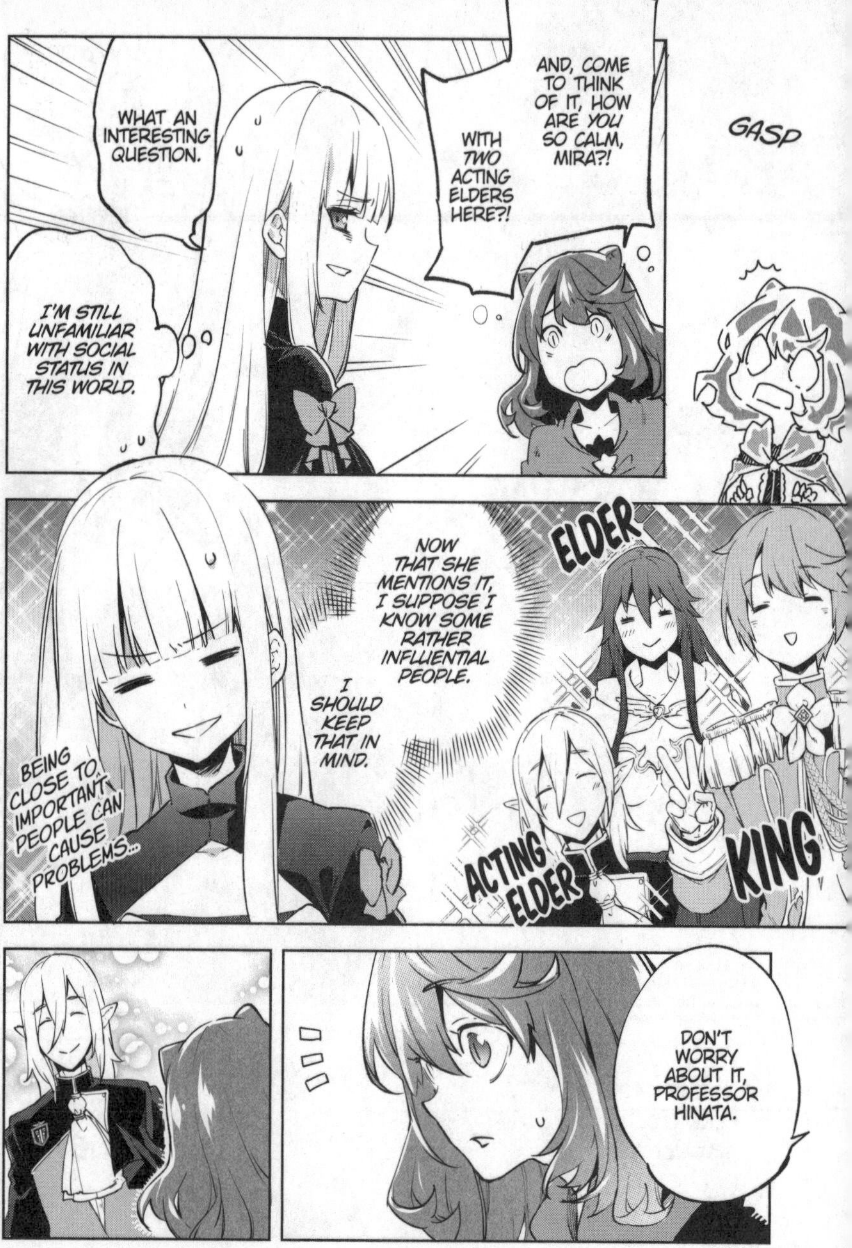
GASP
AND, COME TO THINK OF IT, HOW ARE YOU SO CALM, MIRA?!
WITH TWO ACTING ELDERS HERE?!
WHAT AN INTERESTING QUESTION.
I'M STILL UNFAMILIAR WITH SOCIAL STATUS IN THIS WORLD.
ELDER
KING
NOW THAT SHE MENTIONS IT, I SUPPOSE I KNOW SOME RATHER INFLUENTIAL PEOPLE.
ACTING ELDER
I SHOULD KEEP THAT IN MIND.
BEING CLOSE TO IMPORTANT PEOPLE CAN CAUSE PROBLEMS...
DON'T WORRY ABOUT IT, PROFESSOR HINATA.

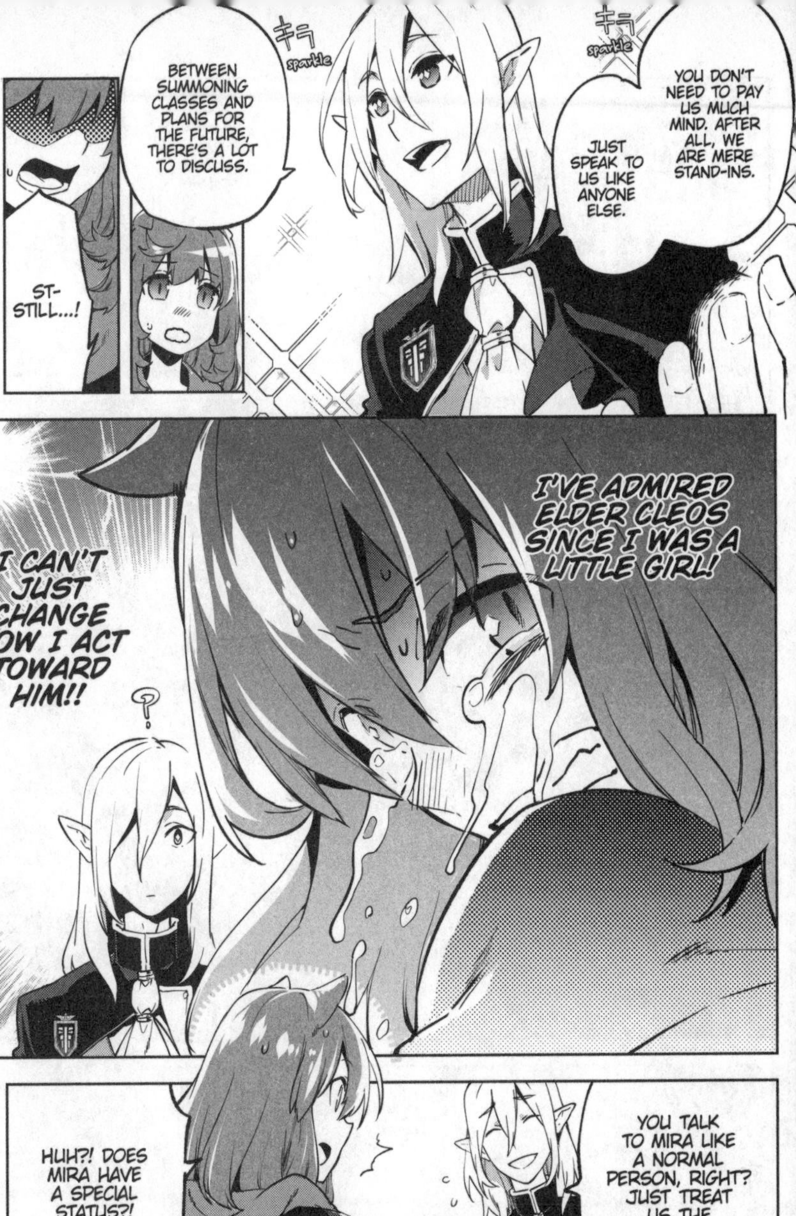
キラ
sparkle
YOU DON'T NEED TO PAY US MUCH MIND. AFTER ALL, WE ARE MERE STAND-INS.
JUST SPEAK TO US LIKE ANYONE ELSE.
キラ
sparkle
BETWEEN SUMMONING CLASSES AND PLANS FOR THE FUTURE, THERE'S A LOT TO DISCUSS.
ST- STILL...!
I'VE ADMIRED ELDER CLEOS SINCE I WAS A LITTLE GIRL!
I CAN'T JUST CHANGE HOW I ACT TOWARD HIM!!
?
YOU TALK TO MIRA LIKE A NORMAL PERSON, RIGHT? JUST TREAT US THE SAME WAY.
HUH?! DOES MIRA HAVE A SPECIAL STATUS?!

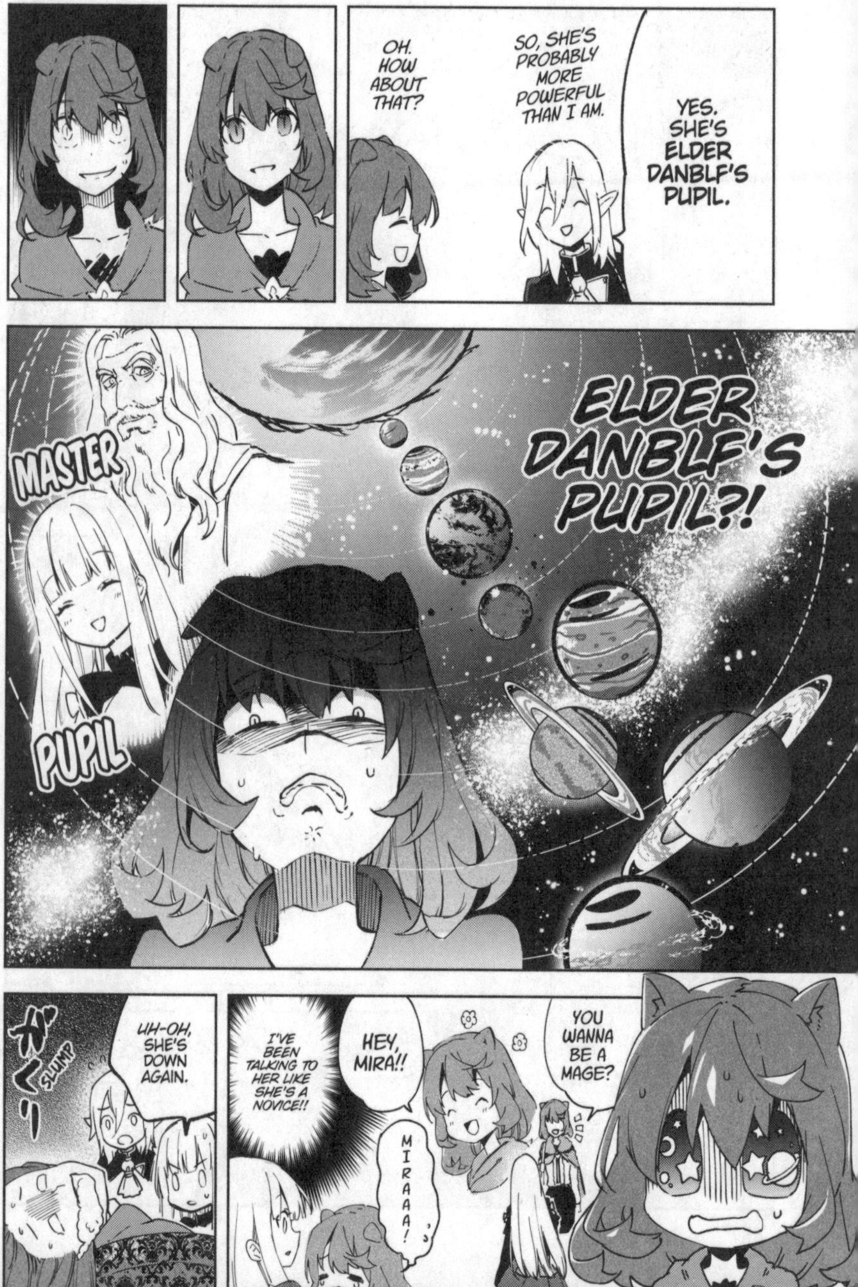
YES. SHE'S ELDER DANBLF'S PUPIL.
SO, SHE'S PROBABLY MORE POWERFUL THAN I AM.
OH. HOW ABOUT THAT?
ELDER DANBLF'S PUPIL?!
MASTER
PUPIL
YOU WANNA BE A MAGE?
HEY, MIRA!!
I'VE BEEN TALKING TO HER LIKE SHE'S A NOVICE!!
MIRAAAA!
UH-OH, SHE'S DOWN AGAIN.
SLUMP

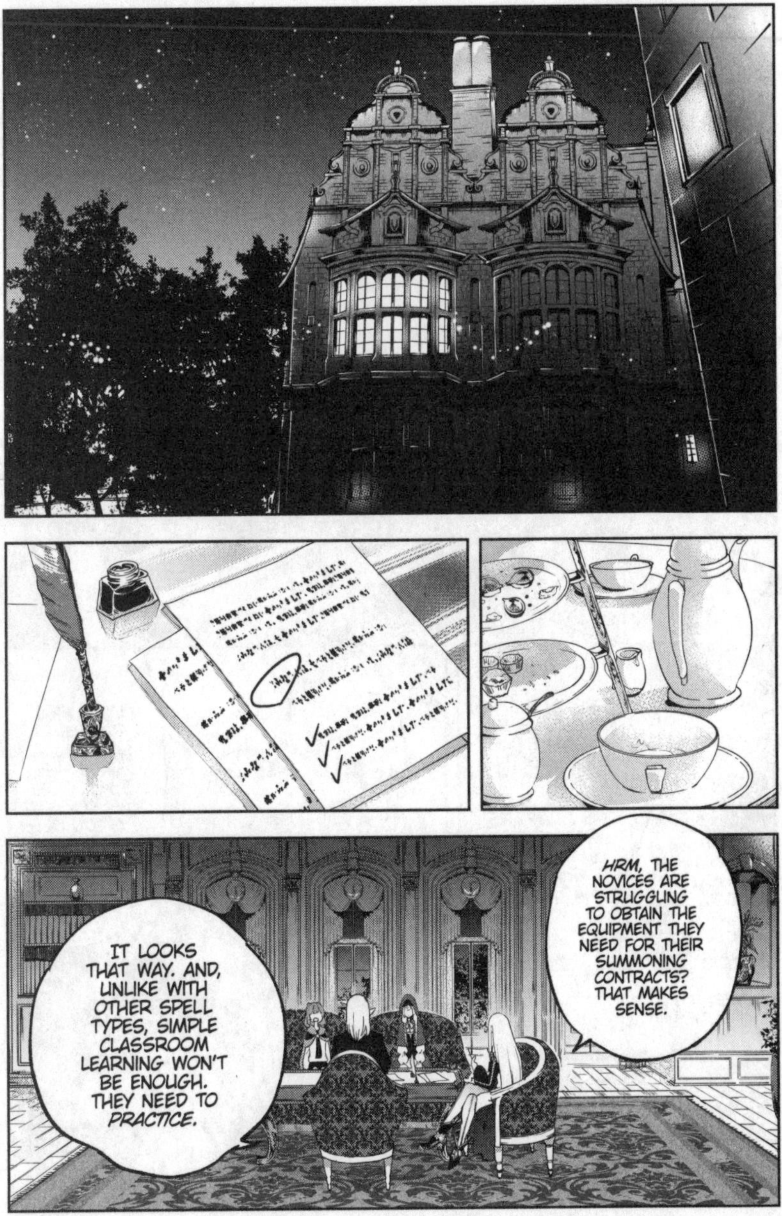
HRM, THE NOVICES ARE STRUGGLING TO OBTAIN THE EQUIPMENT THEY NEED FOR THEIR SUMMONING CONTRACTS? THAT MAKES SENSE.
IT LOOKS THAT WAY. AND, UNLIKE WITH OTHER SPELL TYPES, SIMPLE CLASSROOM LEARNING WON'T BE ENOUGH. THEY NEED TO PRACTICE.

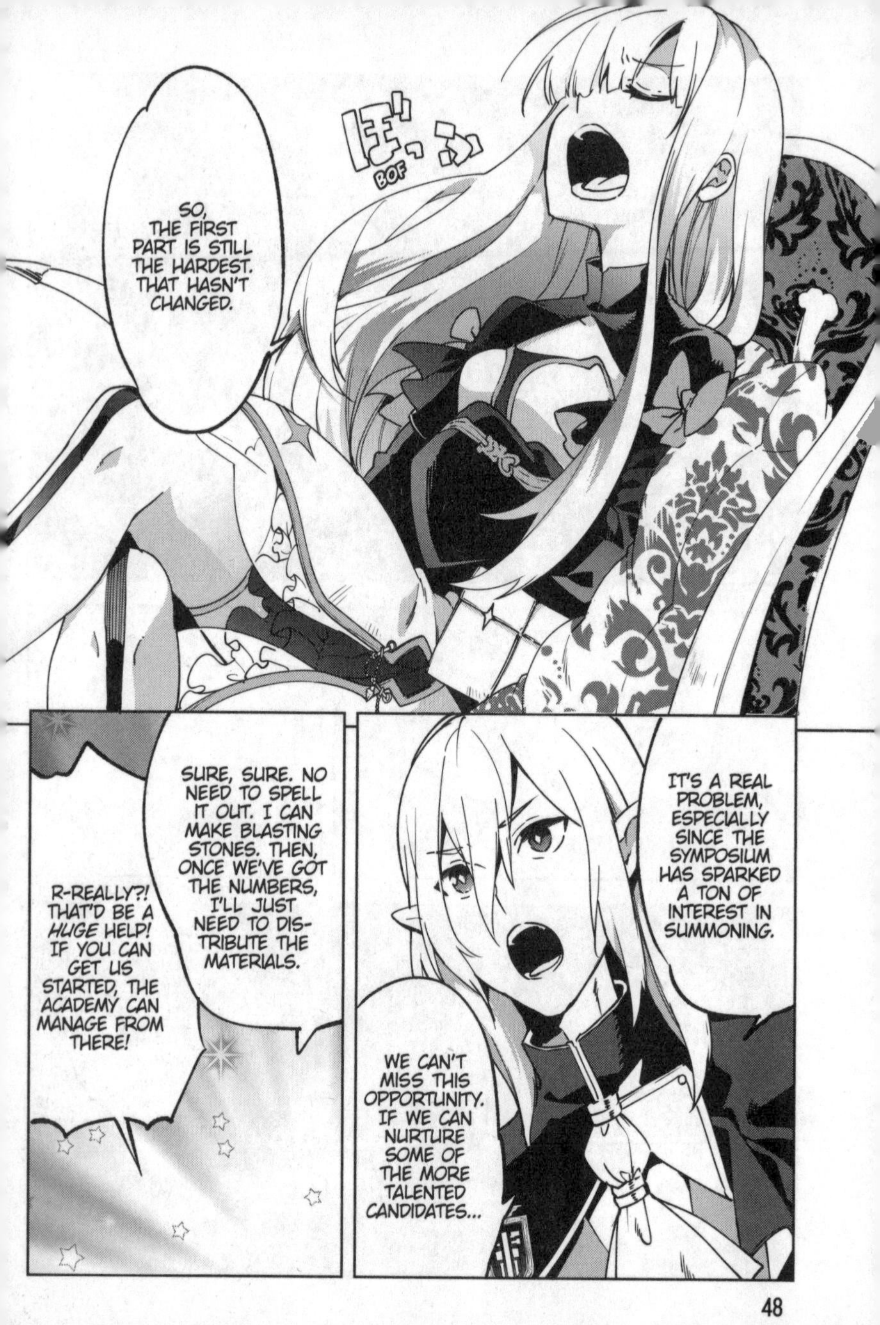
BOF
SO, THE FIRST PART IS STILL THE HARDEST. THAT HASN'T CHANGED.
IT'S A REAL PROBLEM, ESPECIALLY SINCE THE SYMPOSIUM HAS SPARKED A TON OF INTEREST IN SUMMONING.
WE CAN'T MISS THIS OPPORTUNITY. IF WE CAN NURTURE SOME OF THE MORE TALENTED CANDIDATES...
SURE, SURE. NO NEED TO SPELL IT OUT. I CAN MAKE BLASTING STONES. THEN, ONCE WE'VE GOT THE NUMBERS, I'LL JUST NEED TO DIS-TRIBUTE THE MATERIALS.
R-REALLY?! THAT'D BE A *HUGE* HELP! IF YOU CAN GET US STARTED, THE ACADEMY CAN MANAGE FROM THERE!

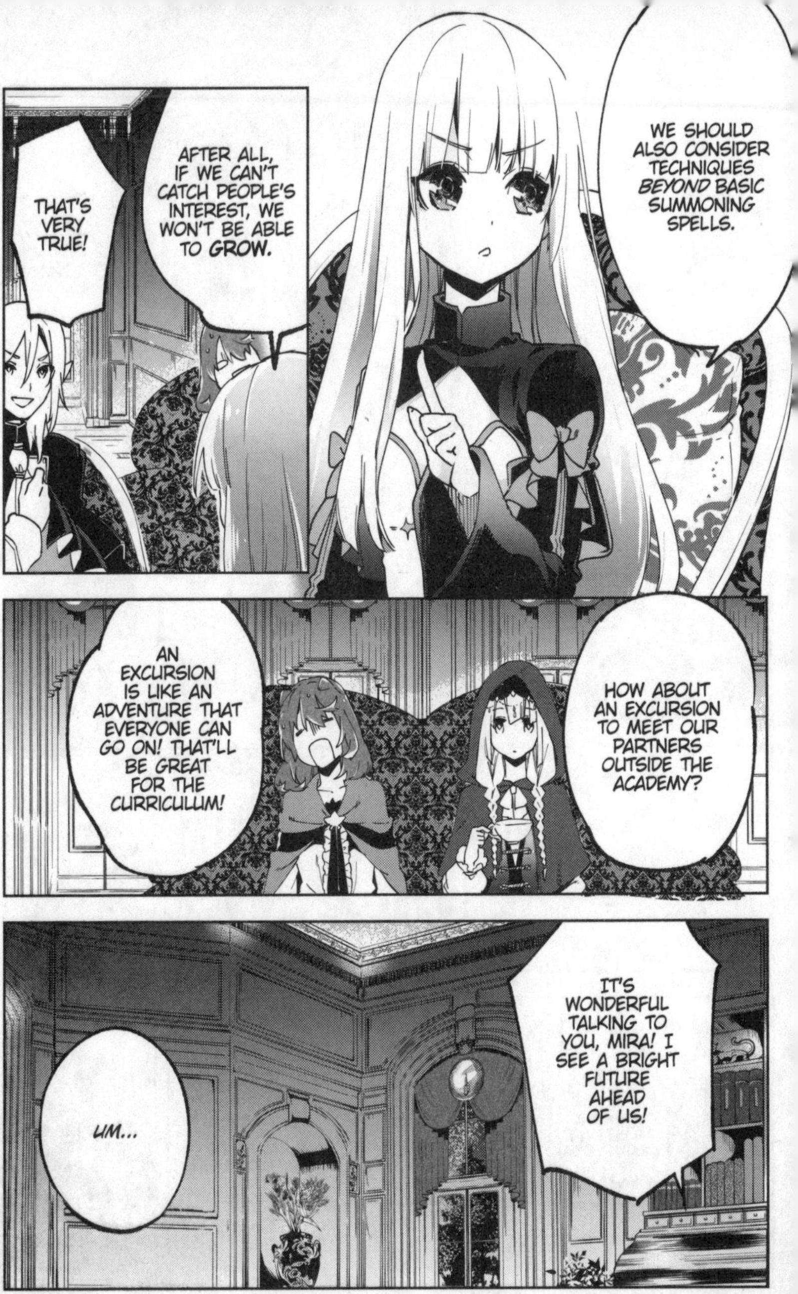
WE SHOULD ALSO CONSIDER TECHNIQUES *BEYOND* BASIC SUMMONING SPELLS.
AFTER ALL, IF WE CAN'T CATCH PEOPLE'S INTEREST, WE WON'T BE ABLE TO **GROW**.
THAT'S VERY TRUE!
HOW ABOUT AN EXCURSION TO MEET OUR PARTNERS OUTSIDE THE ACADEMY?
AN EXCURSION IS LIKE AN ADVENTURE THAT EVERYONE CAN GO ON! THAT'LL BE GREAT FOR THE CURRICULUM!
IT'S WONDERFUL TALKING TO YOU, MIRA! I SEE A BRIGHT FUTURE AHEAD OF US!
UM...

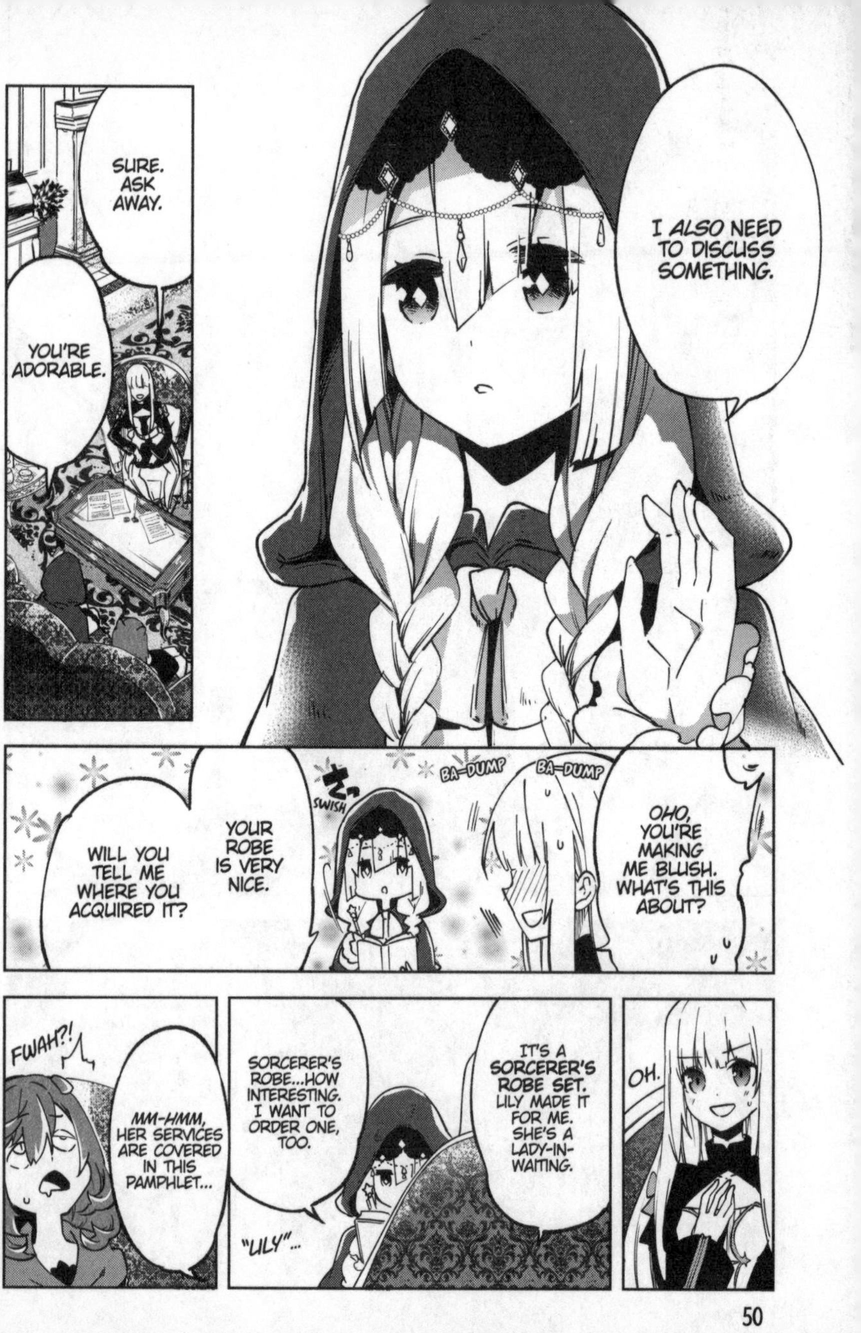
I *ALSO* NEED TO DISCUSS SOMETHING.
SURE. ASK AWAY.
YOU'RE ADORABLE.
BA-DUMP
BA-DUMP
OHO, YOU'RE MAKING ME BLUSH. WHAT'S THIS ABOUT?
SWISH
YOUR ROBE IS VERY NICE.
WILL YOU TELL ME WHERE YOU ACQUIRED IT?
OH.
IT'S A SORCERER'S ROBE SET. LILY MADE IT FOR ME. SHE'S A LADY-IN-WAITING.
SORCERER'S ROBE...HOW INTERESTING. I WANT TO ORDER ONE, TOO.
"LILY"...
FWAH?!
MM-HMM, HER SERVICES ARE COVERED IN THIS PAMPHLET...

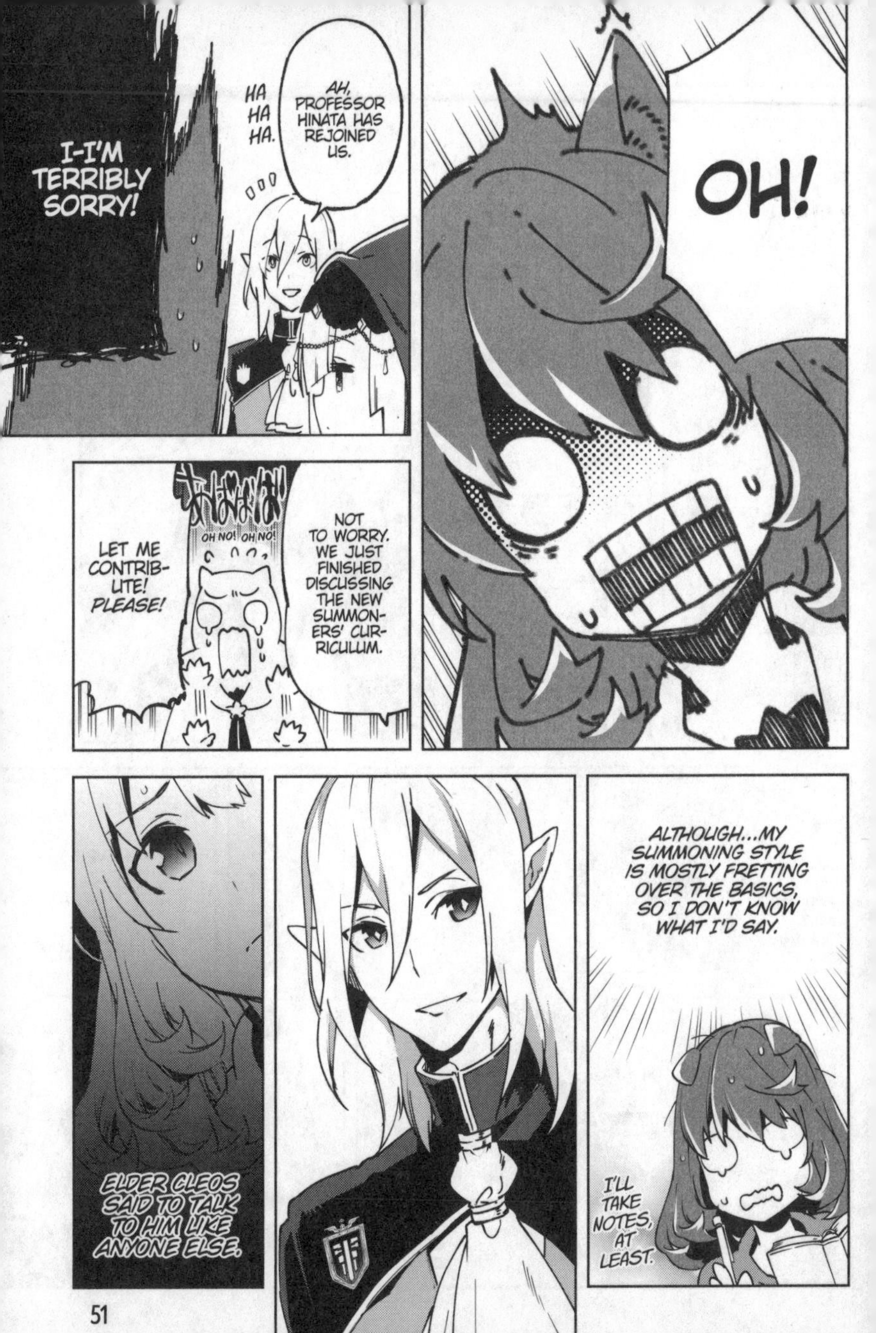
OH!
AH, PROFESSOR HINATA HAS REJOINED US.
HA HA HA.
I-I'M TERRIBLY SORRY!
NOT TO WORRY. WE JUST FINISHED DISCUSSING THE NEW SUMMONERS' CURRICULUM.
OH NO! OH NO!
LET ME CONTRIBUTE! PLEASE!
ALTHOUGH...MY SUMMONING STYLE IS MOSTLY FRETTING OVER THE BASICS, SO I DON'T KNOW WHAT I'D SAY.
I'LL TAKE NOTES, AT LEAST.
ELDER CLEOS SAID TO TALK TO HIM LIKE ANYONE ELSE.

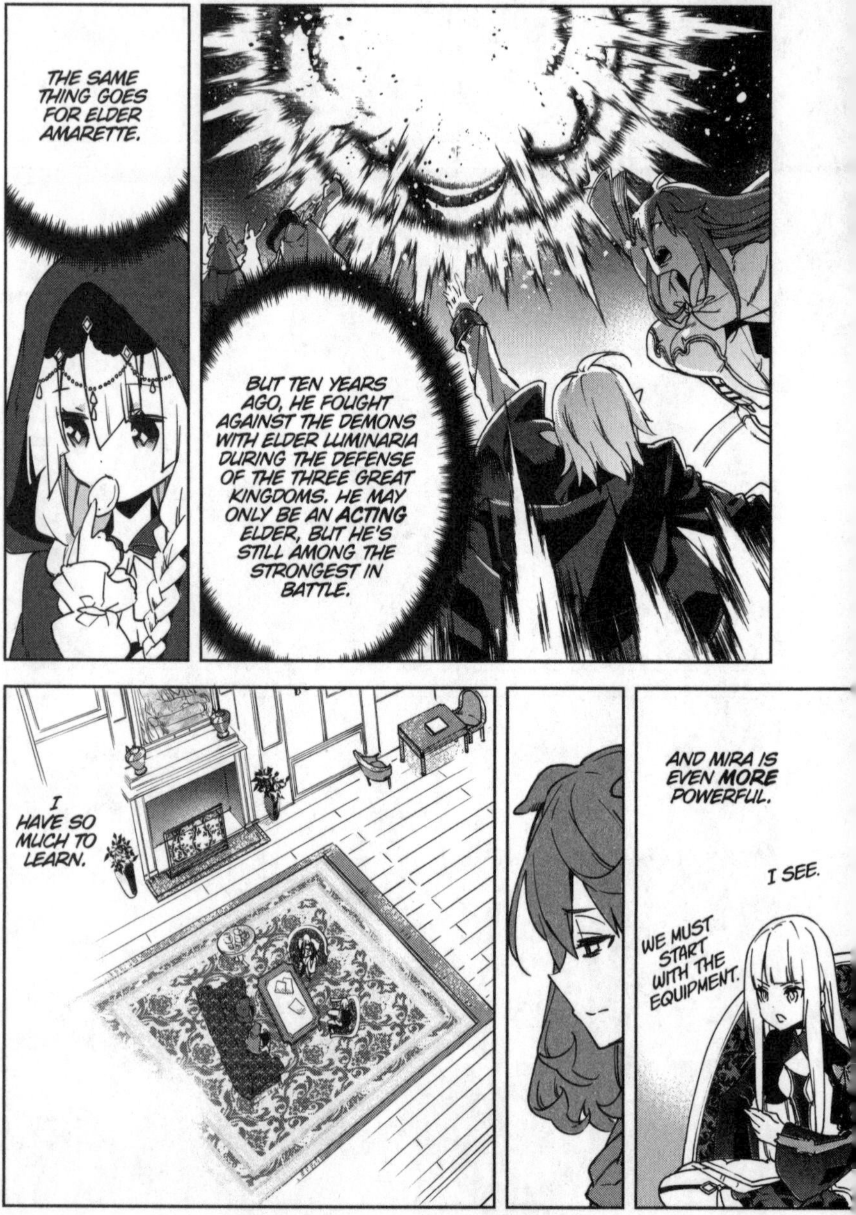
BUT TEN YEARS AGO, HE FOUGHT AGAINST THE DEMONS WITH ELDER LUMINARIA DURING THE DEFENSE OF THE THREE GREAT KINGDOMS. HE MAY ONLY BE AN ACTING ELDER, BUT HE'S STILL AMONG THE STRONGEST IN BATTLE.
THE SAME THING GOES FOR ELDER AMARETTE.
AND MIRA IS EVEN MORE POWERFUL.
I SEE.
WE MUST START WITH THE EQUIPMENT.
I HAVE SO MUCH TO LEARN.

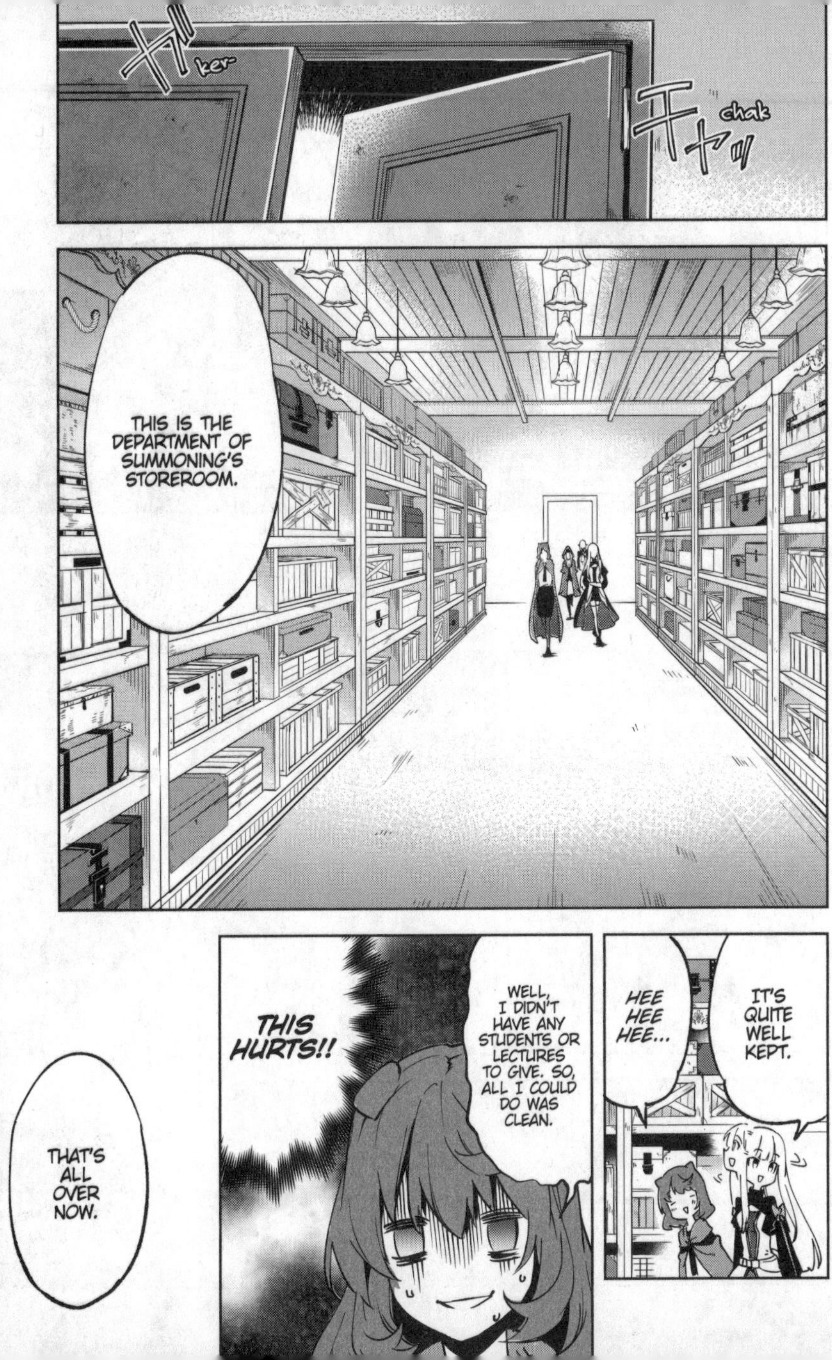
chak
ker-
THIS IS THE DEPARTMENT OF SUMMONING'S STOREROOM.
IT'S QUITE WELL KEPT.
HEE HEE HEE...
WELL, I DIDN'T HAVE ANY STUDENTS OR LECTURES TO GIVE. SO, ALL I COULD DO WAS CLEAN.
THIS HURTS!!
THAT'S ALL OVER NOW.

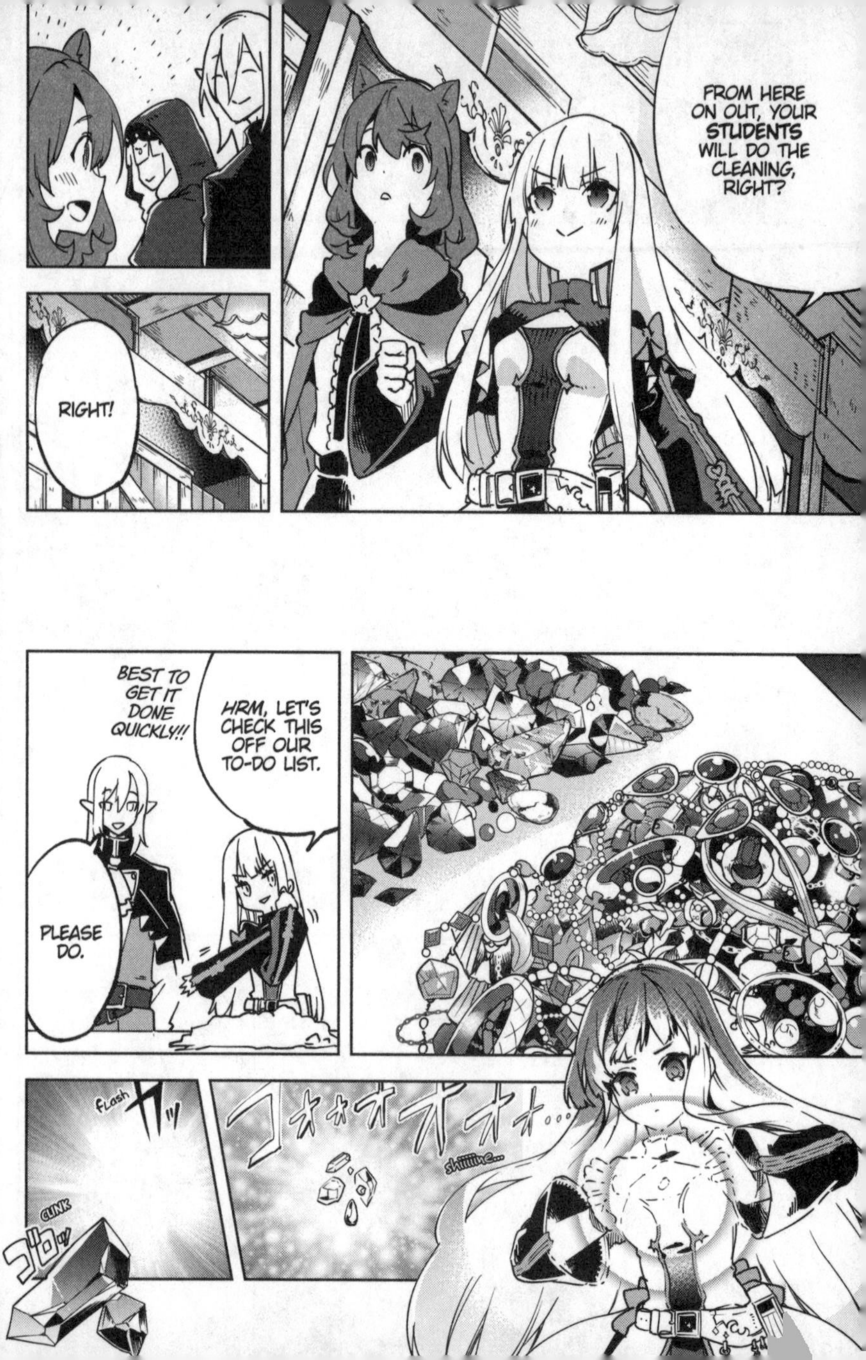
FROM HERE ON OUT, YOUR STUDENTS WILL DO THE CLEANING, RIGHT?
RIGHT!
HRM, LET'S CHECK THIS OFF OUR TO-DO LIST.
BEST TO GET IT DONE QUICKLY!!
PLEASE DO.
shiiiiine...
FLash
ガッ
CLINK
ゴロッ

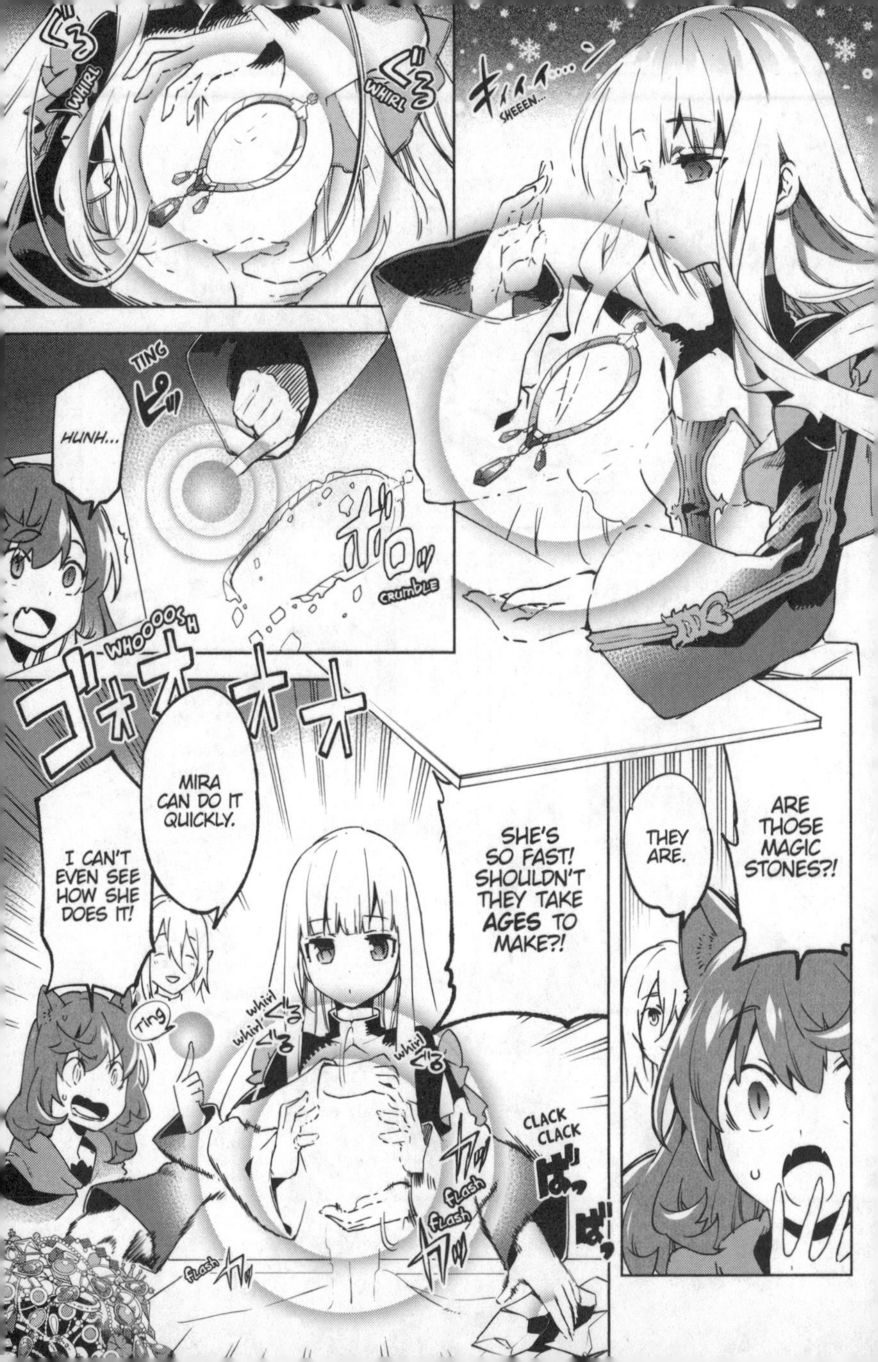
キィィ…ン
SHEEEN...
ぐる
WHIRL
ぐる
WHIRL
TING
ピッ
HUNH...
ボロッ
CRUMBLE
ゴォォォォ
WHOOOOSH
ARE THOSE MAGIC STONES?!
THEY ARE.
SHE'S SO FAST! SHOULDN'T THEY TAKE AGES TO MAKE?!
MIRA CAN DO IT QUICKLY.
I CAN'T EVEN SEE HOW SHE DOES IT!
whirl ぐる
whirl ぐる
whirl ぐる
Ting
CLACK CLACK
ぱっぱっ
FLASH
FLASH
FLASH

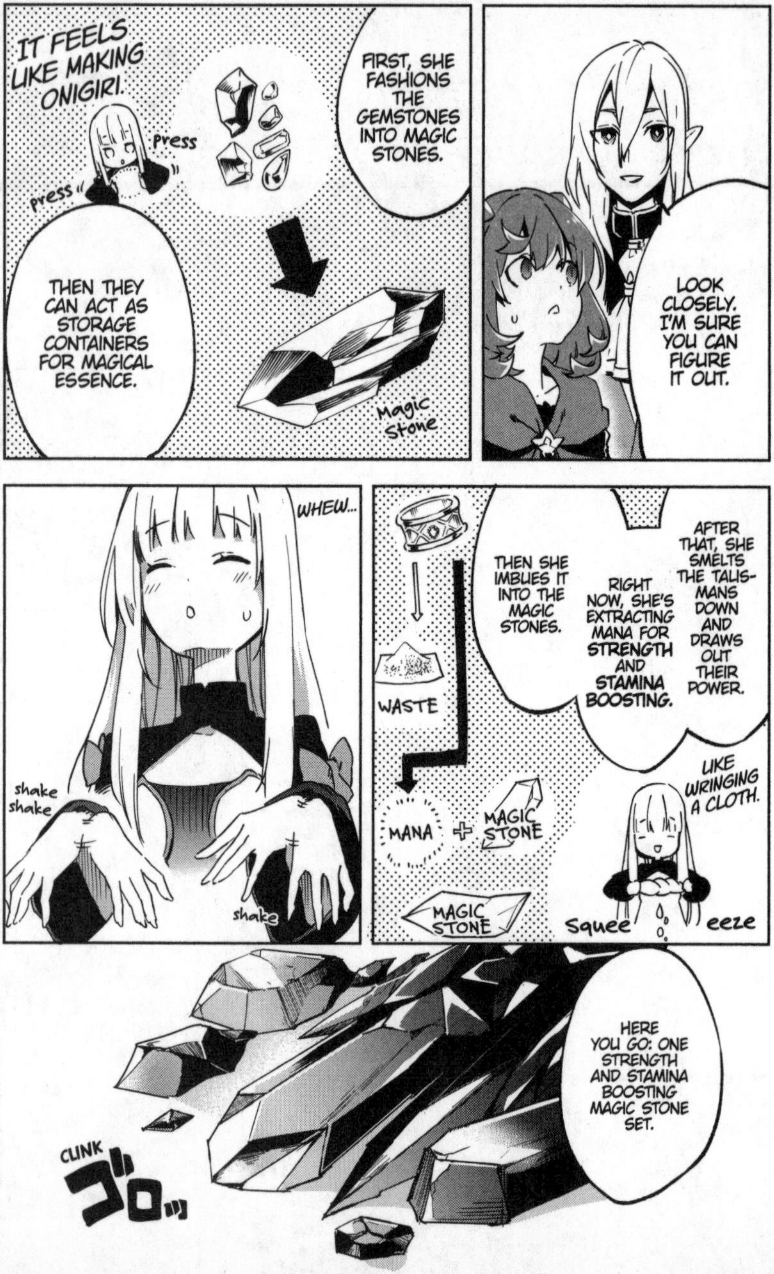
LOOK CLOSELY. I'M SURE YOU CAN FIGURE IT OUT.
FIRST, SHE FASHIONS THE GEMSTONES INTO MAGIC STONES.
IT FEELS LIKE MAKING ONIGIRI.
press
press
THEN THEY CAN ACT AS STORAGE CONTAINERS FOR MAGICAL ESSENCE.
Magic Stone
AFTER THAT, SHE SMELTS THE TALIS-MANS DOWN AND DRAWS OUT THEIR POWER.
RIGHT NOW, SHE'S EXTRACTING MANA FOR STRENGTH AND STAMINA BOOSTING.
THEN SHE IMBUES IT INTO THE MAGIC STONES.
WASTE
MANA + MAGIC STONE
MAGIC STONE
LIKE WRINGING A CLOTH.
Squee eeze
WHEW...
shake shake
shake
HERE YOU GO: ONE STRENGTH AND STAMINA BOOSTING MAGIC STONE SET.
CLINK
ゴロッ

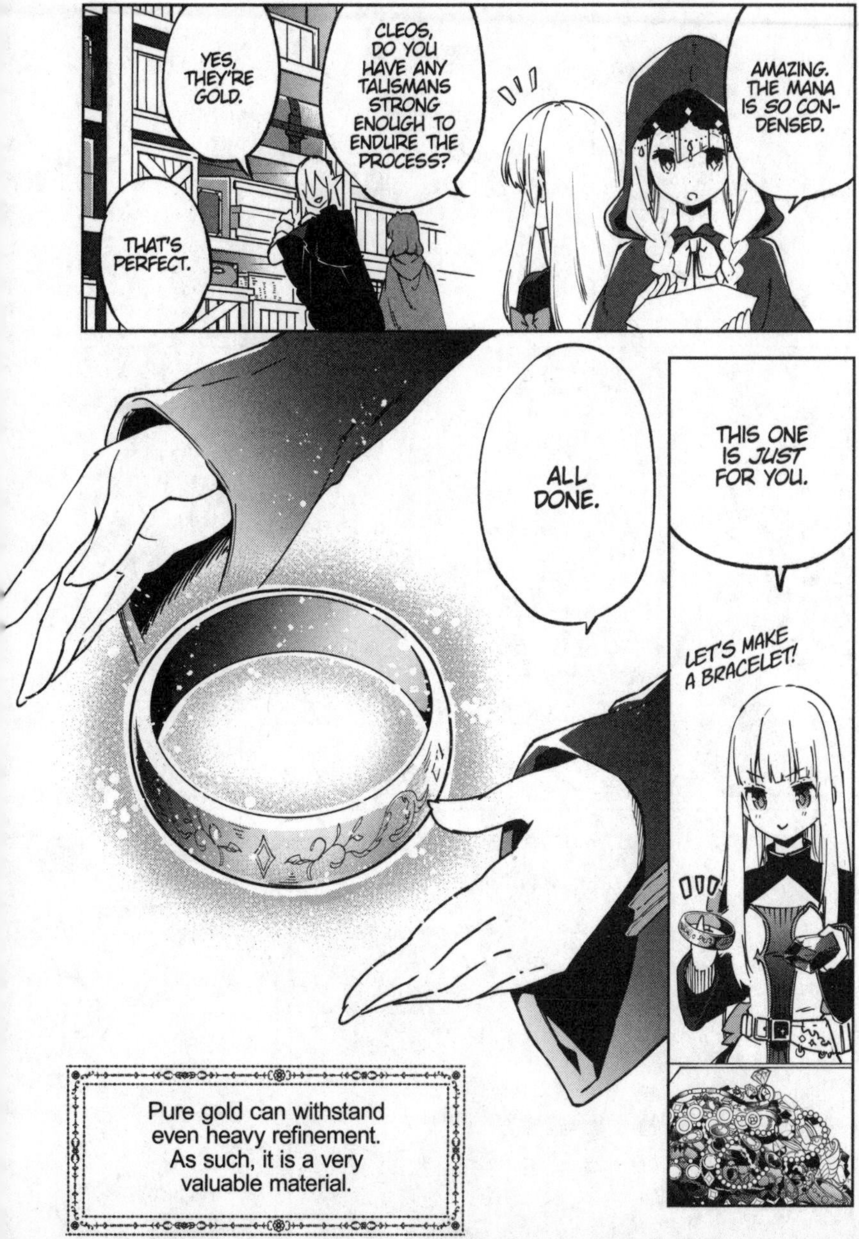
AMAZING. THE MANA IS SO CONDENSED.
CLEOS, DO YOU HAVE ANY TALISMANS STRONG ENOUGH TO ENDURE THE PROCESS?
YES, THEY'RE GOLD.
THAT'S PERFECT.
THIS ONE IS *JUST* FOR YOU.
LET'S MAKE A BRACELET!
ALL DONE.
Pure gold can withstand even heavy refinement. As such, it is a very valuable material.

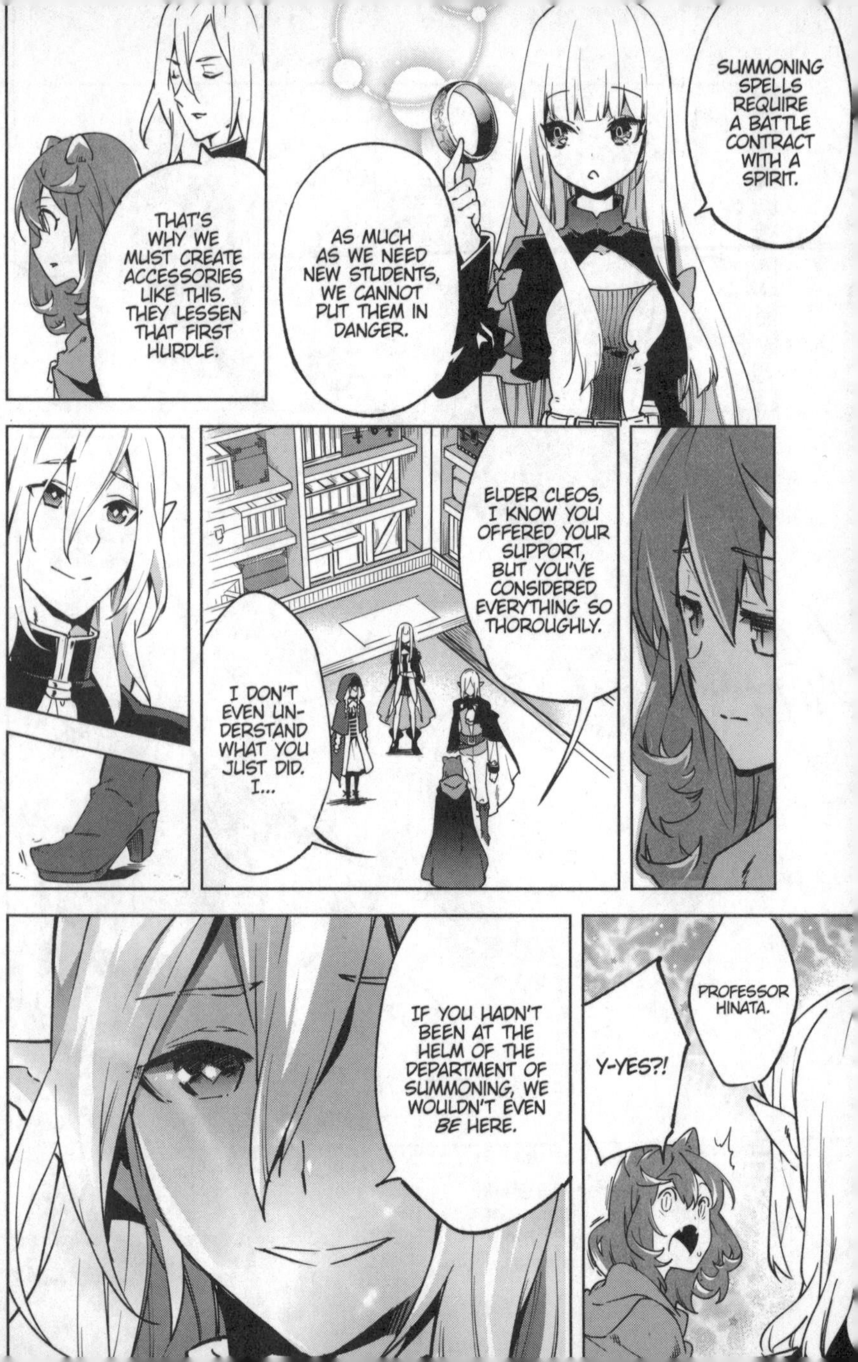
SUMMONING SPELLS REQUIRE A BATTLE CONTRACT WITH A SPIRIT.
AS MUCH AS WE NEED NEW STUDENTS, WE CANNOT PUT THEM IN DANGER.
THAT'S WHY WE MUST CREATE ACCESSORIES LIKE THIS. THEY LESSEN THAT FIRST HURDLE.
ELDER CLEOS, I KNOW YOU OFFERED YOUR SUPPORT, BUT YOU'VE CONSIDERED EVERYTHING SO THOROUGHLY.
I DON'T EVEN UNDERSTAND WHAT YOU JUST DID. I...
PROFESSOR HINATA.
Y-YES?!
IF YOU HADN'T BEEN AT THE HELM OF THE DEPARTMENT OF SUMMONING, WE WOULDN'T EVEN *BE* HERE.

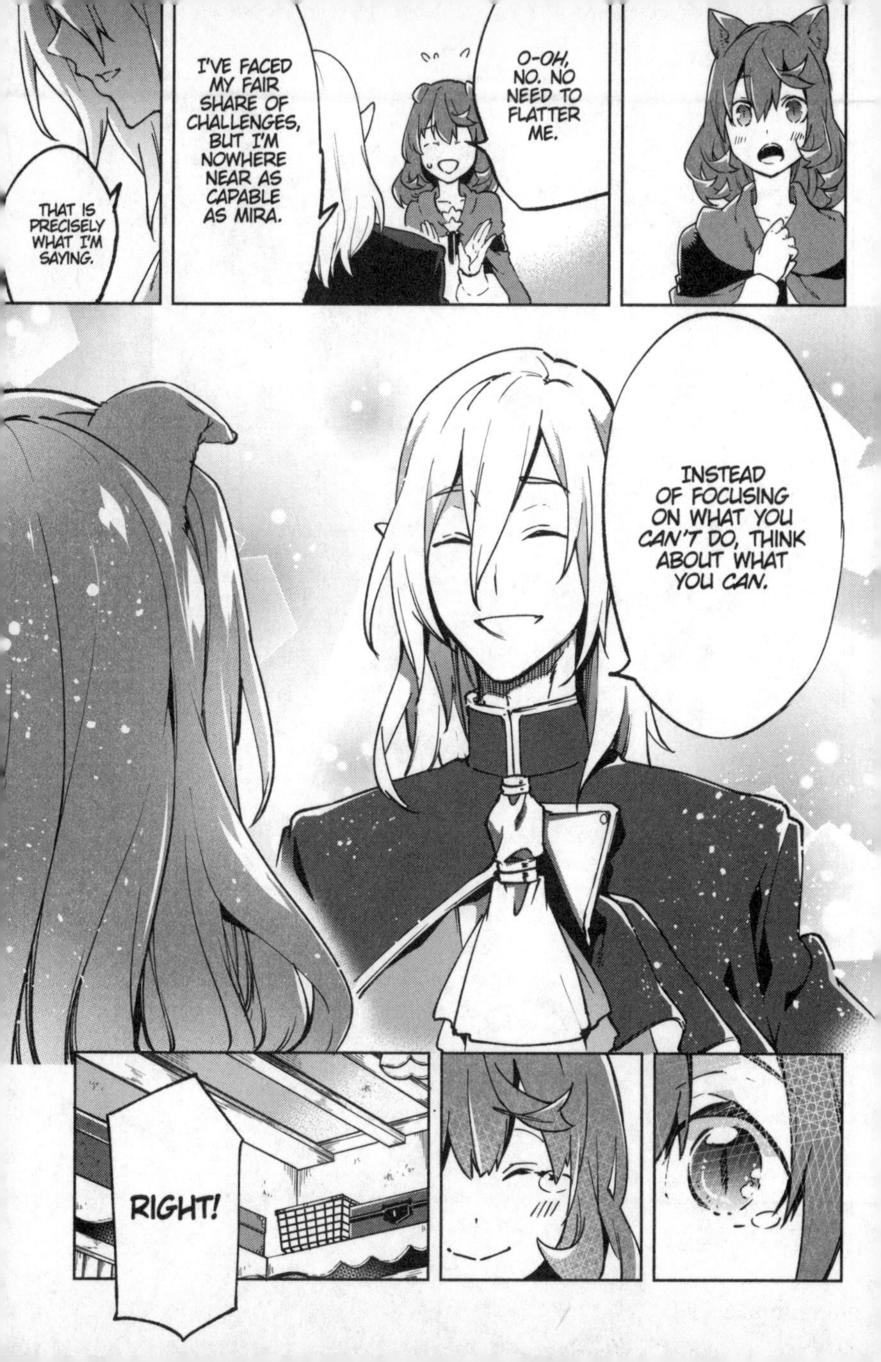
O-OH, NO. NO NEED TO FLATTER ME.
I'VE FACED MY FAIR SHARE OF CHALLENGES, BUT I'M NOWHERE NEAR AS CAPABLE AS MIRA.
THAT IS PRECISELY WHAT I'M SAYING.
INSTEAD OF FOCUSING ON WHAT YOU CAN'T DO, THINK ABOUT WHAT YOU CAN.
RIGHT!

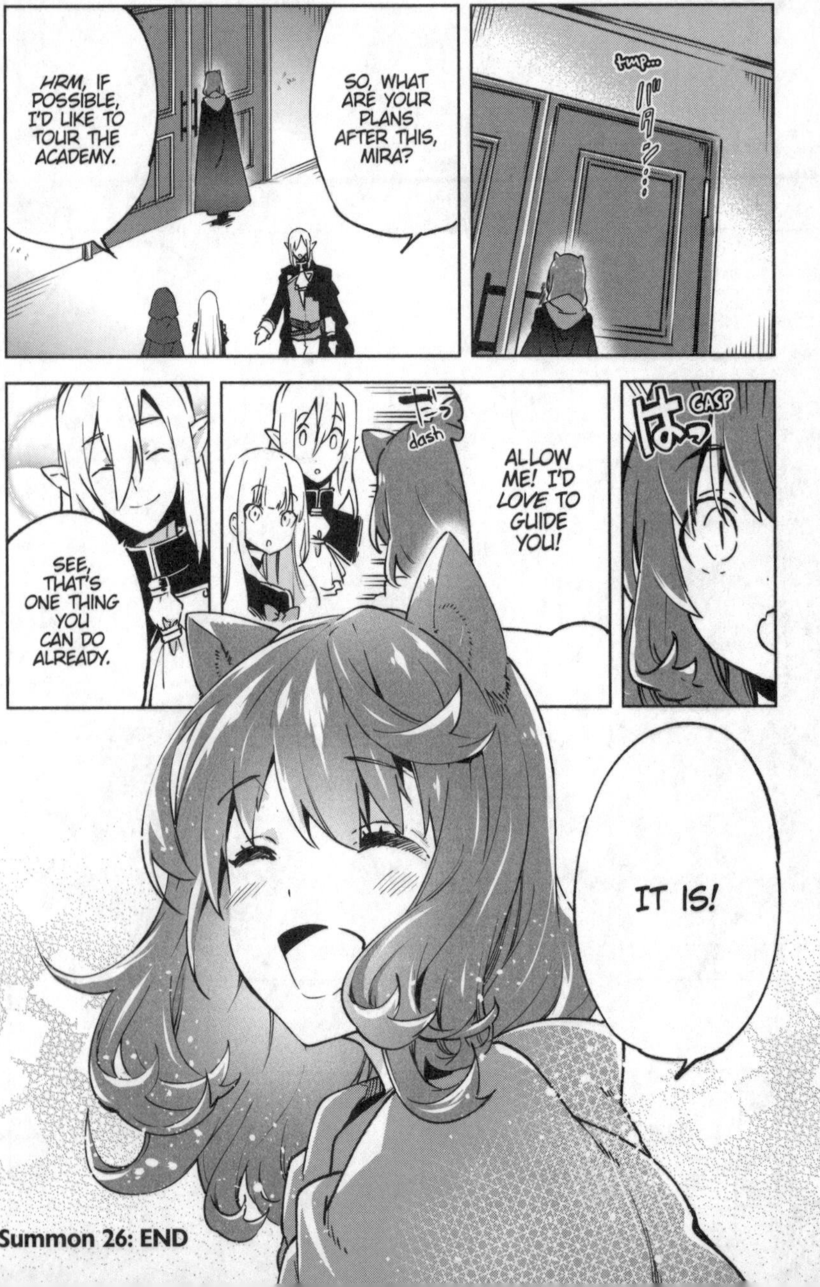
tmp...
バタン...
SO, WHAT ARE YOUR PLANS AFTER THIS, MIRA?
HRM, IF POSSIBLE, I'D LIKE TO TOUR THE ACADEMY.
はっ
GASP
dash
ALLOW ME! I'D *LOVE* TO GUIDE YOU!
SEE, THAT'S ONE THING YOU CAN DO ALREADY.
IT IS!

Summon 26: END

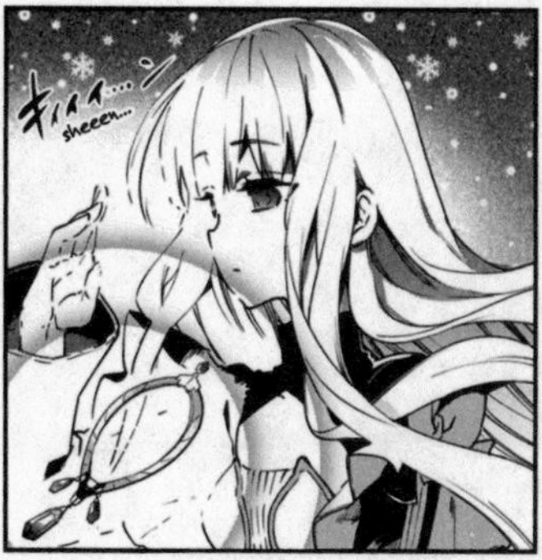
キィィィ…ン
sheeen…

She
Professed
Herself
Pupil of the
Wise Man

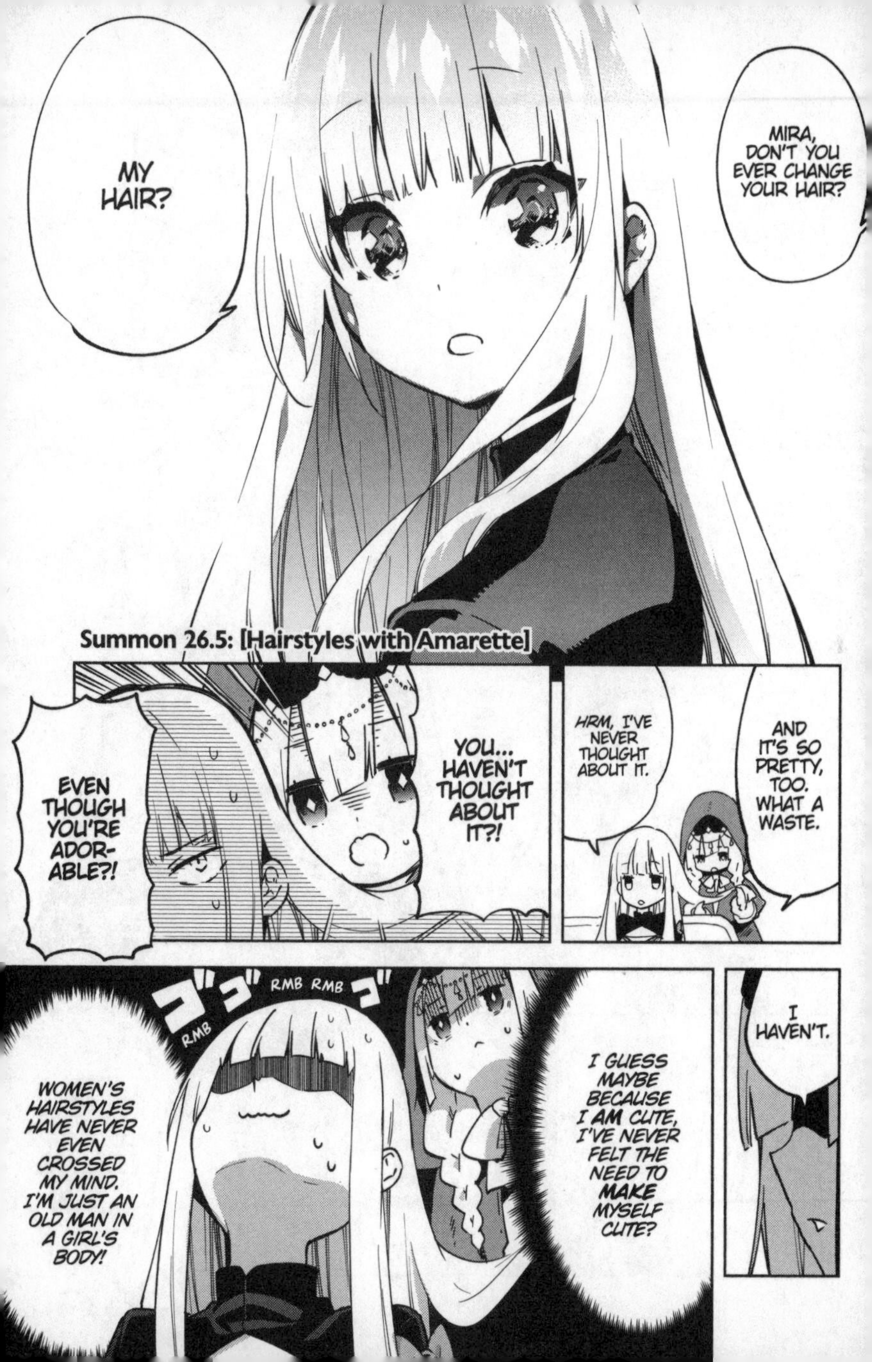
MIRA, DON'T YOU EVER CHANGE YOUR HAIR?
MY HAIR?
Summon 26.5: [Hairstyles with Amarette]
AND IT'S SO PRETTY, TOO. WHAT A WASTE.
HRM, I'VE NEVER THOUGHT ABOUT IT.
YOU... HAVEN'T THOUGHT ABOUT IT?!
EVEN THOUGH YOU'RE ADOR-ABLE?!
I HAVEN'T.
I GUESS MAYBE BECAUSE I AM CUTE, I'VE NEVER FELT THE NEED TO MAKE MYSELF CUTE?
RMB RMB
RMB
WOMEN'S HAIRSTYLES HAVE NEVER EVEN CROSSED MY MIND. I'M JUST AN OLD MAN IN A GIRL'S BODY!

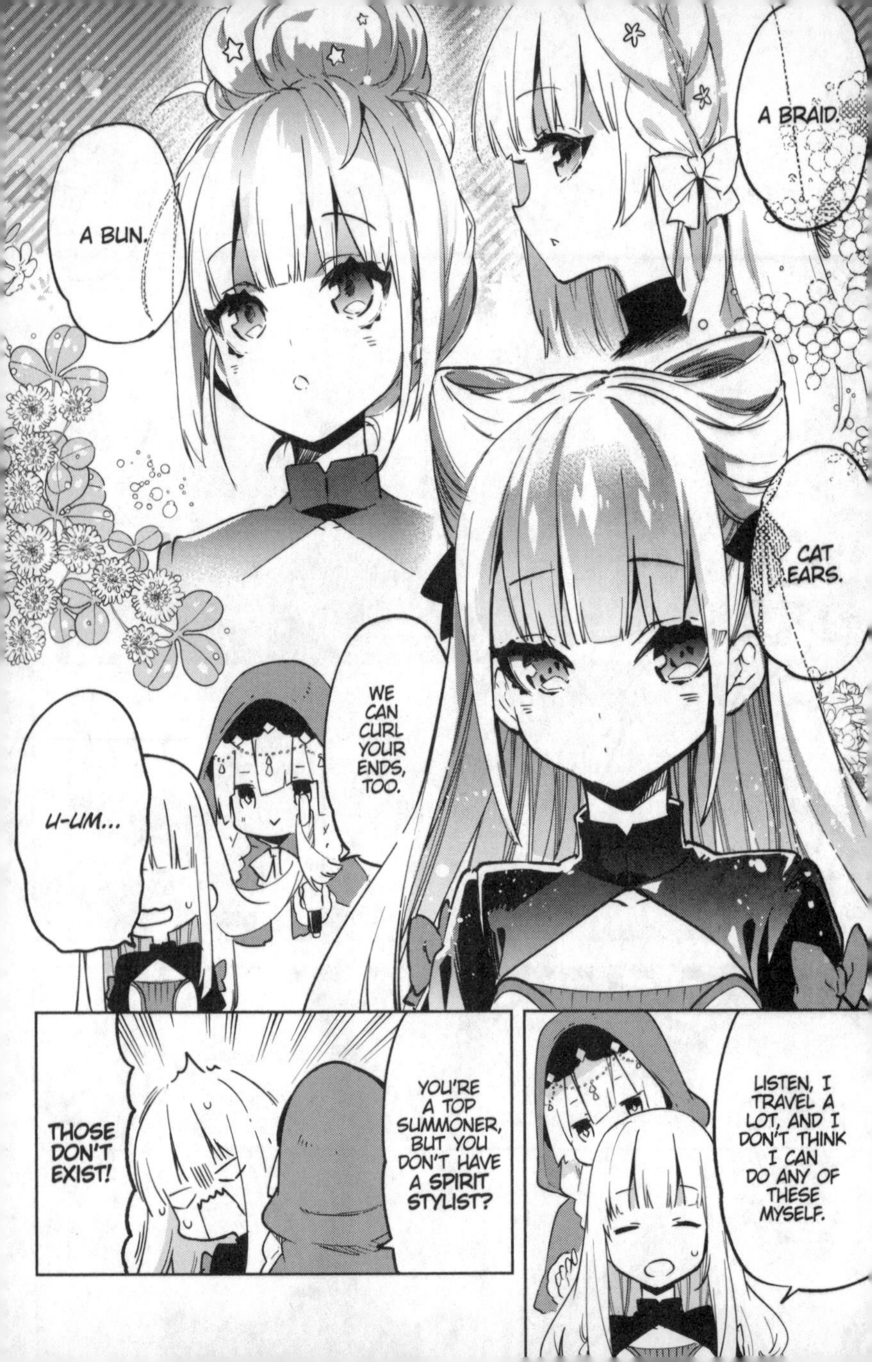
A BRAID.
A BUN.
CAT EARS.
WE CAN CURL YOUR ENDS, TOO.
U-UM...
LISTEN, I TRAVEL A LOT, AND I DON'T THINK I CAN DO ANY OF THESE MYSELF.
YOU'RE A TOP SUMMONER, BUT YOU DON'T HAVE A SPIRIT STYLIST?
THOSE DON'T EXIST!

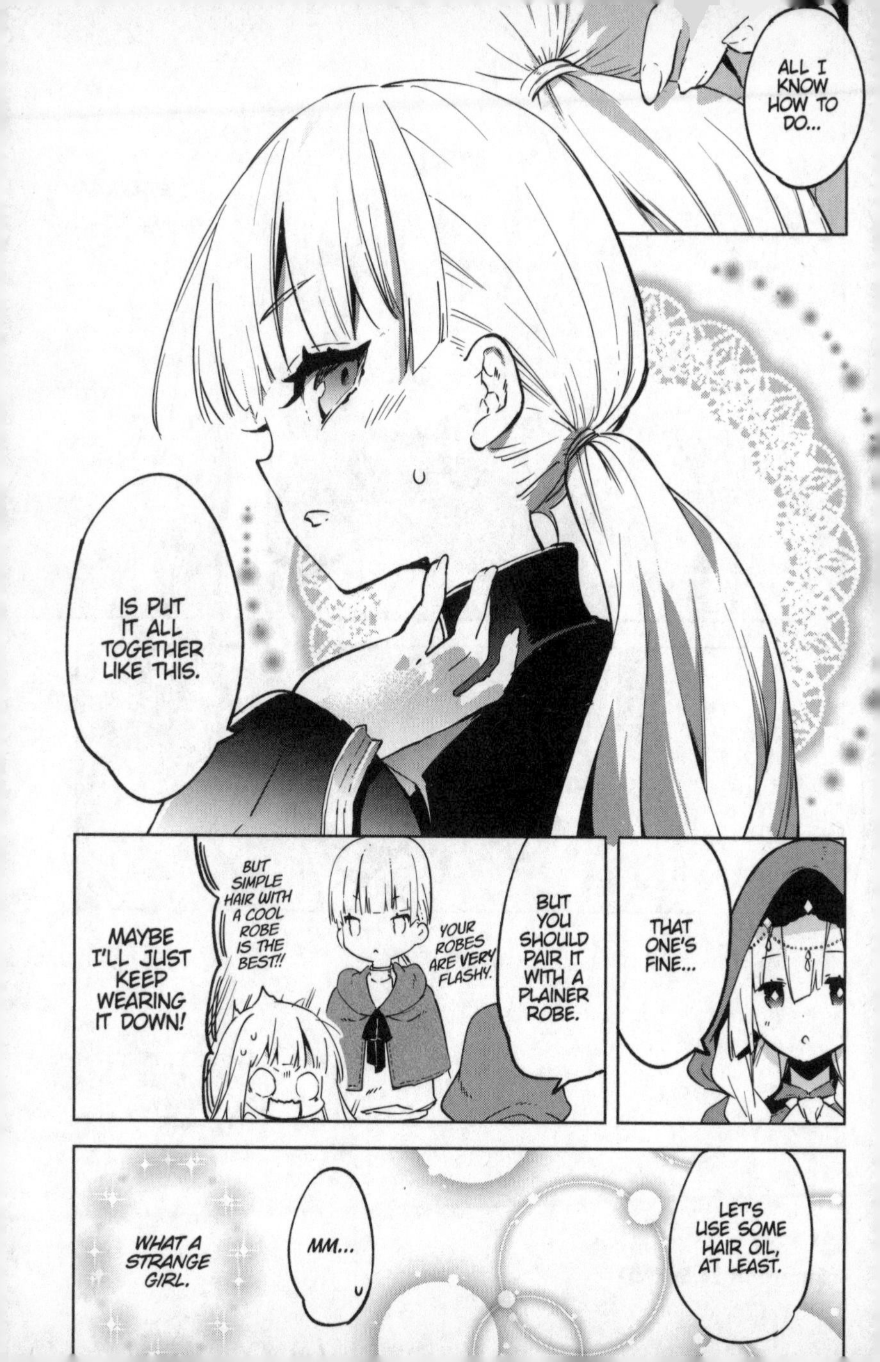
ALL I KNOW HOW TO DO...
IS PUT IT ALL TOGETHER LIKE THIS.
THAT ONE'S FINE...
BUT YOU SHOULD PAIR IT WITH A PLAINER ROBE.
YOUR ROBES ARE VERY FLASHY.
BUT SIMPLE HAIR WITH A COOL ROBE IS THE BEST!!
MAYBE I'LL JUST KEEP WEARING IT DOWN!
LET'S USE SOME HAIR OIL, AT LEAST.
MM...
WHAT A STRANGE GIRL.

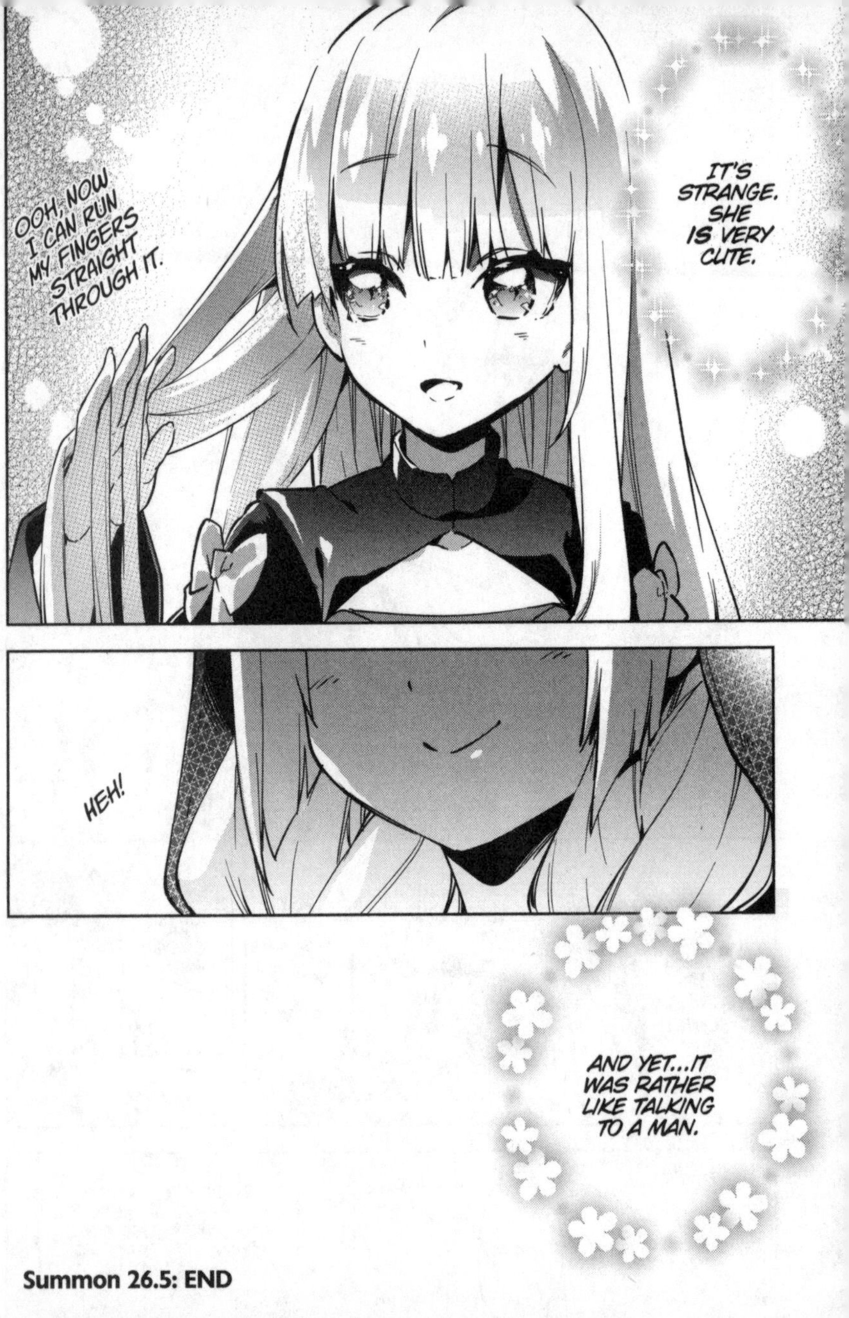
IT'S STRANGE. SHE IS VERY CUTE.
OOH, NOW I CAN RUN MY FINGERS STRAIGHT THROUGH IT.
HEH!
AND YET...IT WAS RATHER LIKE TALKING TO A MAN.

Summon 26.5: END

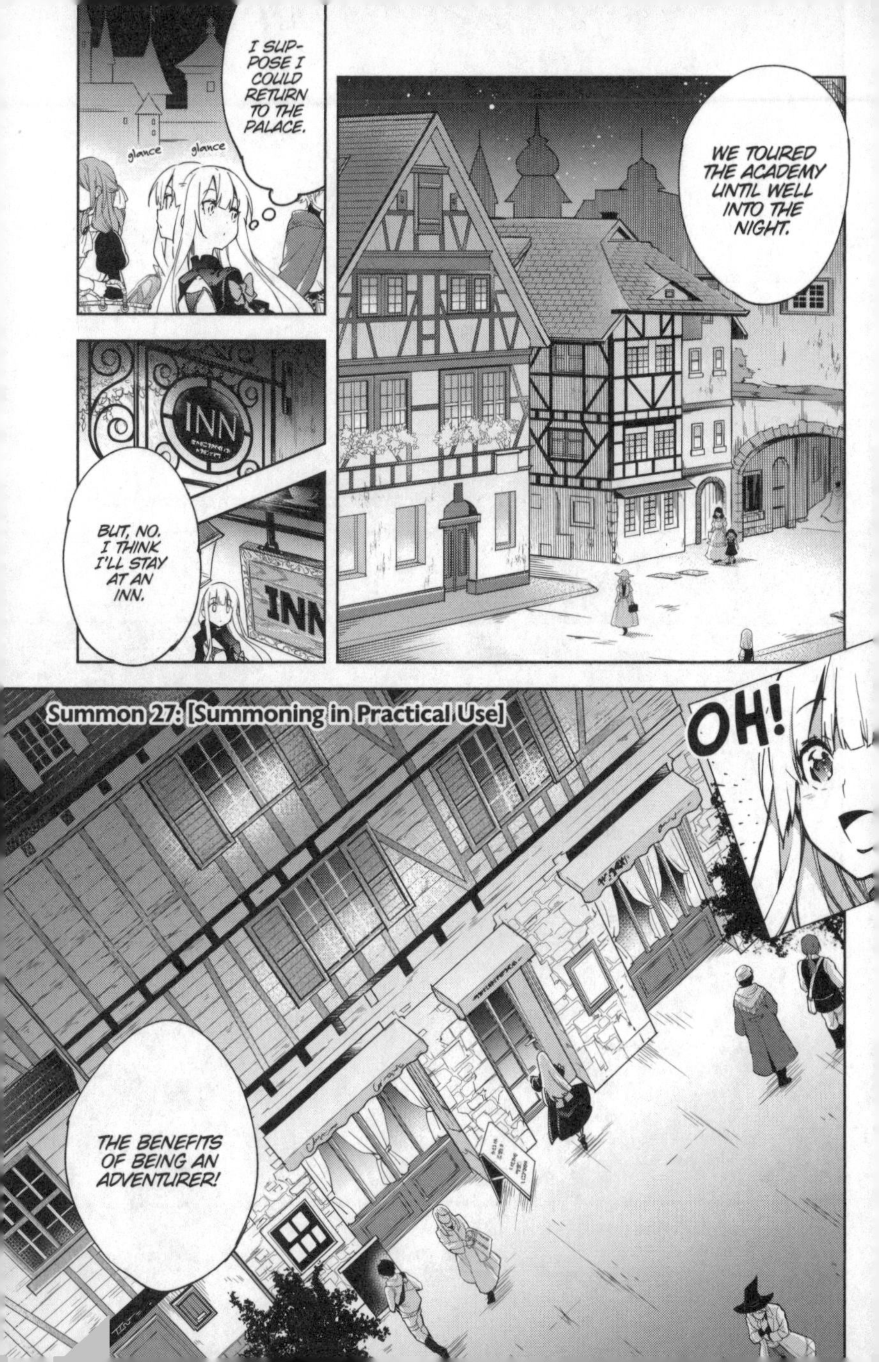
WE TOURED THE ACADEMY UNTIL WELL INTO THE NIGHT.
I SUPPOSE I COULD RETURN TO THE PALACE.
glance
glance
INN
BUT, NO. I THINK I'LL STAY AT AN INN.
INN
Summon 27: [Summoning in Practical Use]
OH!
THE BENEFITS OF BEING AN ADVENTURER!

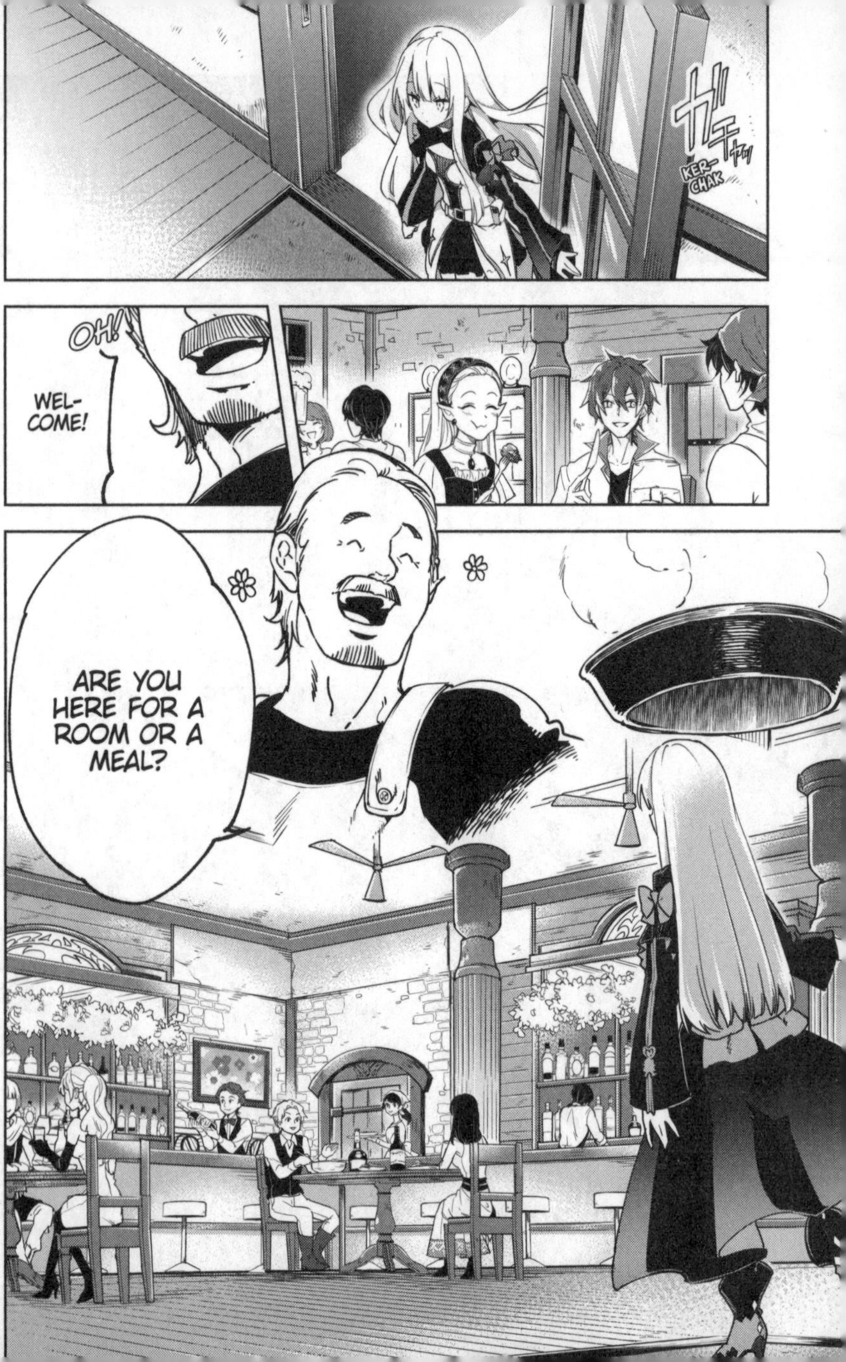
ガチャッ
KER-CHAK
OH!
WEL-COME!
ARE YOU HERE FOR A ROOM OR A MEAL?

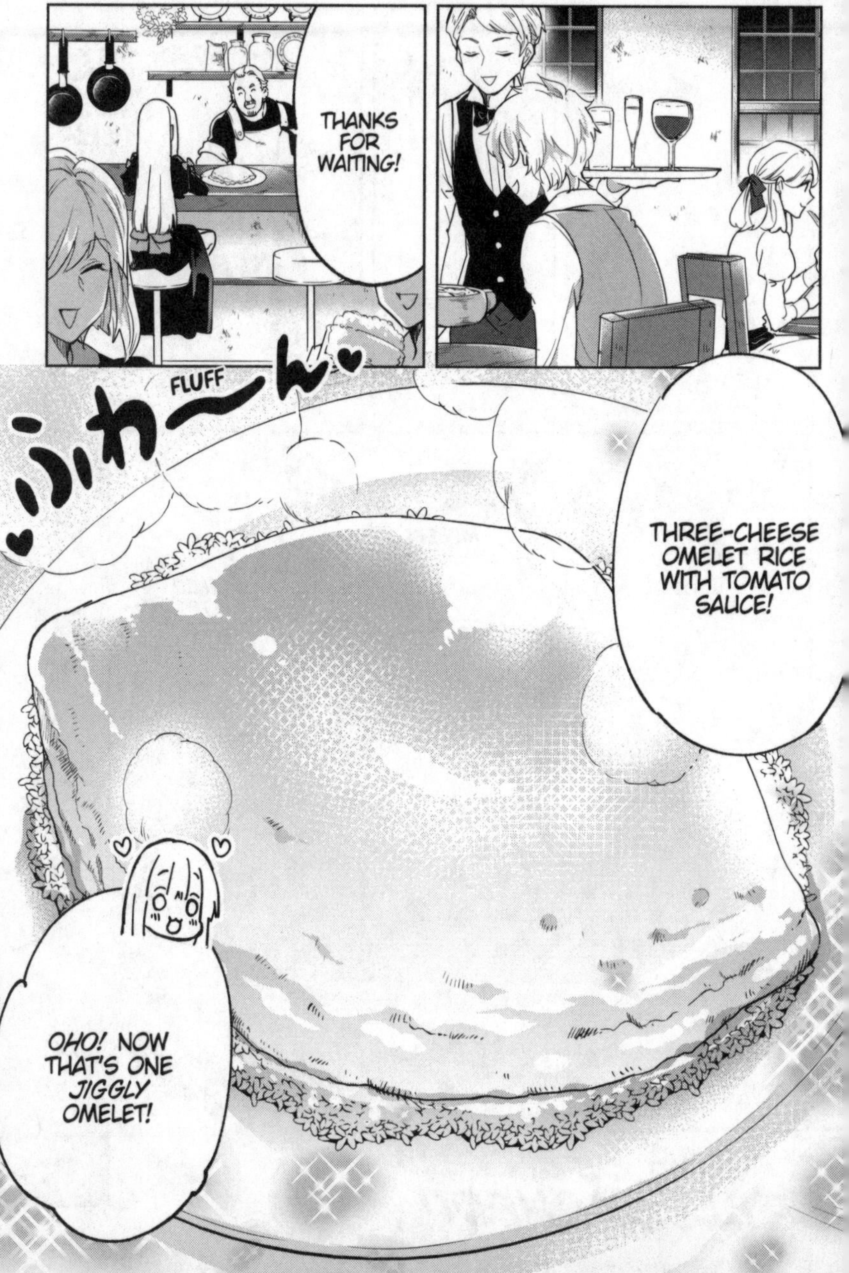
THANKS FOR WAITING!
THREE-CHEESE OMELET RICE WITH TOMATO SAUCE!
ふわ〜ん
FLUFF
OHO! NOW THAT'S ONE JIGGLY OMELET!

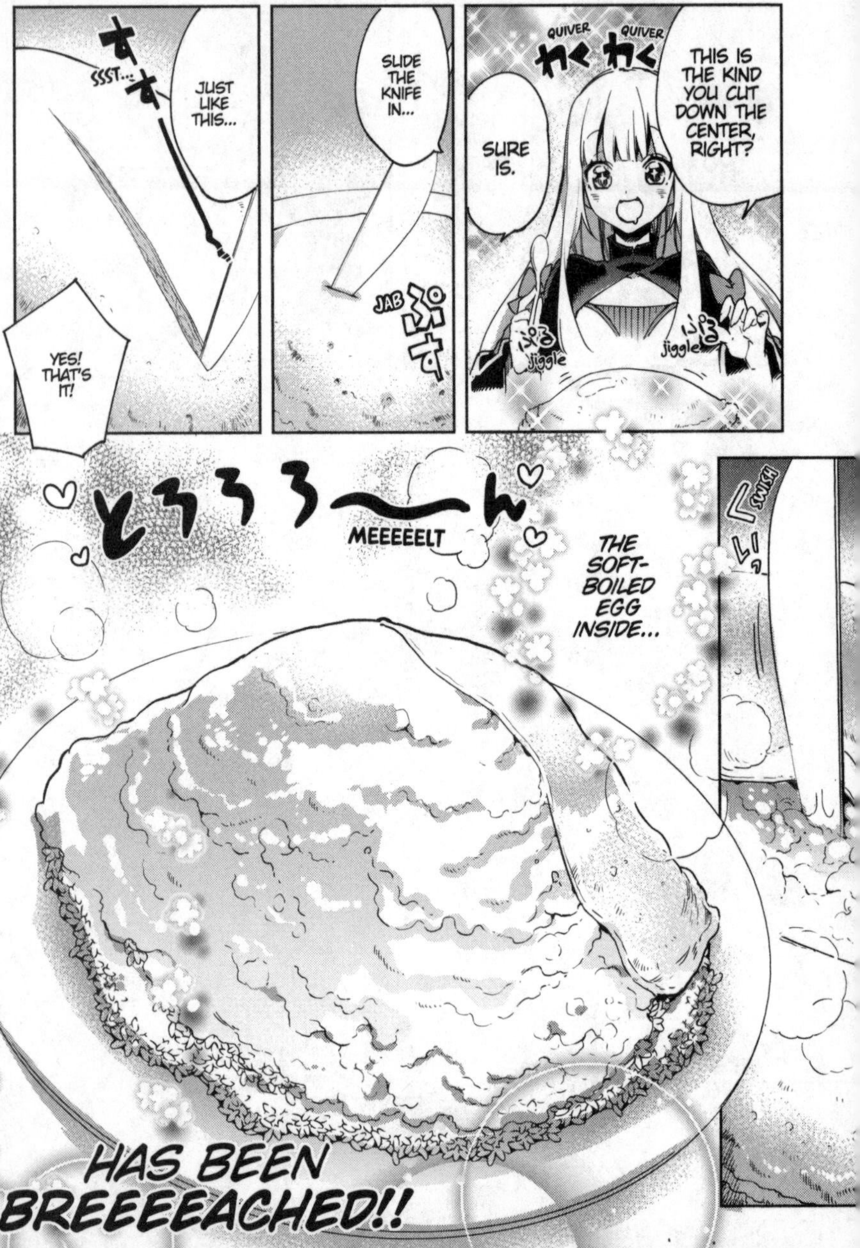
QUIVER QUIVER
わくわく
THIS IS THE KIND YOU CUT DOWN THE CENTER, RIGHT?
SURE IS.
ぷる jiggle
ぷる jiggle
SLIDE THE KNIFE IN...
JAB
ぷす
SSST...
JUST LIKE THIS...
YES! THAT'S IT!
SWISH
THE SOFT-BOILED EGG INSIDE...
とろろろ〜〜ん
MEEEEELT
HAS BEEN BREEEEEACHED!!

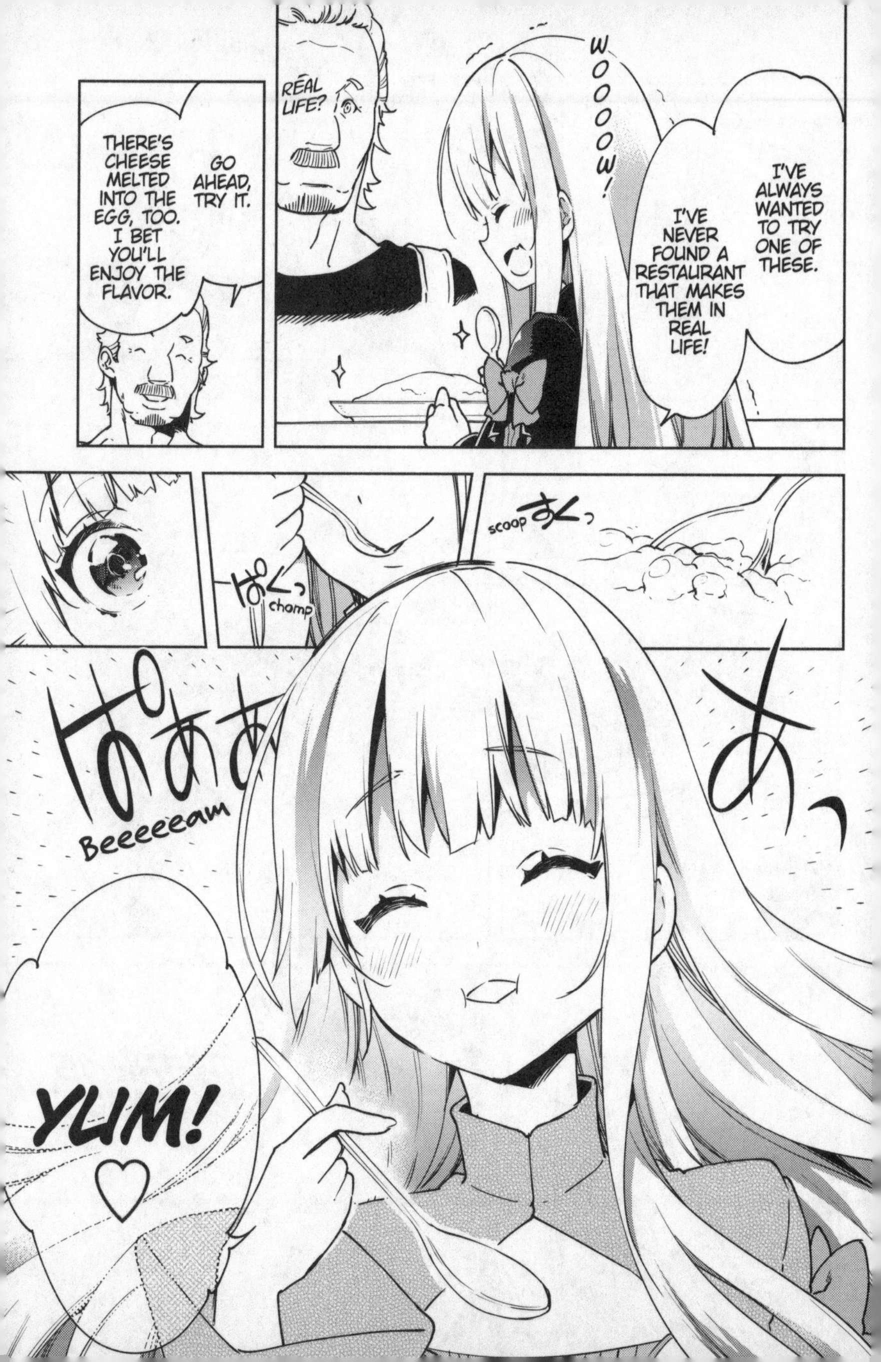

WOOOOOW!
I'VE ALWAYS WANTED TO TRY ONE OF THESE.
I'VE NEVER FOUND A RESTAURANT THAT MAKES THEM IN REAL LIFE!
REAL LIFE?
GO AHEAD, TRY IT.
THERE'S CHEESE MELTED INTO THE EGG, TOO. I BET YOU'LL ENJOY THE FLAVOR.
scoop すくっ
ぱくっ champ
あっ
ぱああ
Beeeeeam
YUM! ♥

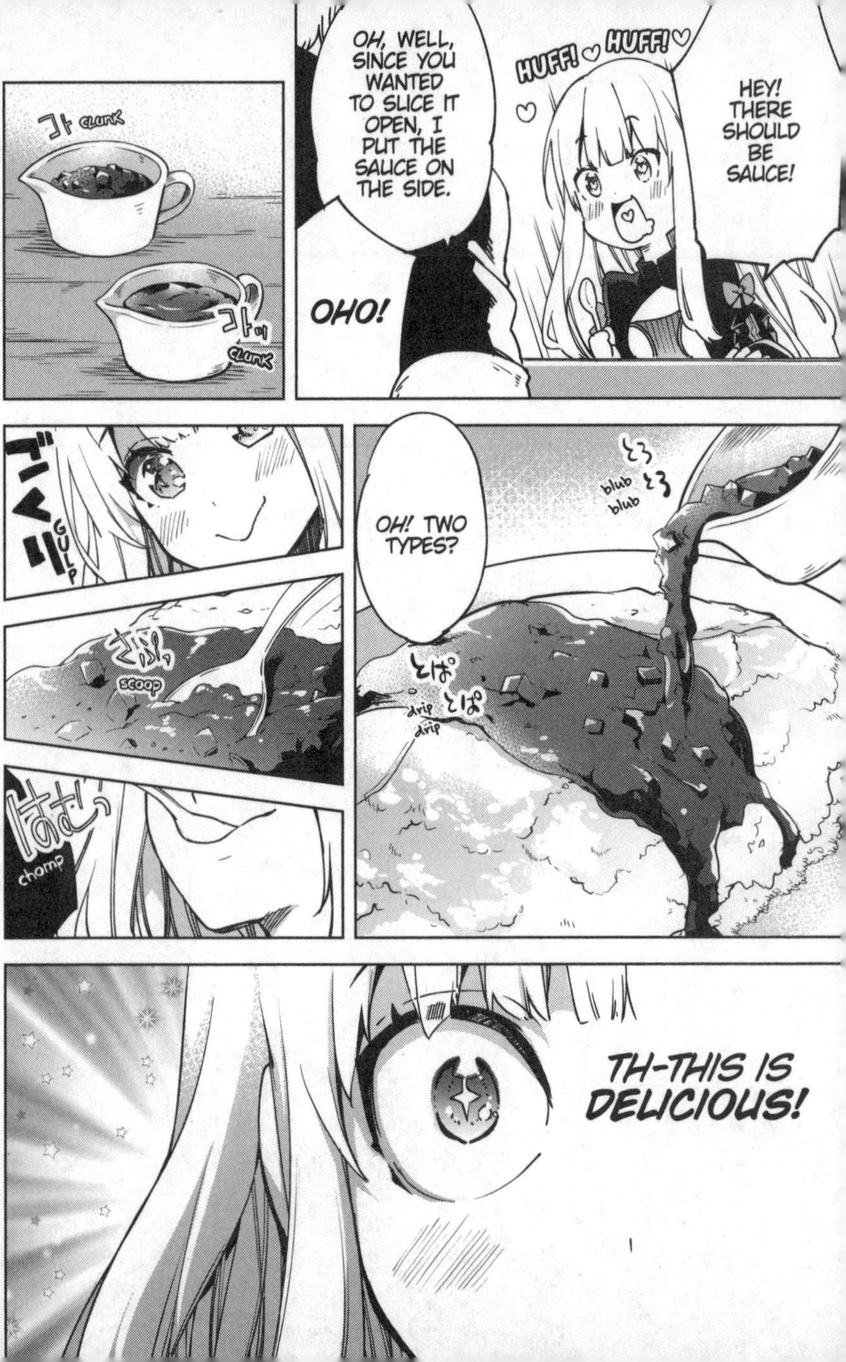
HUFF! ♡ HUFF! ♡
HEY! THERE SHOULD BE SAUCE!
OH, WELL, SINCE YOU WANTED TO SLICE IT OPEN, I PUT THE SAUCE ON THE SIDE.
OHO!
CLUNK
CLUNK
blub blub
OH! TWO TYPES?
drip drip
GULP
scoop
champ
TH-THIS IS DELICIOUS!

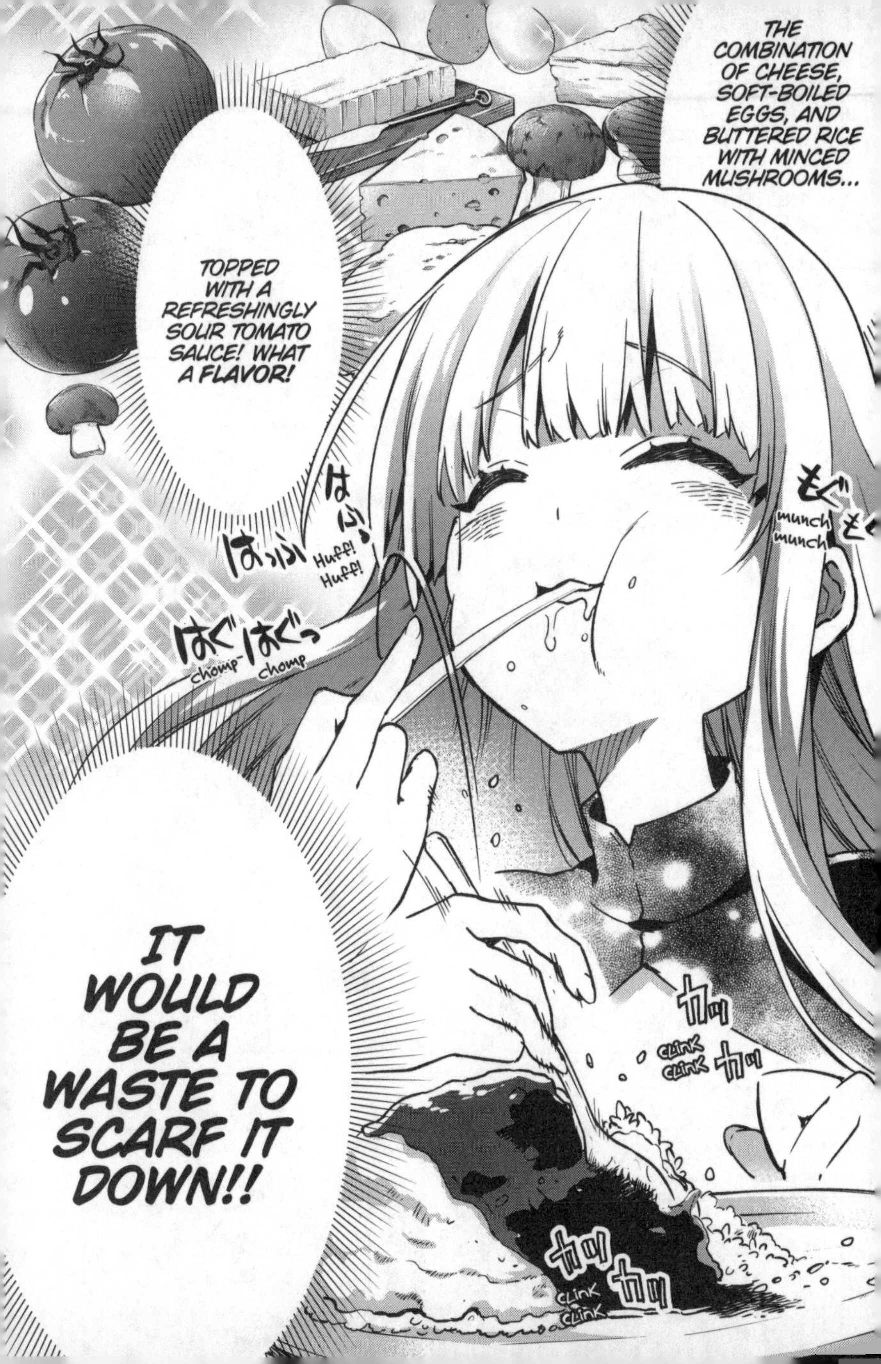
THE COMBINATION OF CHEESE, SOFT-BOILED EGGS, AND BUTTERED RICE WITH MINCED MUSHROOMS...
TOPPED WITH A REFRESHINGLY SOUR TOMATO SAUCE! WHAT A FLAVOR!
もぐもぐ
munch munch
はふっ
Huff! Huff!
はっふ
はぐはぐっ
chomp-chomp
カッカッ
CLINK CLINK
IT WOULD BE A WASTE TO SCARF IT DOWN!!
カッカッ
CLINK CLINK

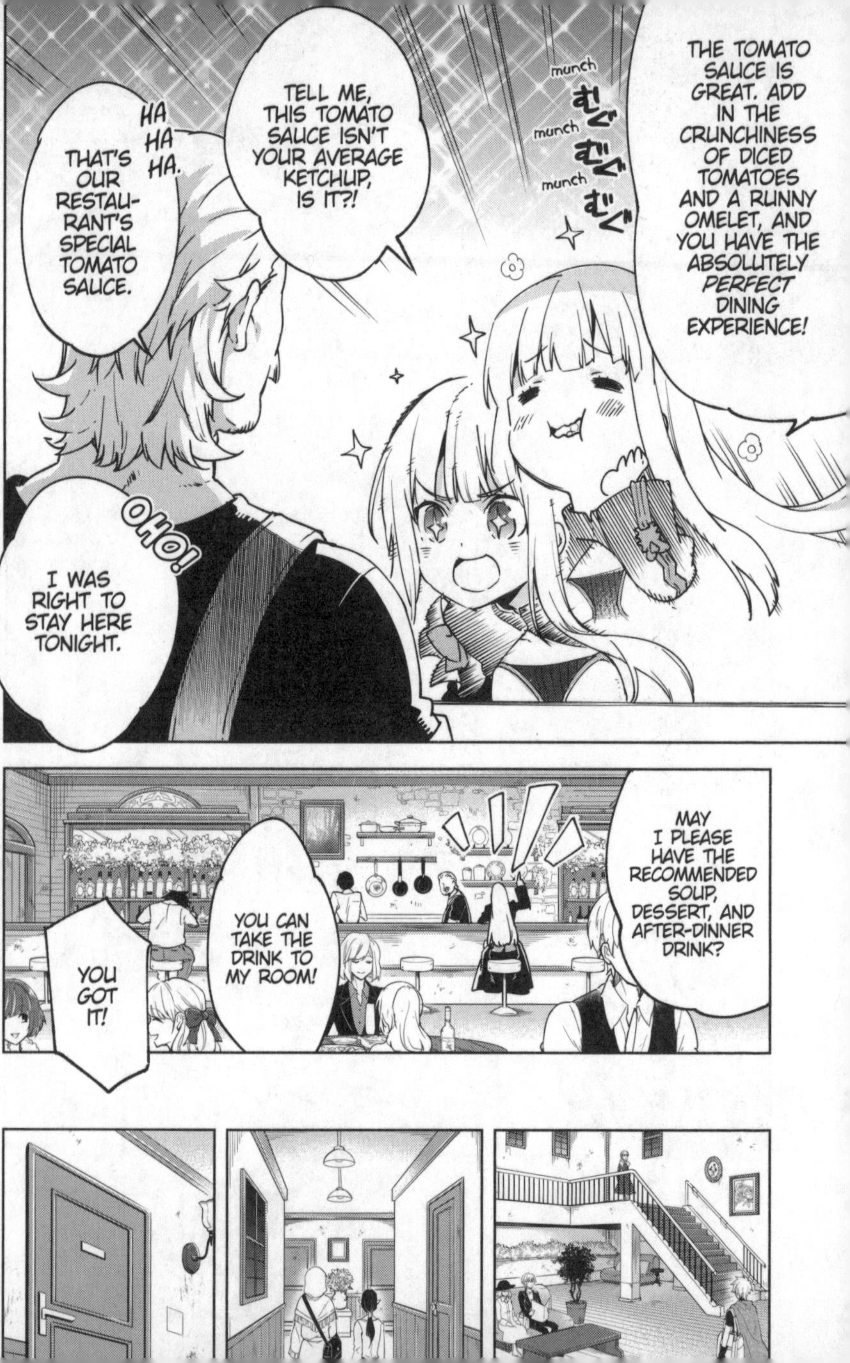
THE TOMATO SAUCE IS GREAT. ADD IN THE CRUNCHINESS OF DICED TOMATOES AND A RUNNY OMELET, AND YOU HAVE THE ABSOLUTELY *PERFECT* DINING EXPERIENCE!
munch むぐ
munch むぐ
munch むぐ
TELL ME, THIS TOMATO SAUCE ISN'T YOUR AVERAGE KETCHUP, IS IT?!
HA HA HA.
THAT'S OUR RESTAU-RANT'S SPECIAL TOMATO SAUCE.
OHO!
I WAS RIGHT TO STAY HERE TONIGHT.
MAY I PLEASE HAVE THE RECOMMENDED SOUP, DESSERT, AND AFTER-DINNER DRINK?
YOU CAN TAKE THE DRINK TO MY ROOM!
YOU GOT IT!

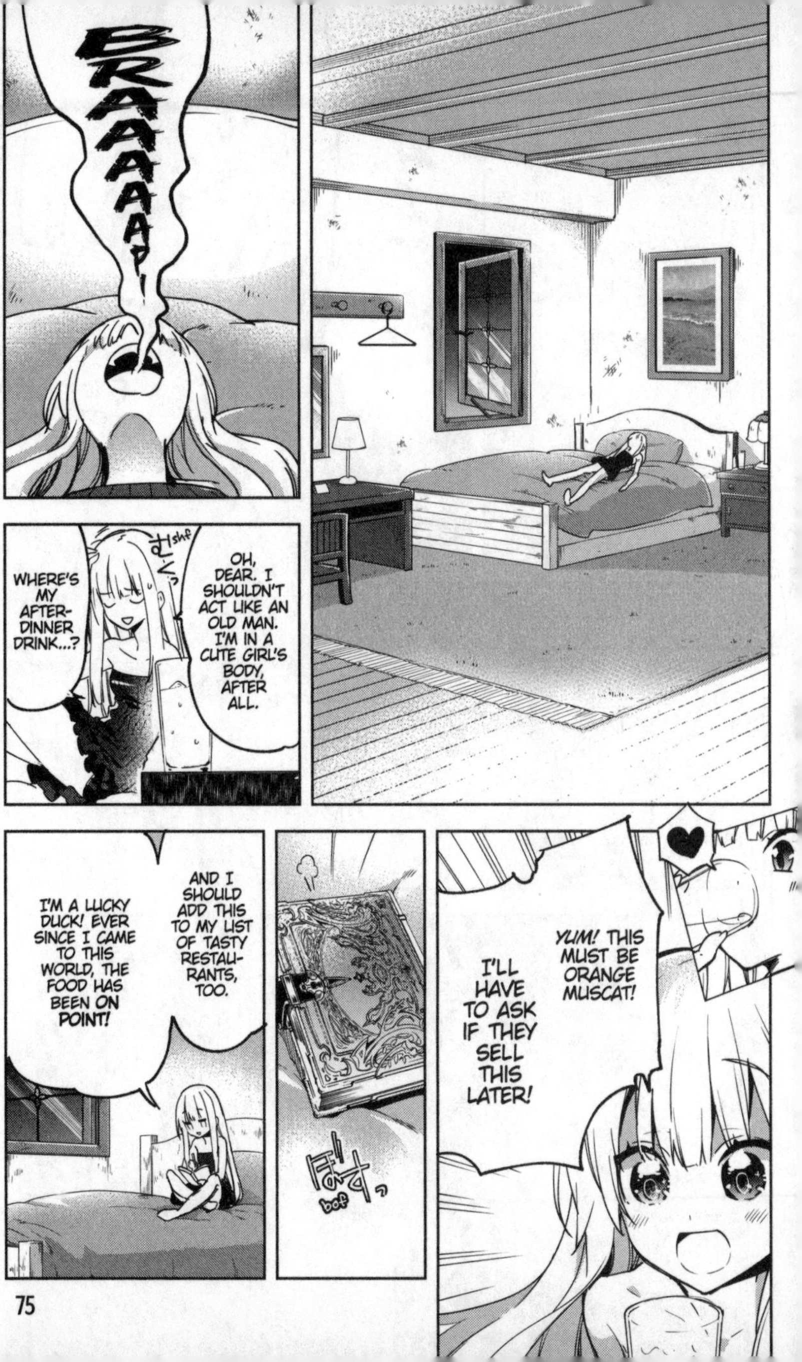
BRAAAAAAP!
OH, DEAR. I SHOULDN'T ACT LIKE AN OLD MAN. I'M IN A CUTE GIRL'S BODY, AFTER ALL.
shf
WHERE'S MY AFTER-DINNER DRINK...?
YUM! THIS MUST BE ORANGE MUSCAT!
I'LL HAVE TO ASK IF THEY SELL THIS LATER!
bof
I'M A LUCKY DUCK! EVER SINCE I CAME TO THIS WORLD, THE FOOD HAS BEEN ON POINT!
AND I SHOULD ADD THIS TO MY LIST OF TASTY RESTAU-RANTS, TOO.

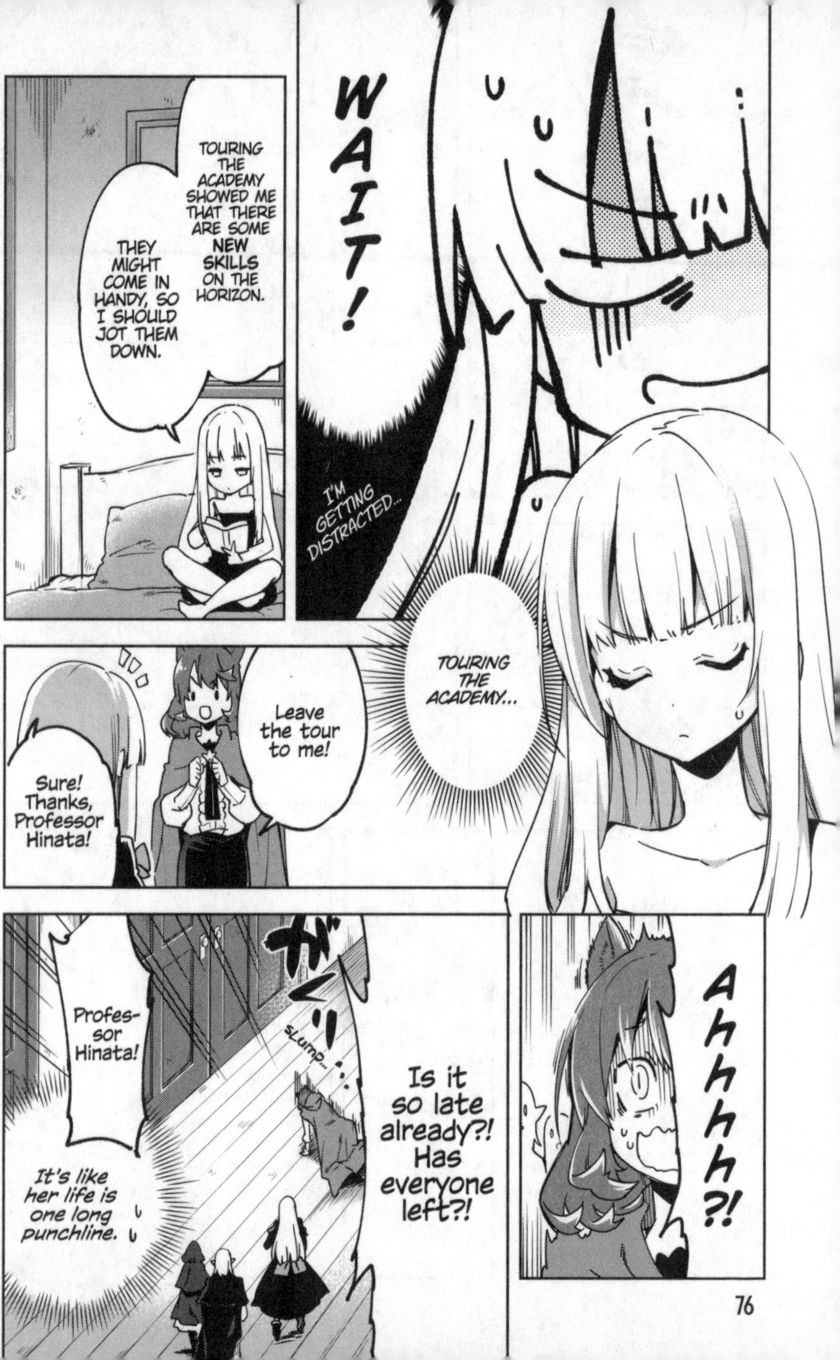
WAIT!
I'M GETTING DISTRACTED...
TOURING THE ACADEMY...
TOURING THE ACADEMY SHOWED ME THAT THERE ARE SOME NEW SKILLS ON THE HORIZON.
THEY MIGHT COME IN HANDY, SO I SHOULD JOT THEM DOWN.
Leave the tour to me!
Sure! Thanks, Professor Hinata!
Ahhhh?!
SLUMP...
Is it so late already?! Has everyone left?!
Profes-sor Hinata!
It's like her life is one long punchline.

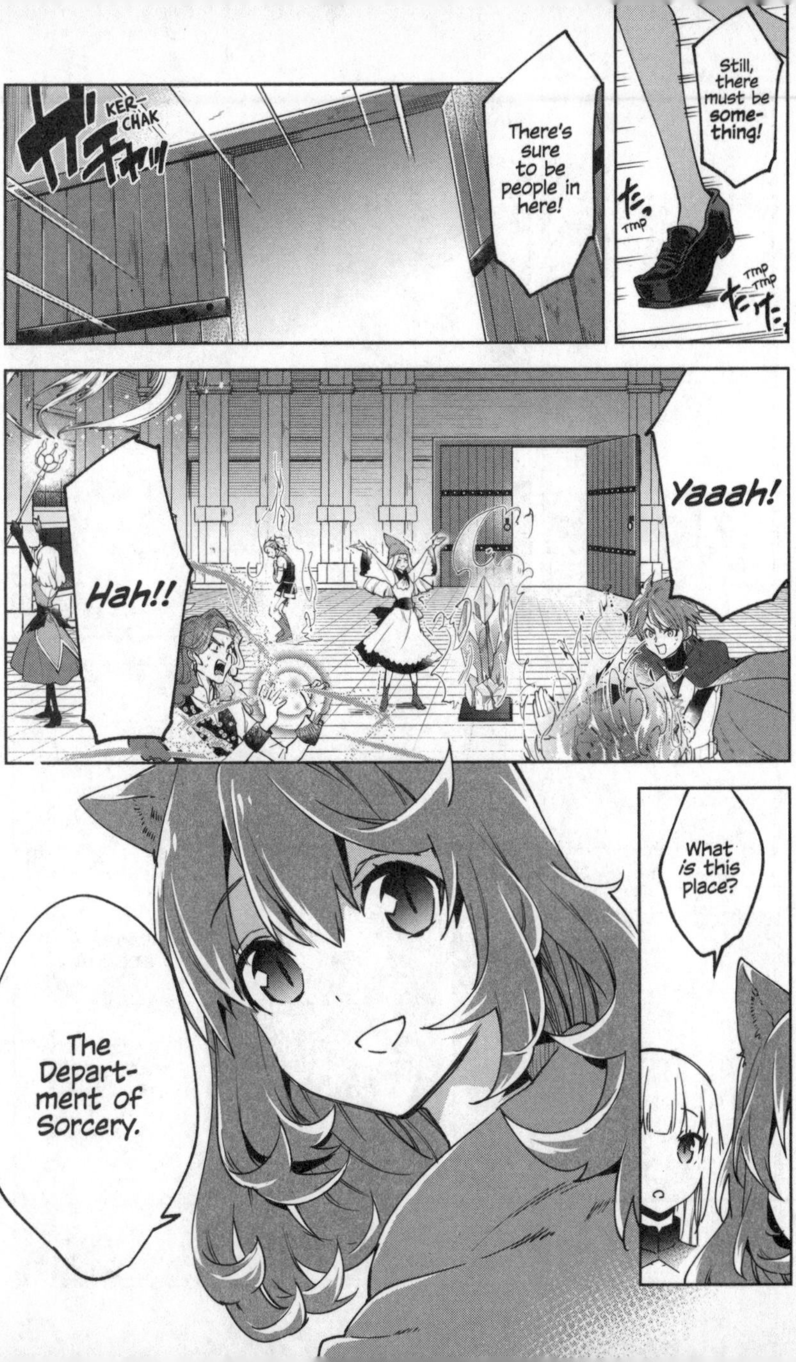
Still, there must be something!
TMP
TMP TMP
There's sure to be people in here!
KER-CHAK
Yaaah!
Hah!!
What is this place?
The Department of Sorcery.

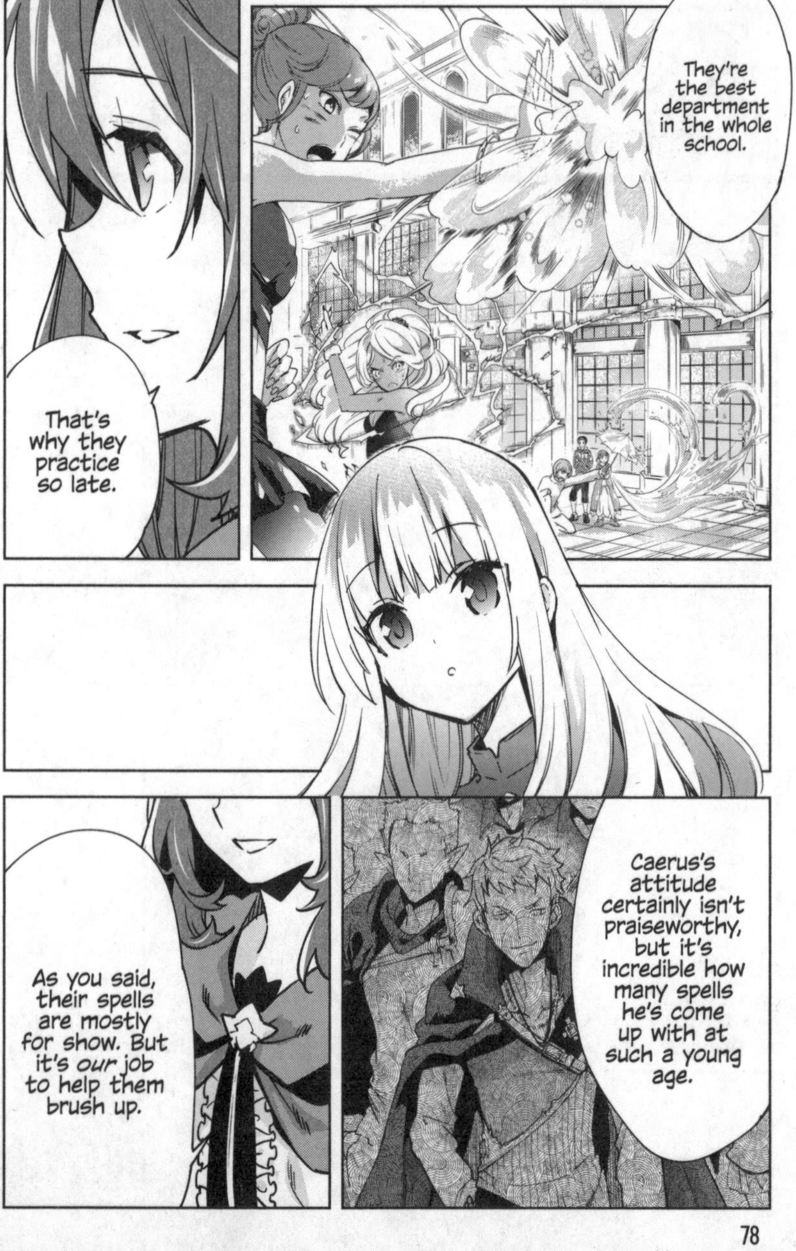
They're the best department in the whole school.
That's why they practice so late.
Caerus's attitude certainly isn't praiseworthy, but it's incredible how many spells he's come up with at such a young age.
As you said, their spells are mostly for show. But it's *our* job to help them brush up.

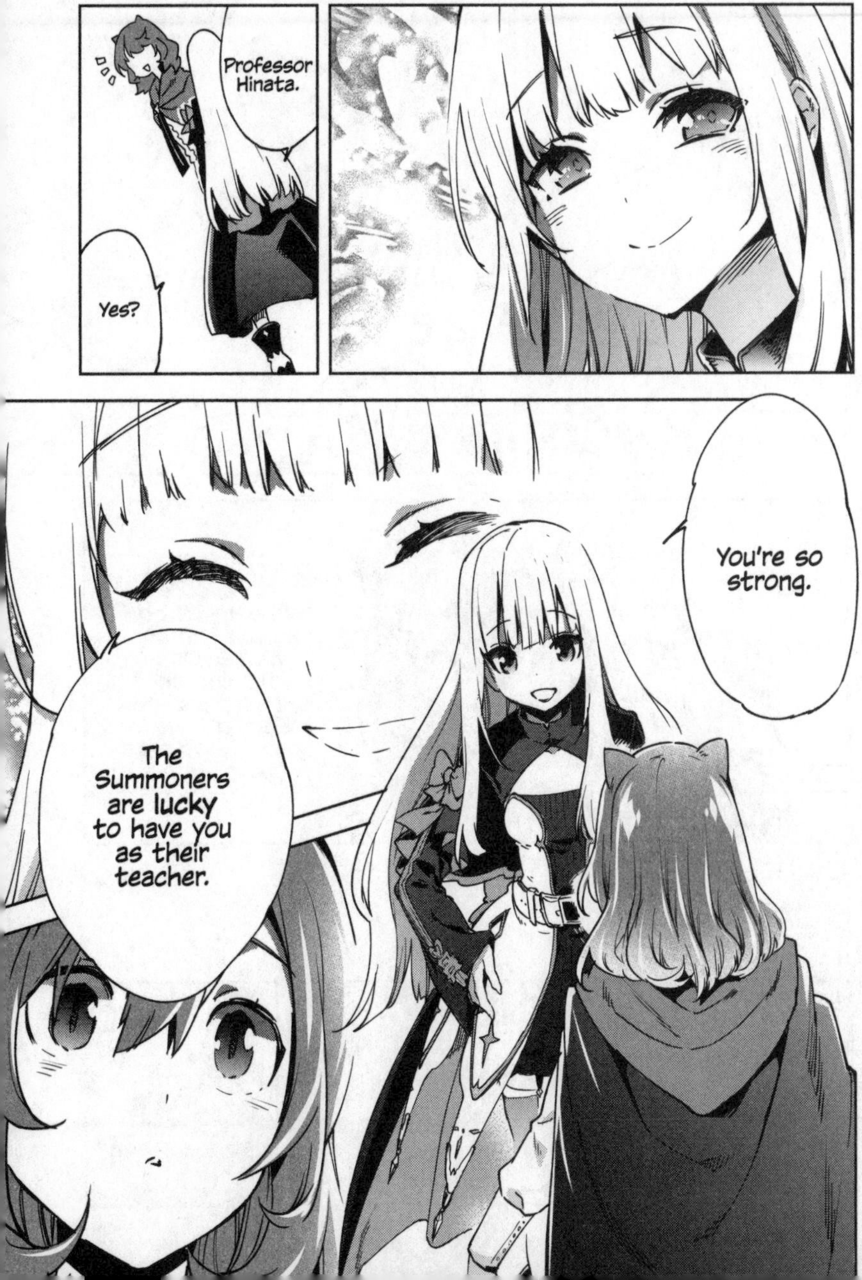
Professor Hinata.
Yes?
You're so strong.
The Summoners are lucky to have you as their teacher.

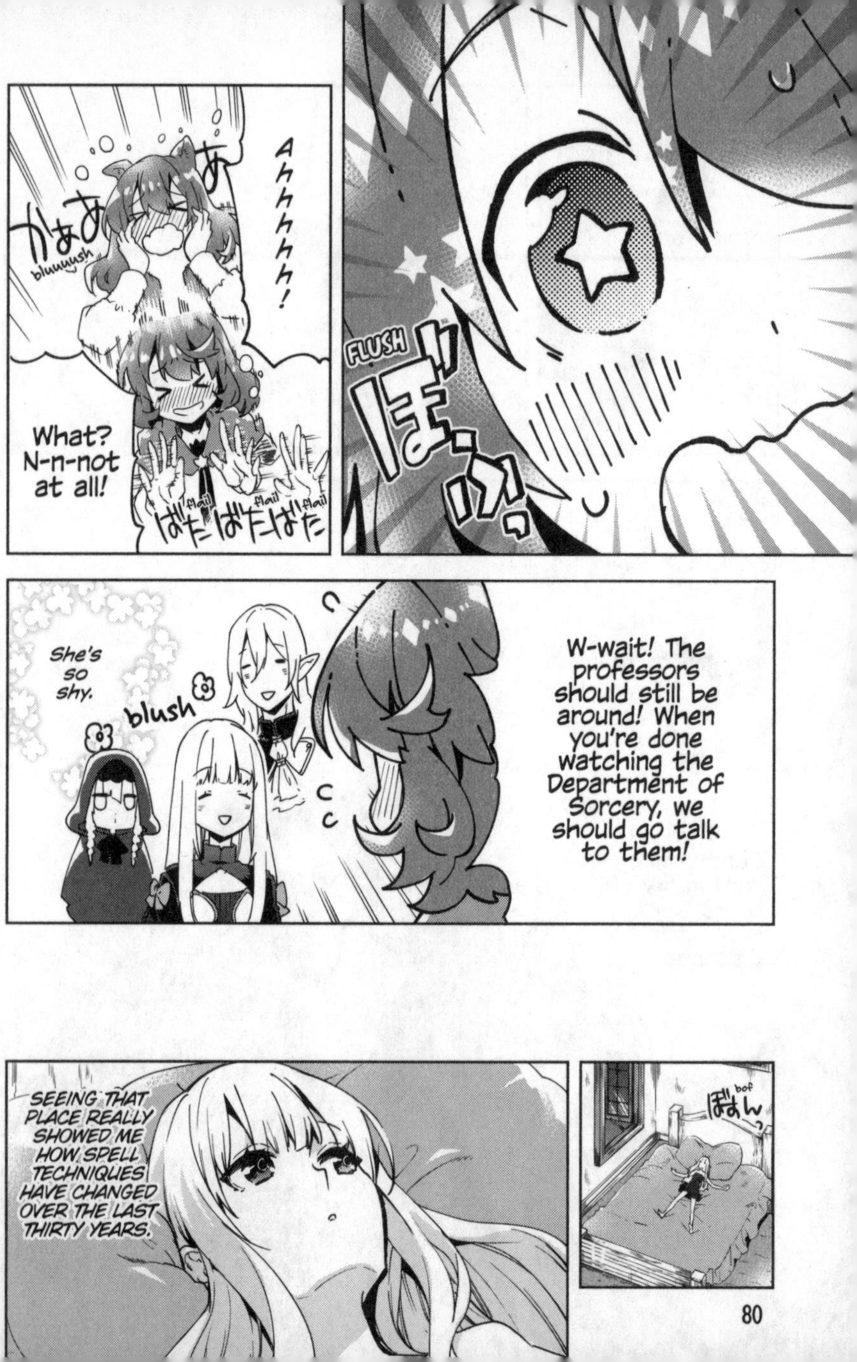
FLUSH
ぼっ
Ahhhhhh!
bluuush
What? N-n-not at all!
flail flail flail
ばたばたばた
W-wait! The professors should still be around! When you're done watching the Department of Sorcery, we should go talk to them!
She's so shy.
blush
bof
ぼすん
SEEING THAT PLACE REALLY SHOWED ME HOW SPELL TECHNIQUES HAVE CHANGED OVER THE LAST THIRTY YEARS.

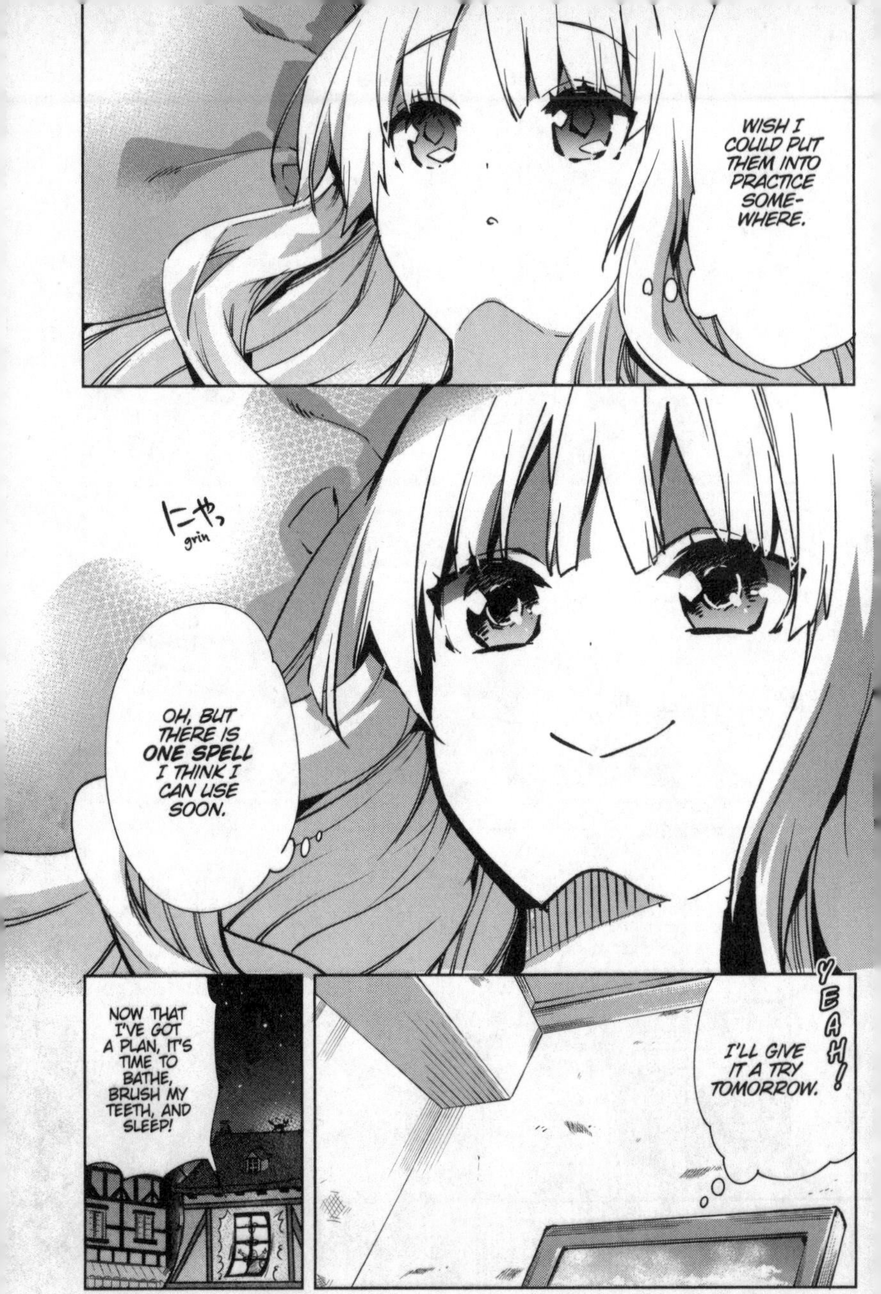
WISH I COULD PUT THEM INTO PRACTICE SOME-WHERE.
にやっ
grin
OH, BUT THERE IS ONE SPELL I THINK I CAN USE SOON.
YEAH!
I'LL GIVE IT A TRY TOMORROW.
NOW THAT I'VE GOT A PLAN, IT'S TIME TO BATHE, BRUSH MY TEETH, AND SLEEP!

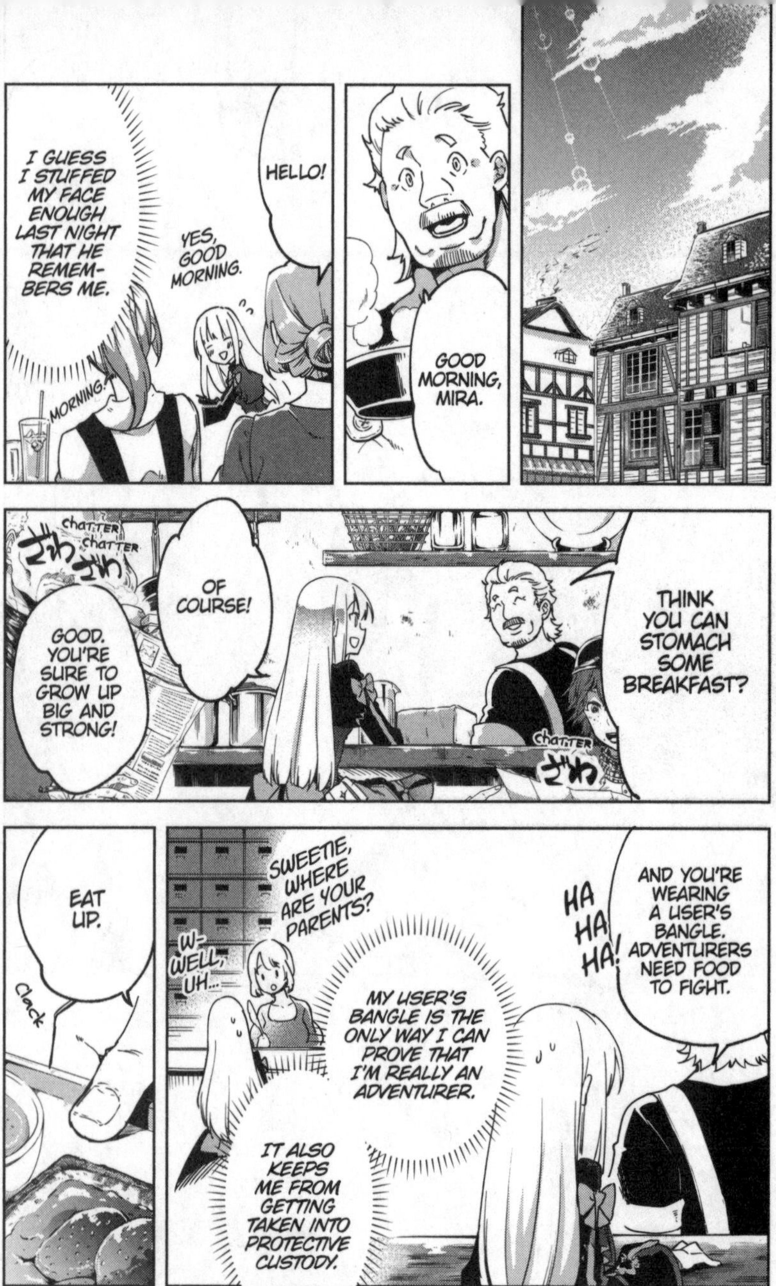

HELLO!
GOOD MORNING, MIRA.
YES, GOOD MORNING.
I GUESS I STUFFED MY FACE ENOUGH LAST NIGHT THAT HE REMEMBERS ME.
MORNING.
THINK YOU CAN STOMACH SOME BREAKFAST?
CHATTER ざわ
OF COURSE!
CHATTER CHATTER ざわざわ
GOOD. YOU'RE SURE TO GROW UP BIG AND STRONG!
AND YOU'RE WEARING A USER'S BANGLE. ADVENTURERS NEED FOOD TO FIGHT.
HA HA HA!
SWEETIE, WHERE ARE YOUR PARENTS?
W-WELL, UH...
MY USER'S BANGLE IS THE ONLY WAY I CAN PROVE THAT I'M REALLY AN ADVENTURER.
IT ALSO KEEPS ME FROM GETTING TAKEN INTO PROTECTIVE CUSTODY.
EAT UP.
Clack

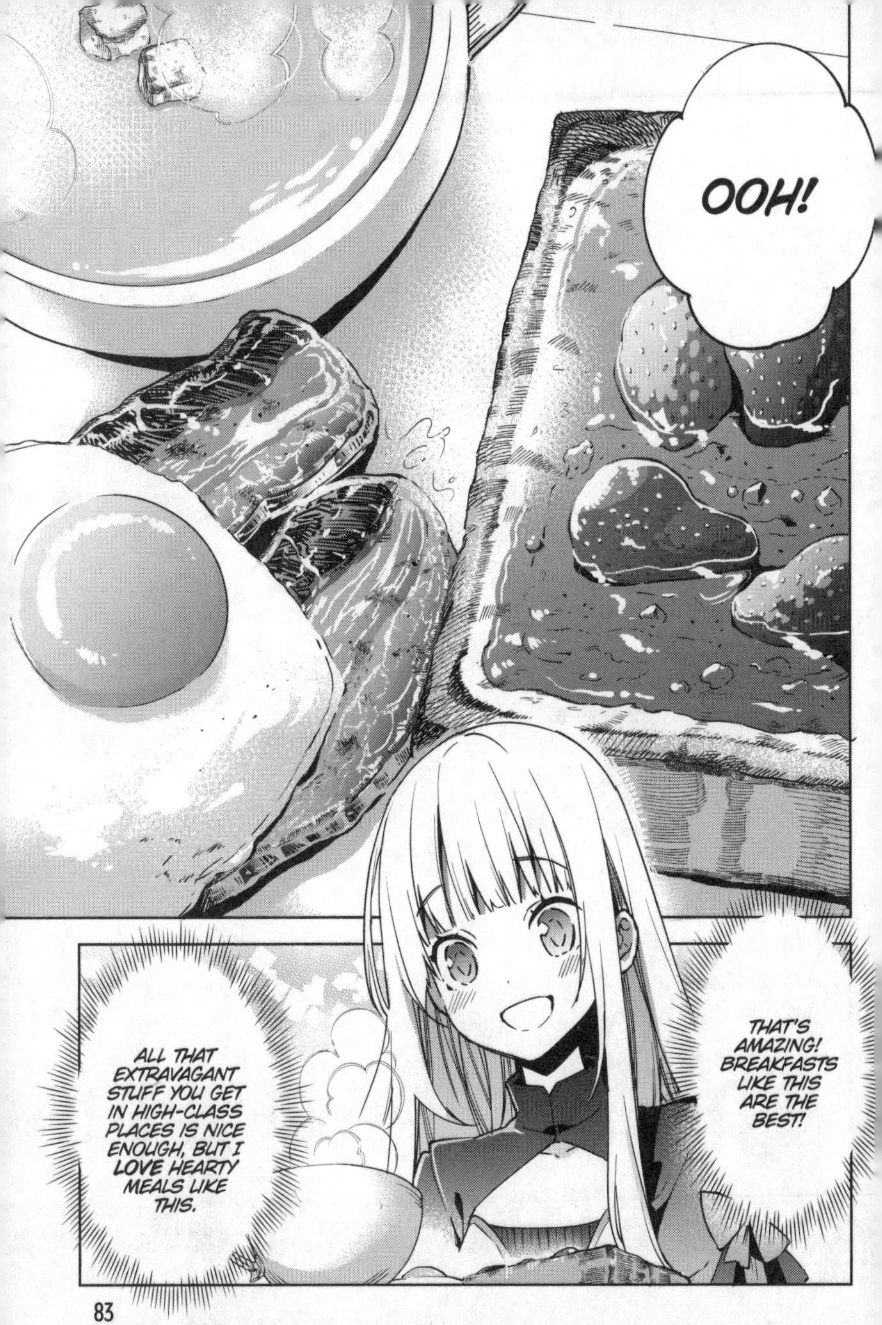
OOH!
THAT'S AMAZING! BREAKFASTS LIKE THIS ARE THE BEST!
ALL THAT EXTRAVAGANT STUFF YOU GET IN HIGH-CLASS PLACES IS NICE ENOUGH, BUT I **LOVE** HEARTY MEALS LIKE THIS.

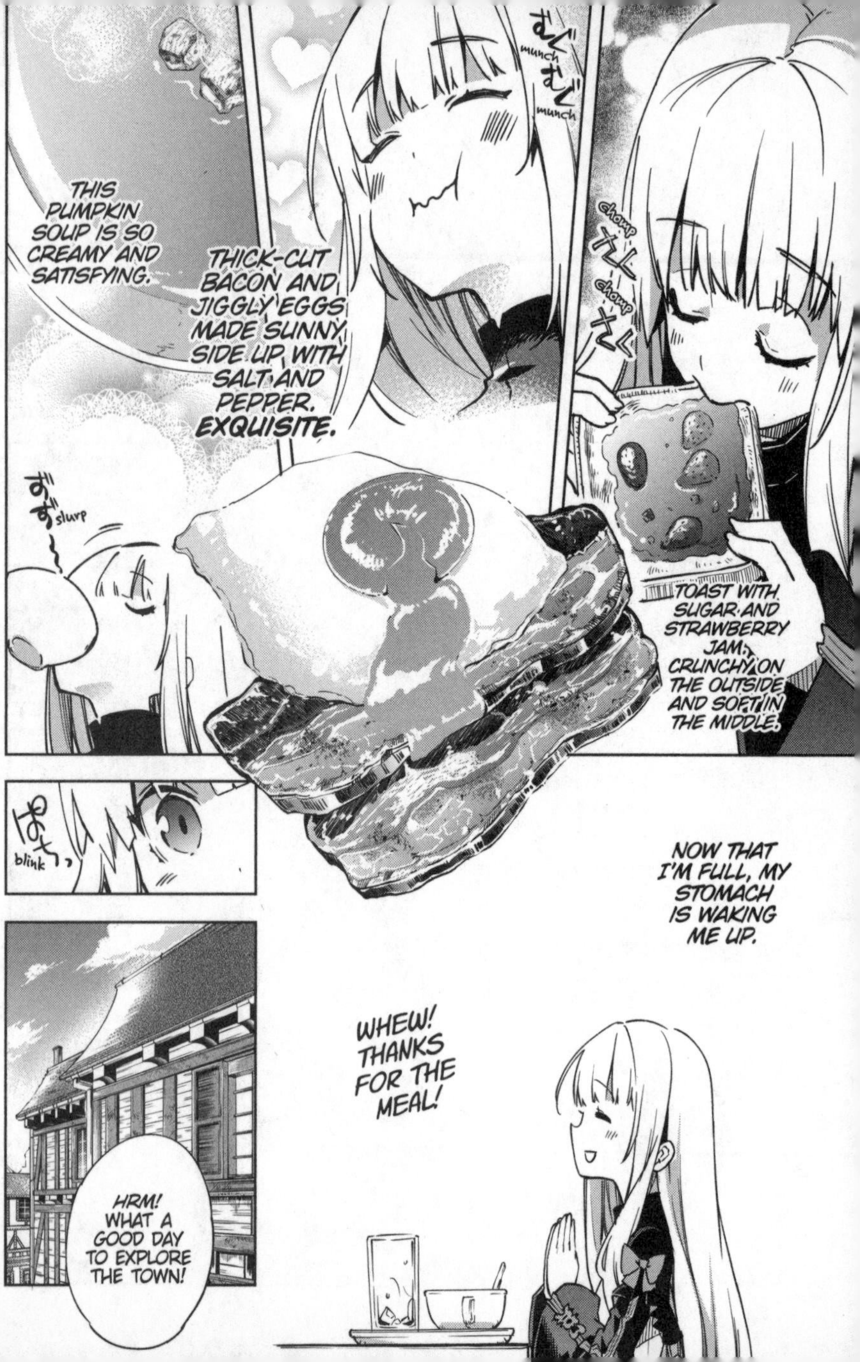
さくさく chomp chomp
TOAST WITH SUGAR AND STRAWBERRY JAM. CRUNCHY ON THE OUTSIDE AND SOFT IN THE MIDDLE.
むぐむぐ munch munch
THICK-CUT BACON AND JIGGLY EGGS MADE SUNNY SIDE UP WITH SALT AND PEPPER. **EXQUISITE.**
THIS PUMPKIN SOUP IS SO CREAMY AND SATISFYING.
ずず～ slurp
ぱちっ blink
NOW THAT I'M FULL, MY STOMACH IS WAKING ME UP.
WHEW! THANKS FOR THE MEAL!
HRM! WHAT A GOOD DAY TO EXPLORE THE TOWN!

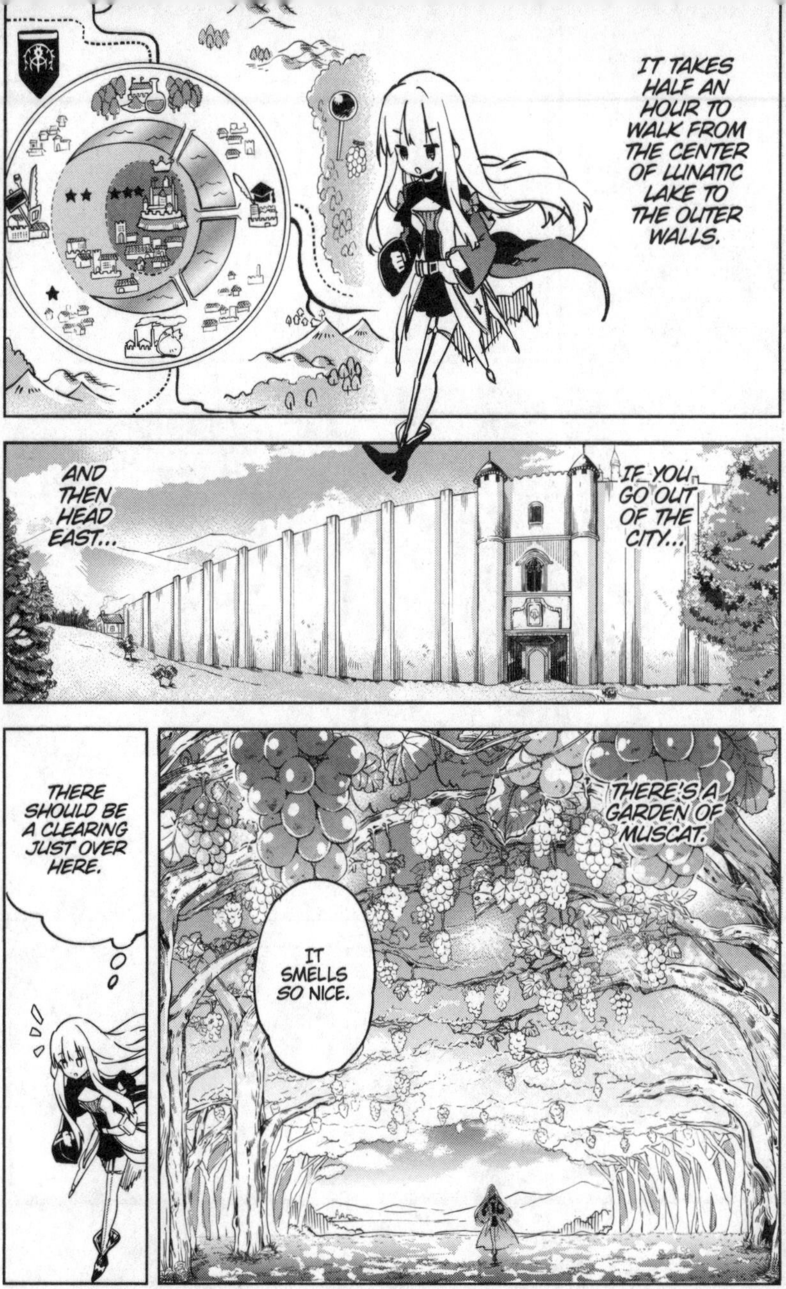
IT TAKES HALF AN HOUR TO WALK FROM THE CENTER OF LUNATIC LAKE TO THE OUTER WALLS.
IF YOU GO OUT OF THE CITY...
AND THEN HEAD EAST...
THERE'S A GARDEN OF MUSCAT.
IT SMELLS SO NICE.
THERE SHOULD BE A CLEARING JUST OVER HERE.

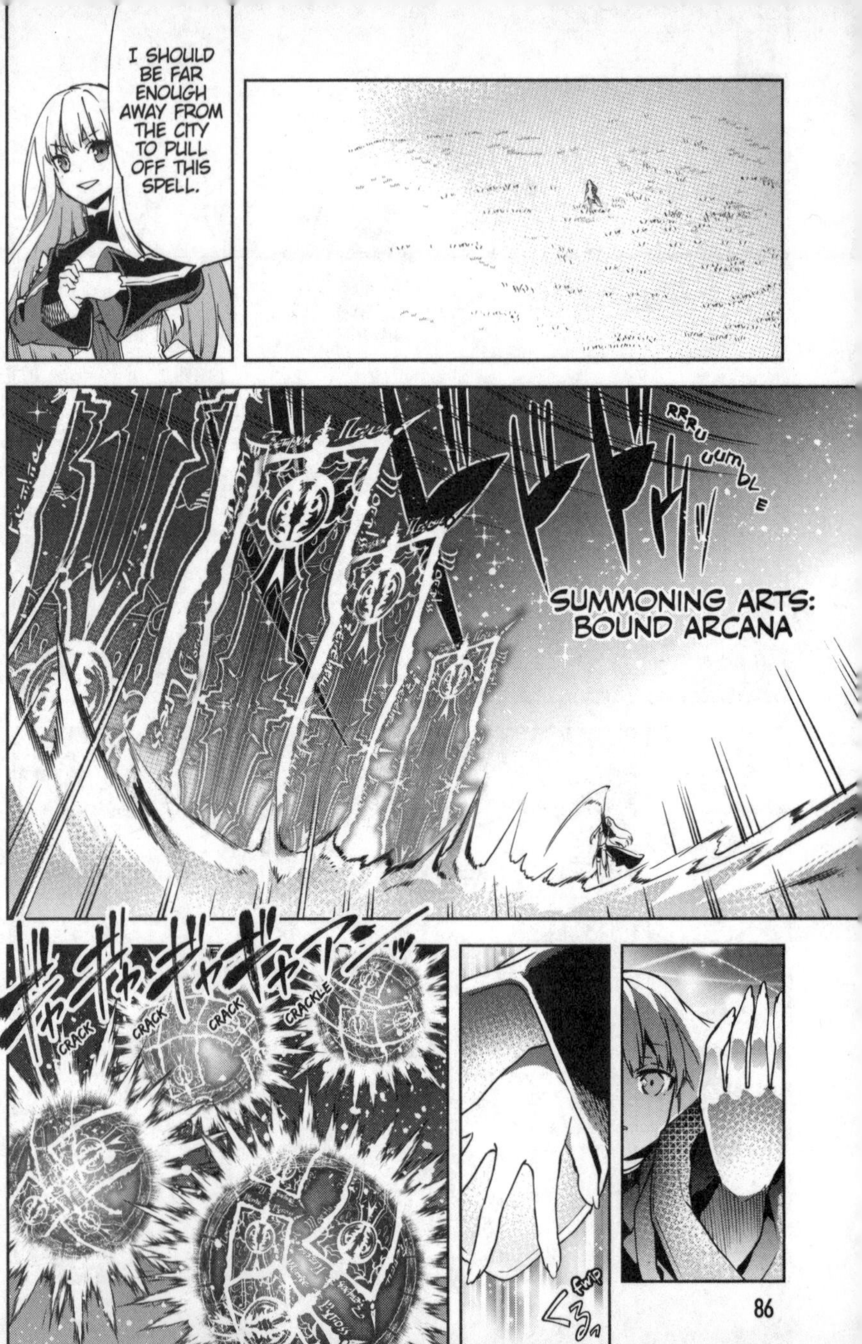
I SHOULD BE FAR ENOUGH AWAY FROM THE CITY TO PULL OFF THIS SPELL.
RRRUMBLE
SUMMONING ARTS: BOUND ARCANA
FWIP
CRACK
CRACK
CRACK
CRACKLE

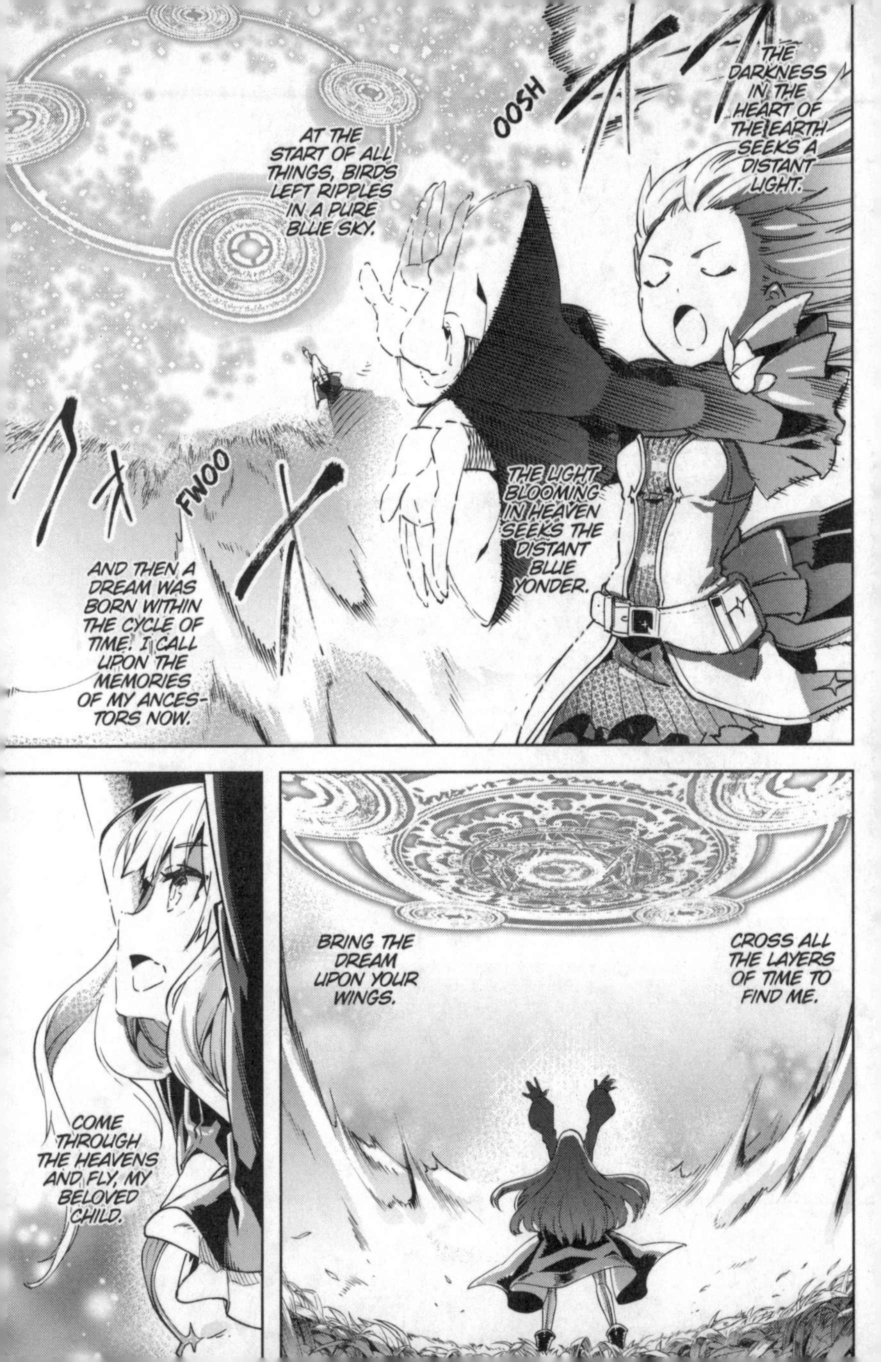
THE DARKNESS IN THE HEART OF THE EARTH SEEKS A DISTANT LIGHT.
OOSH
AT THE START OF ALL THINGS, BIRDS LEFT RIPPLES IN A PURE BLUE SKY.
THE LIGHT BLOOMING IN HEAVEN SEEKS THE DISTANT BLUE YONDER.
FWOO
AND THEN A DREAM WAS BORN WITHIN THE CYCLE OF TIME. I CALL UPON THE MEMORIES OF MY ANCES-TORS NOW.
CROSS ALL THE LAYERS OF TIME TO FIND ME.
BRING THE DREAM UPON YOUR WINGS.
COME THROUGH THE HEAVENS AND FLY, MY BELOVED CHILD.

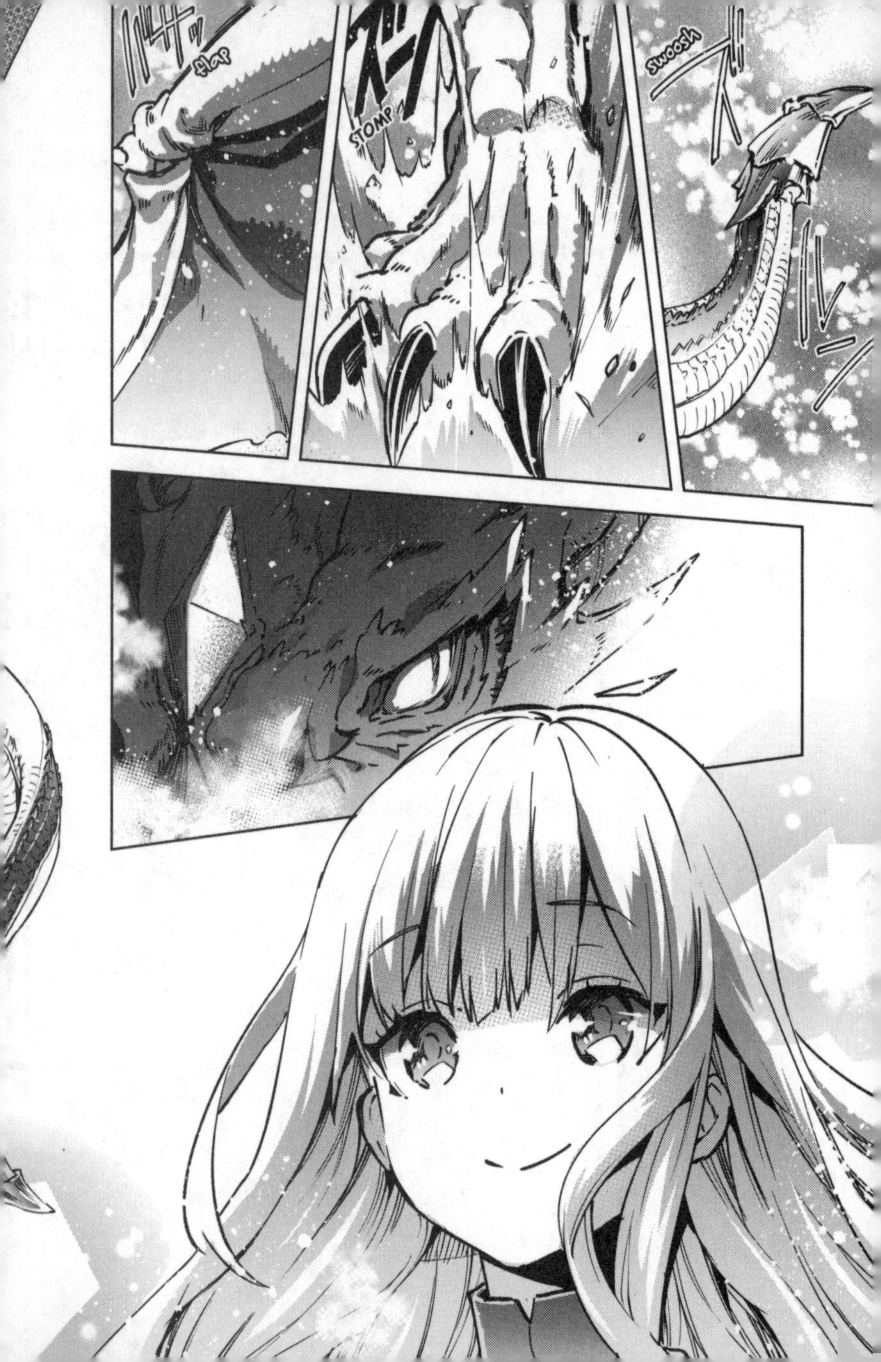
swoosh
STOMP
flap

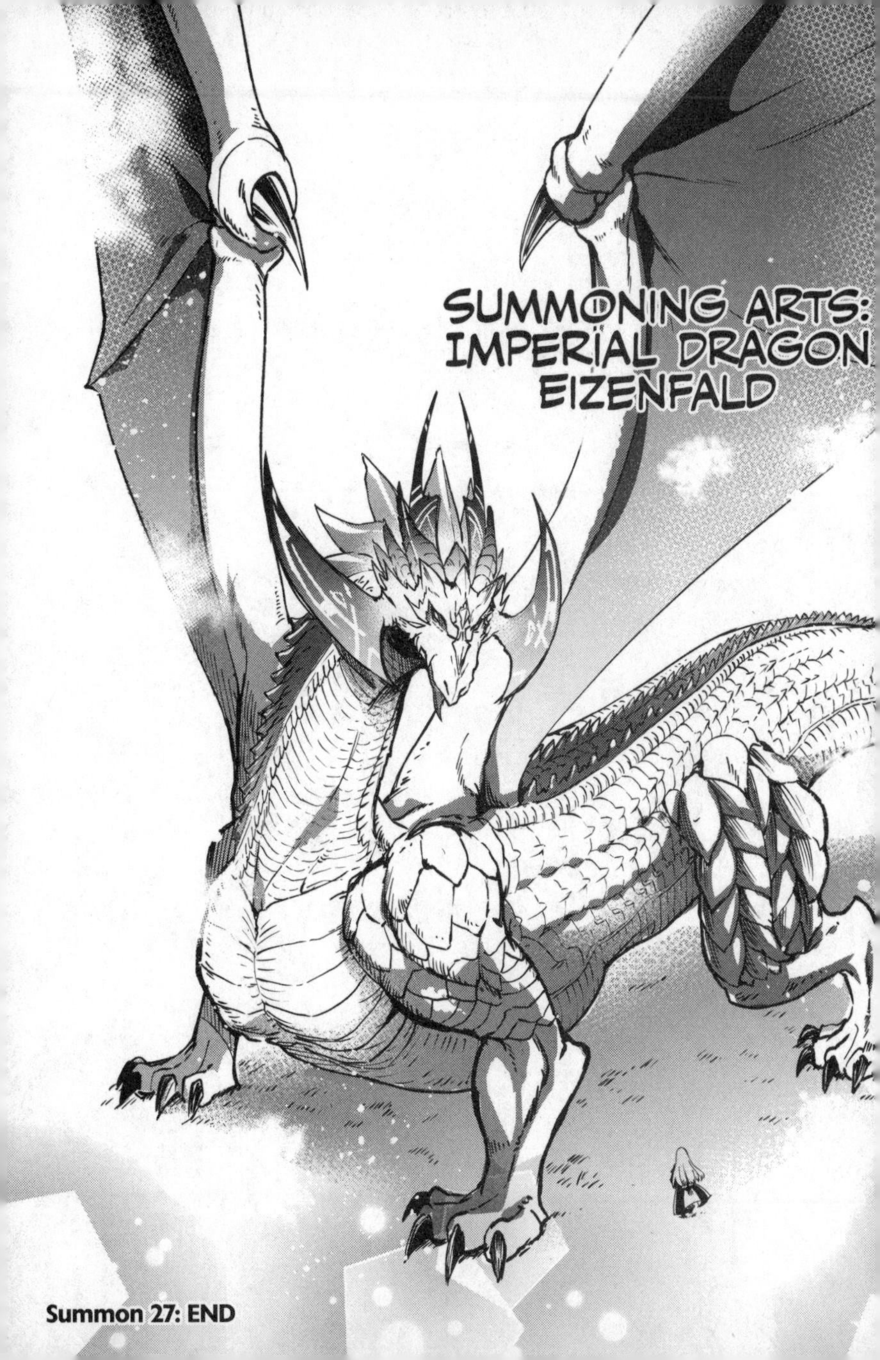
SUMMONING ARTS:
IMPERIAL DRAGON
EIZENFALD
Summon 27: END

She
Professed
Herself
Pupil of the
Wise Man

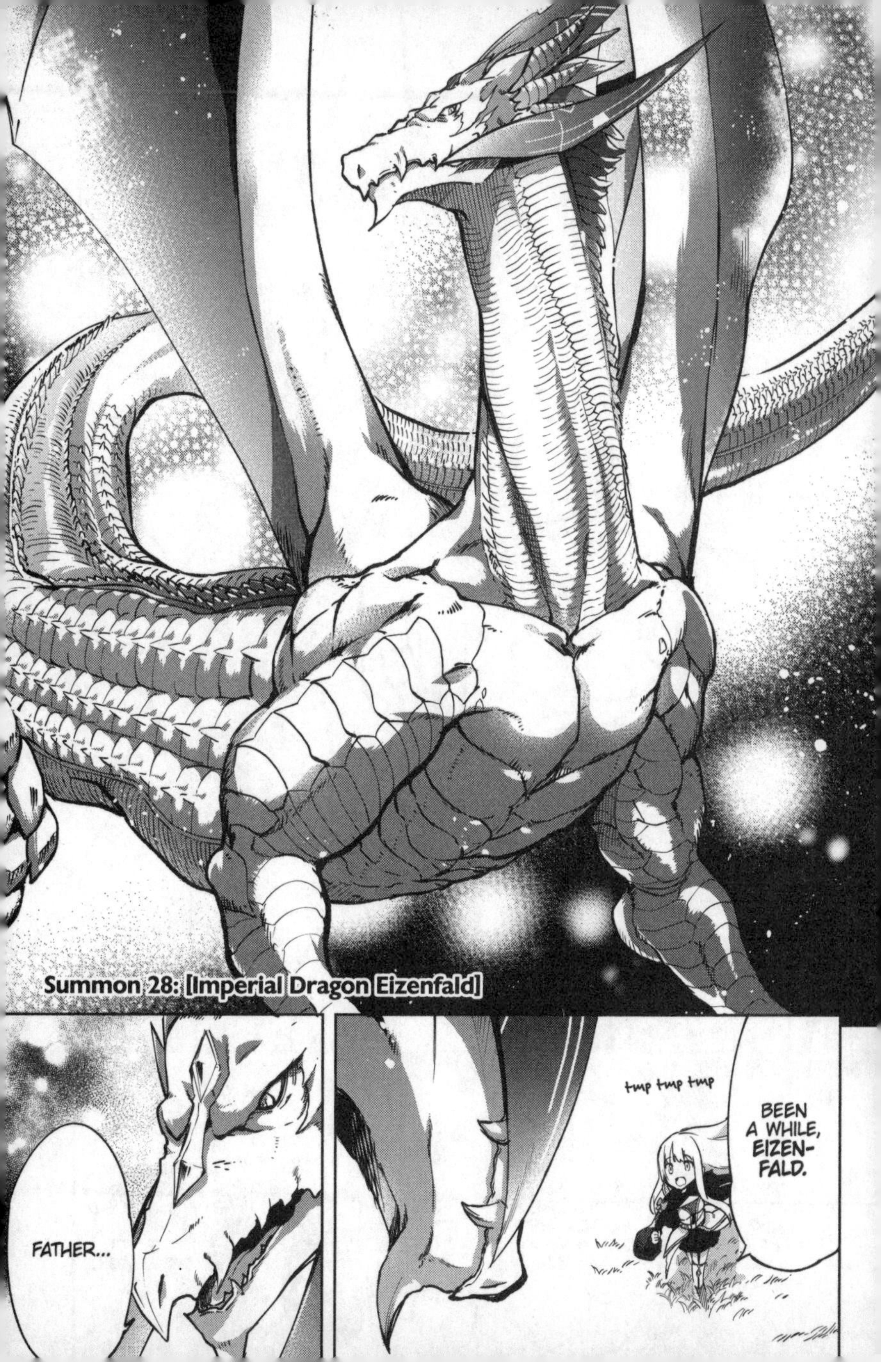
Summon 28: [Imperial Dragon Eizenfald]
tmp tmp tmp
BEEN A WHILE, EIZEN-FALD.
FATHER...

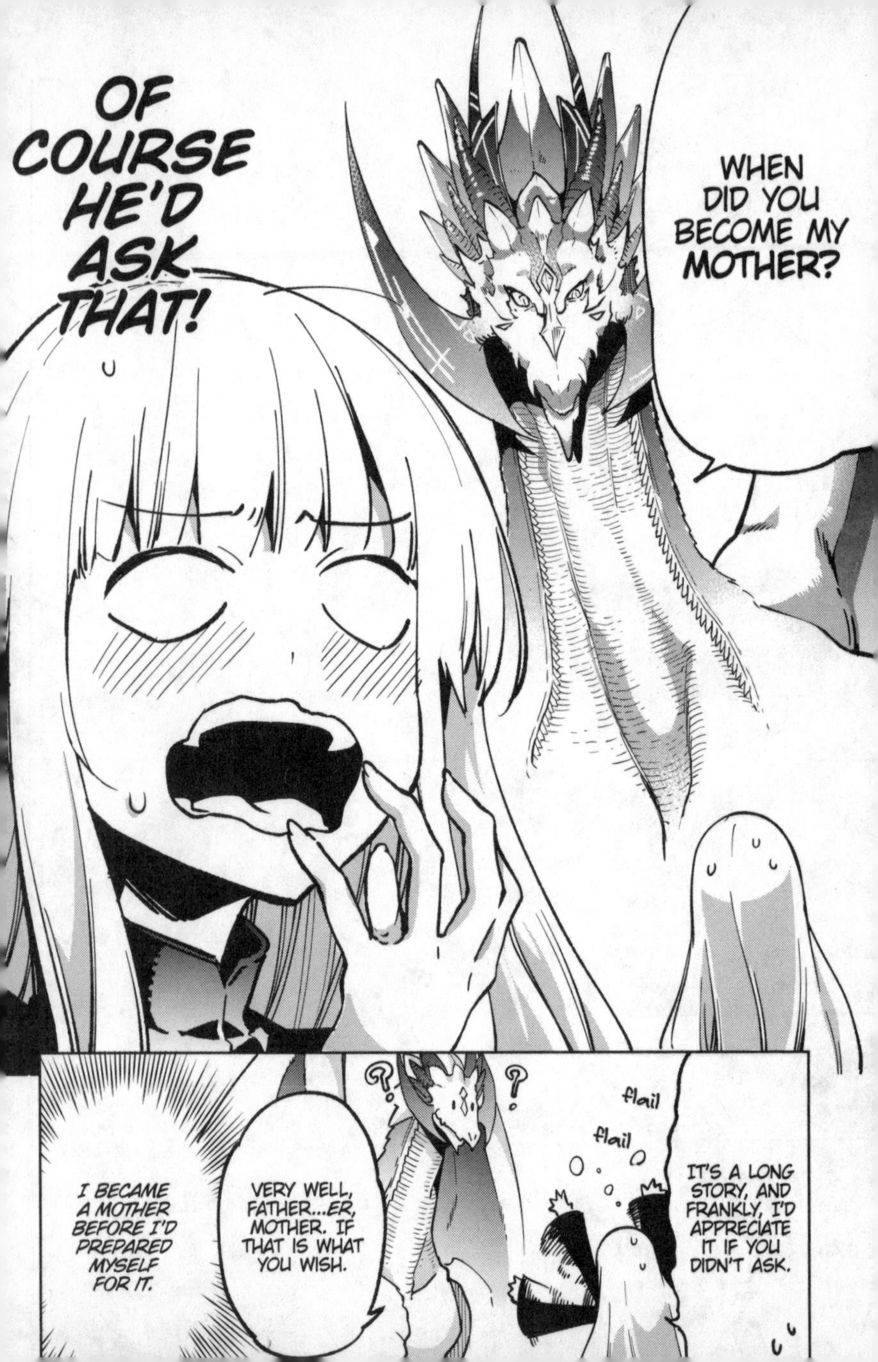
WHEN DID YOU BECOME MY MOTHER?
OF COURSE HE'D ASK THAT!
IT'S A LONG STORY, AND FRANKLY, I'D APPRECIATE IT IF YOU DIDN'T ASK.
flail
flail
VERY WELL, FATHER...ER, MOTHER. IF THAT IS WHAT YOU WISH.
I BECAME A MOTHER BEFORE I'D PREPARED MYSELF FOR IT.

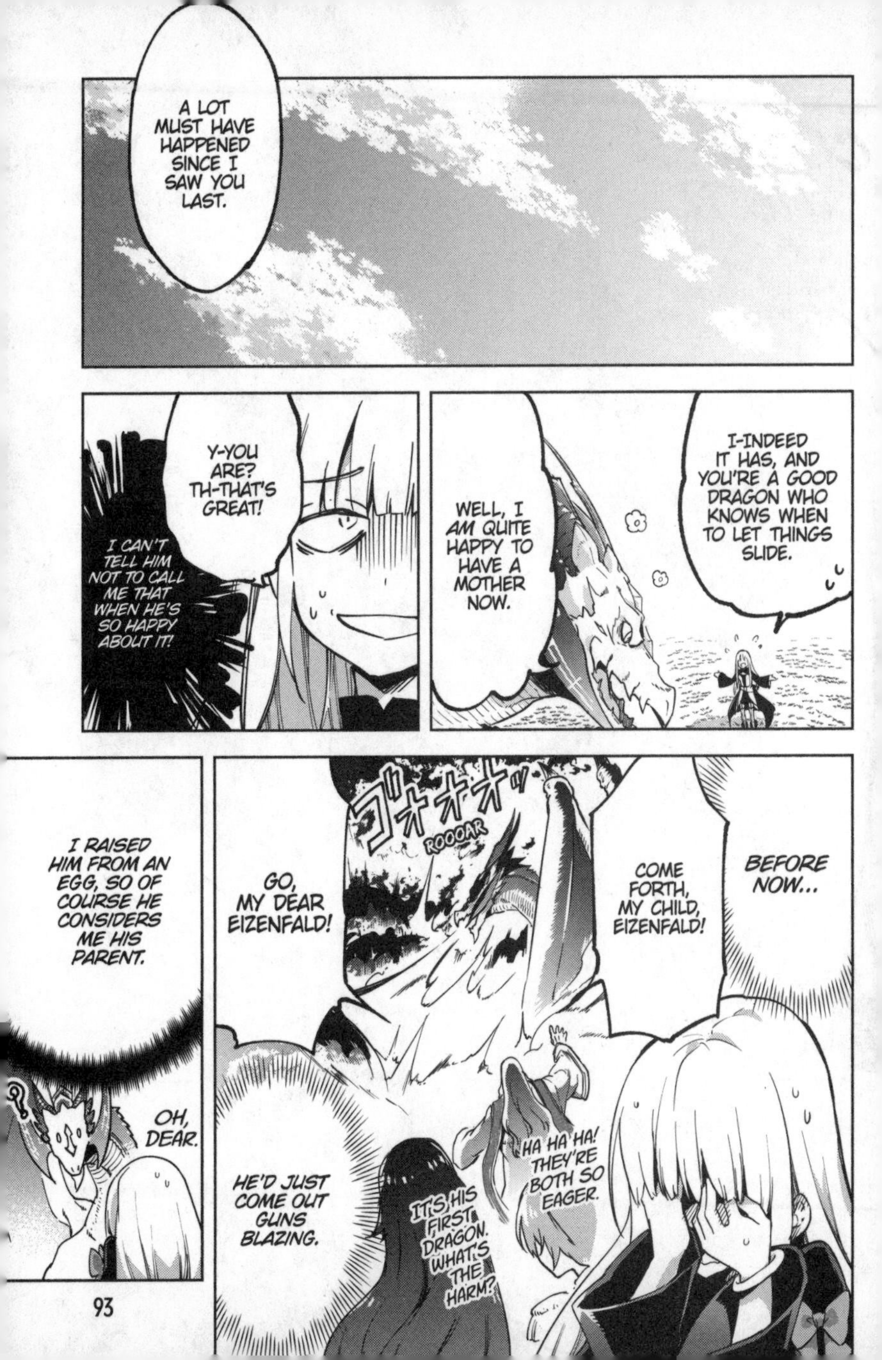
A LOT MUST HAVE HAPPENED SINCE I SAW YOU LAST.
I-INDEED IT HAS, AND YOU'RE A GOOD DRAGON WHO KNOWS WHEN TO LET THINGS SLIDE.
WELL, I AM QUITE HAPPY TO HAVE A MOTHER NOW.
Y-YOU ARE? TH-THAT'S GREAT!
I CAN'T TELL HIM NOT TO CALL ME THAT WHEN HE'S SO HAPPY ABOUT IT!
BEFORE NOW...
COME FORTH, MY CHILD, EIZENFALD!
ROOOAR
GO, MY DEAR EIZENFALD!
HA HA HA! THEY'RE BOTH SO EAGER.
IT'S HIS FIRST DRAGON. WHAT'S THE HARM?
HE'D JUST COME OUT GUNS BLAZING.
I RAISED HIM FROM AN EGG, SO OF COURSE HE CONSIDERS ME HIS PARENT.
OH, DEAR.

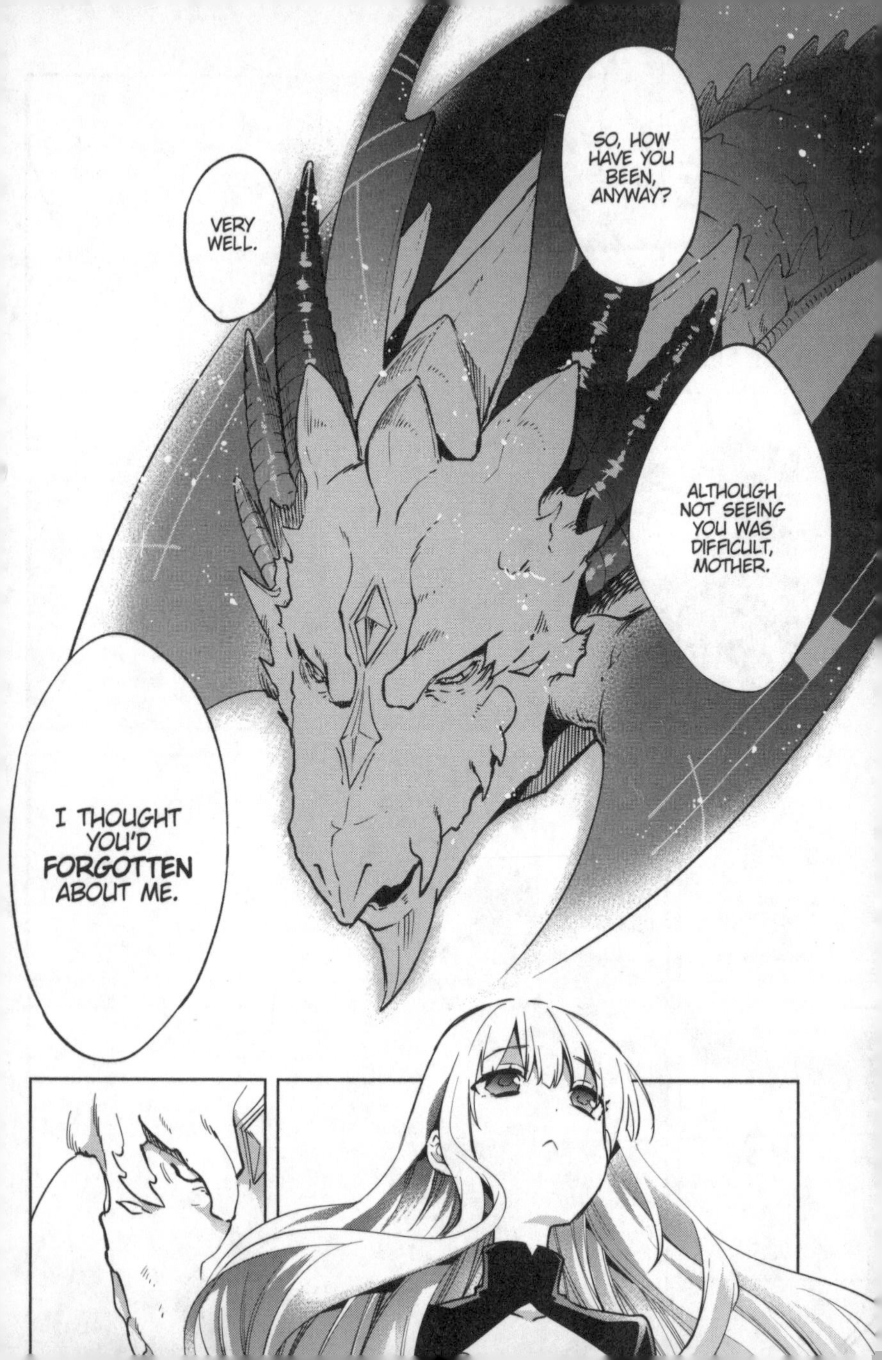
SO, HOW HAVE YOU BEEN, ANYWAY?
VERY WELL.
ALTHOUGH NOT SEEING YOU WAS DIFFICULT, MOTHER.
I THOUGHT YOU'D **FORGOTTEN** ABOUT ME.

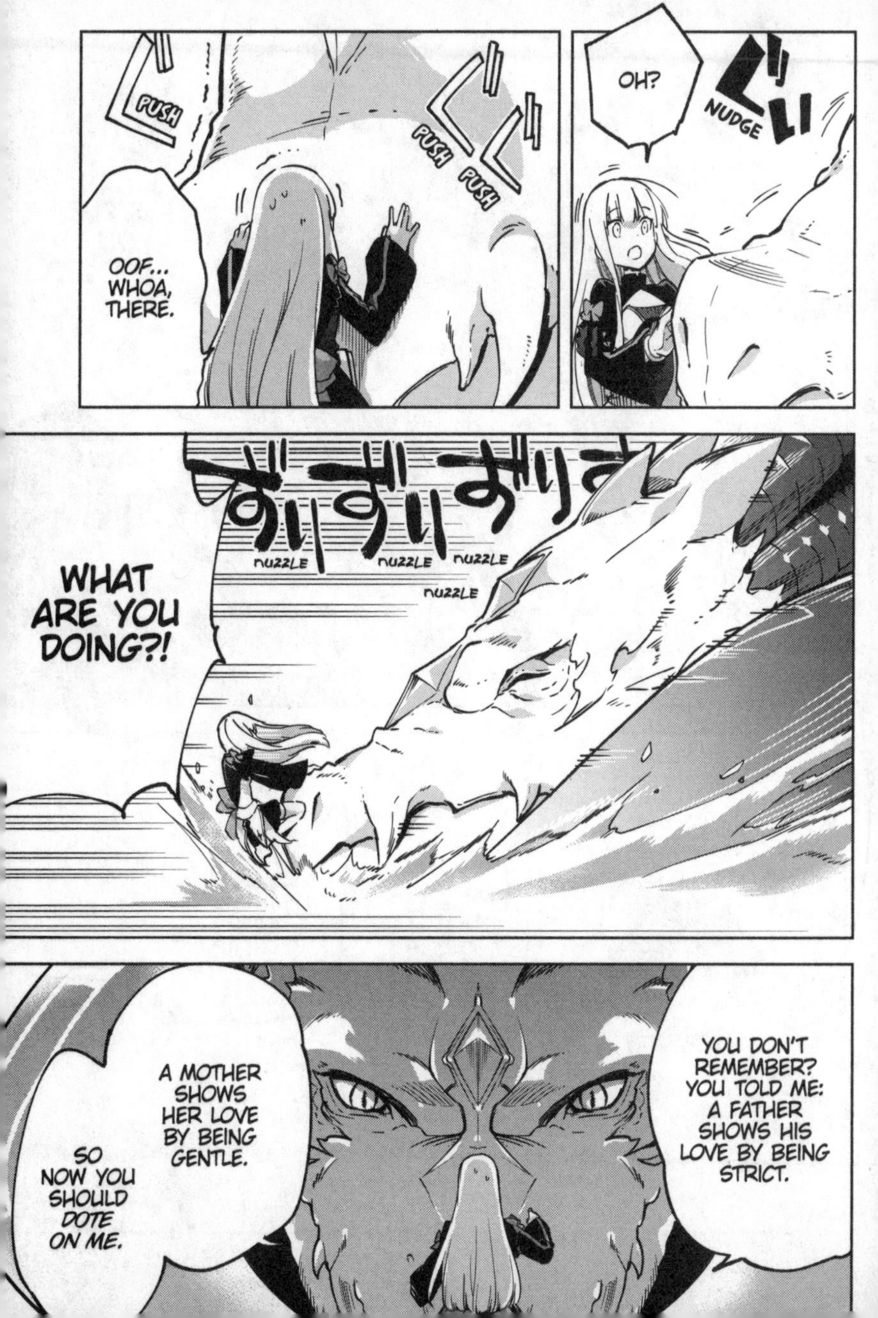
OH?
NUDGE
PUSH
PUSH
PUSH
OOF... WHOA, THERE.
nuzzle
nuzzle
nuzzle
nuzzle
WHAT ARE YOU DOING?!
YOU DON'T REMEMBER? YOU TOLD ME: A FATHER SHOWS HIS LOVE BY BEING STRICT.
A MOTHER SHOWS HER LOVE BY BEING GENTLE.
SO NOW YOU SHOULD DOTE ON ME.

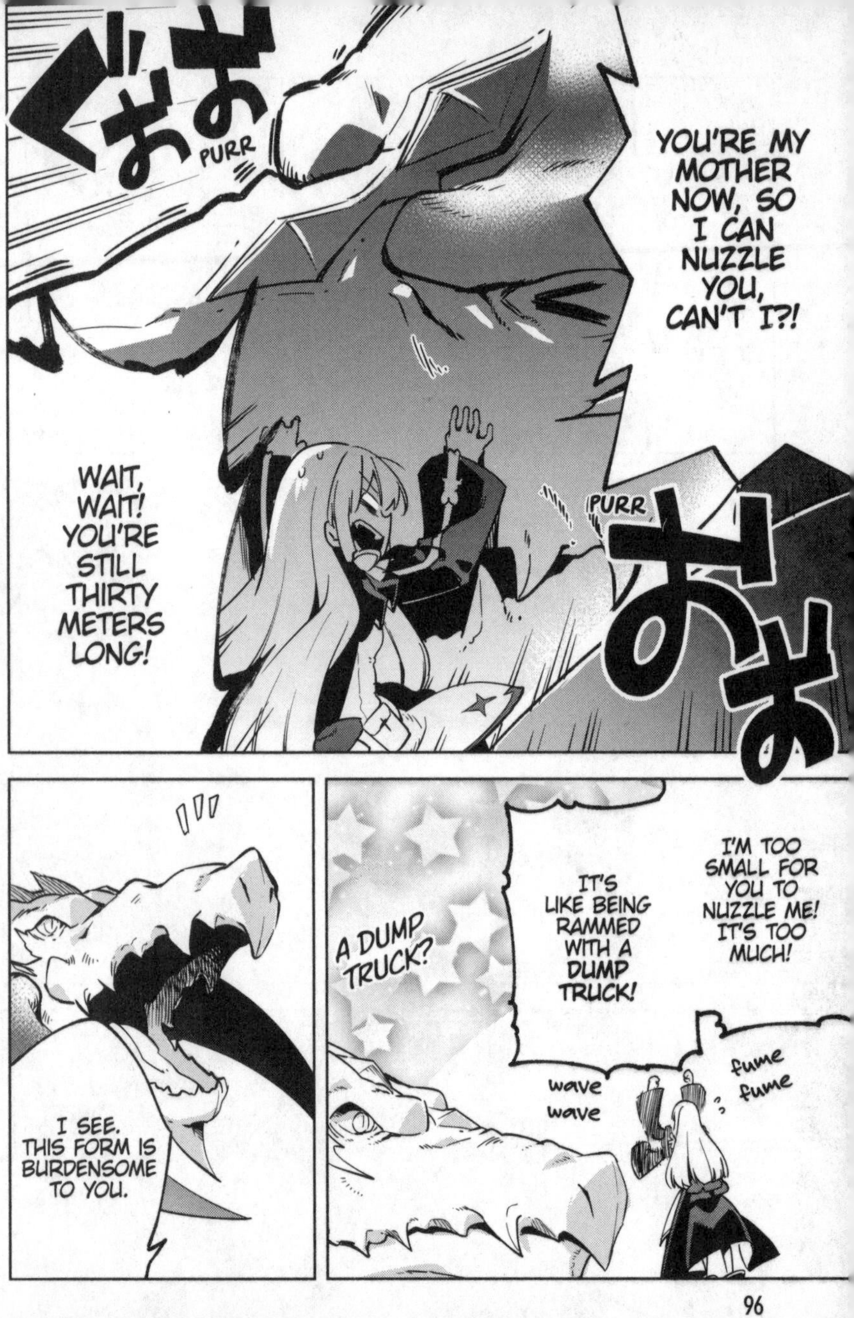
YOU'RE MY MOTHER NOW, SO I CAN NUZZLE YOU, CAN'T I?!
ぐおお
PURR
おお
PURR
WAIT, WAIT! YOU'RE STILL THIRTY METERS LONG!
I'M TOO SMALL FOR YOU TO NUZZLE ME! IT'S TOO MUCH!
IT'S LIKE BEING RAMMED WITH A DUMP TRUCK!
A DUMP TRUCK?
fume fume
wave wave
I SEE. THIS FORM IS BURDENSOME TO YOU.

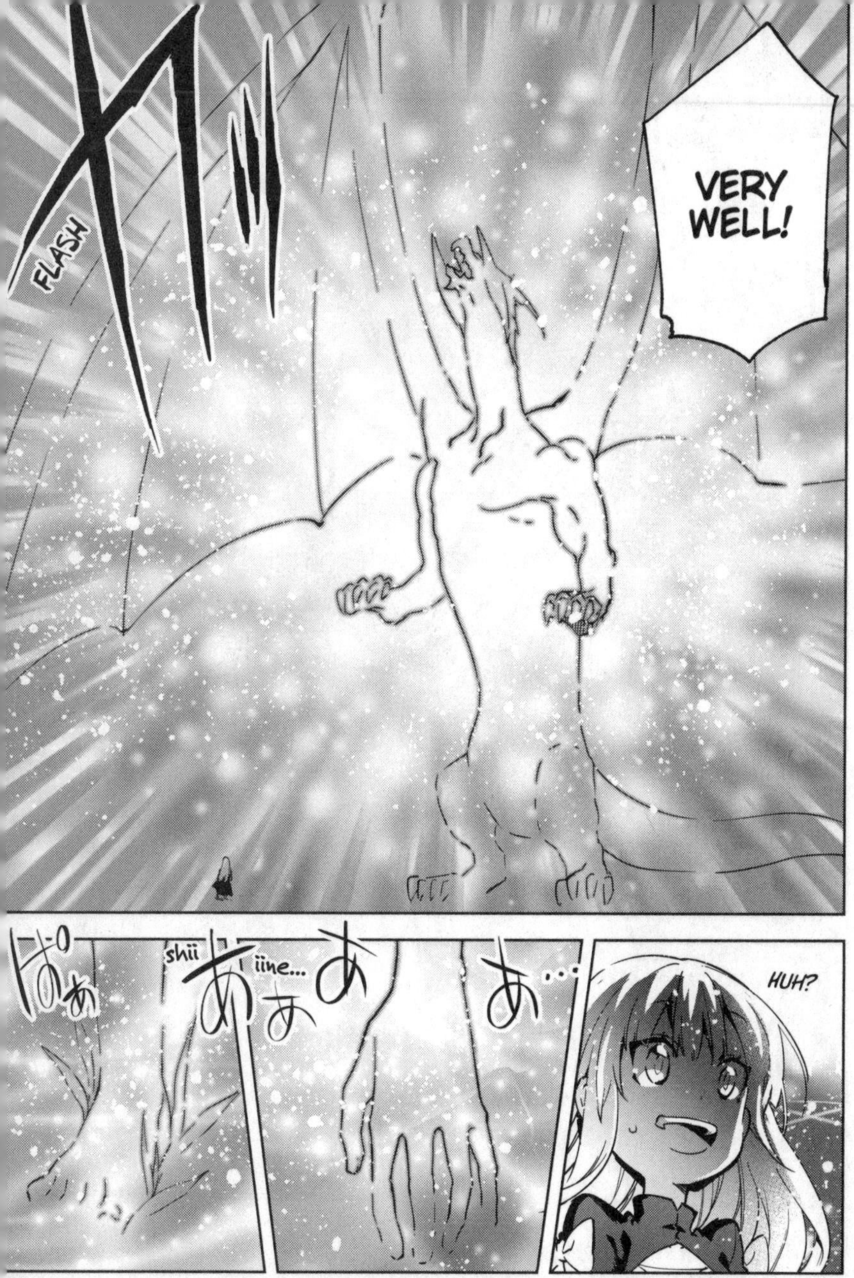
VERY WELL!
FLASH
HUH?
iine...
shii

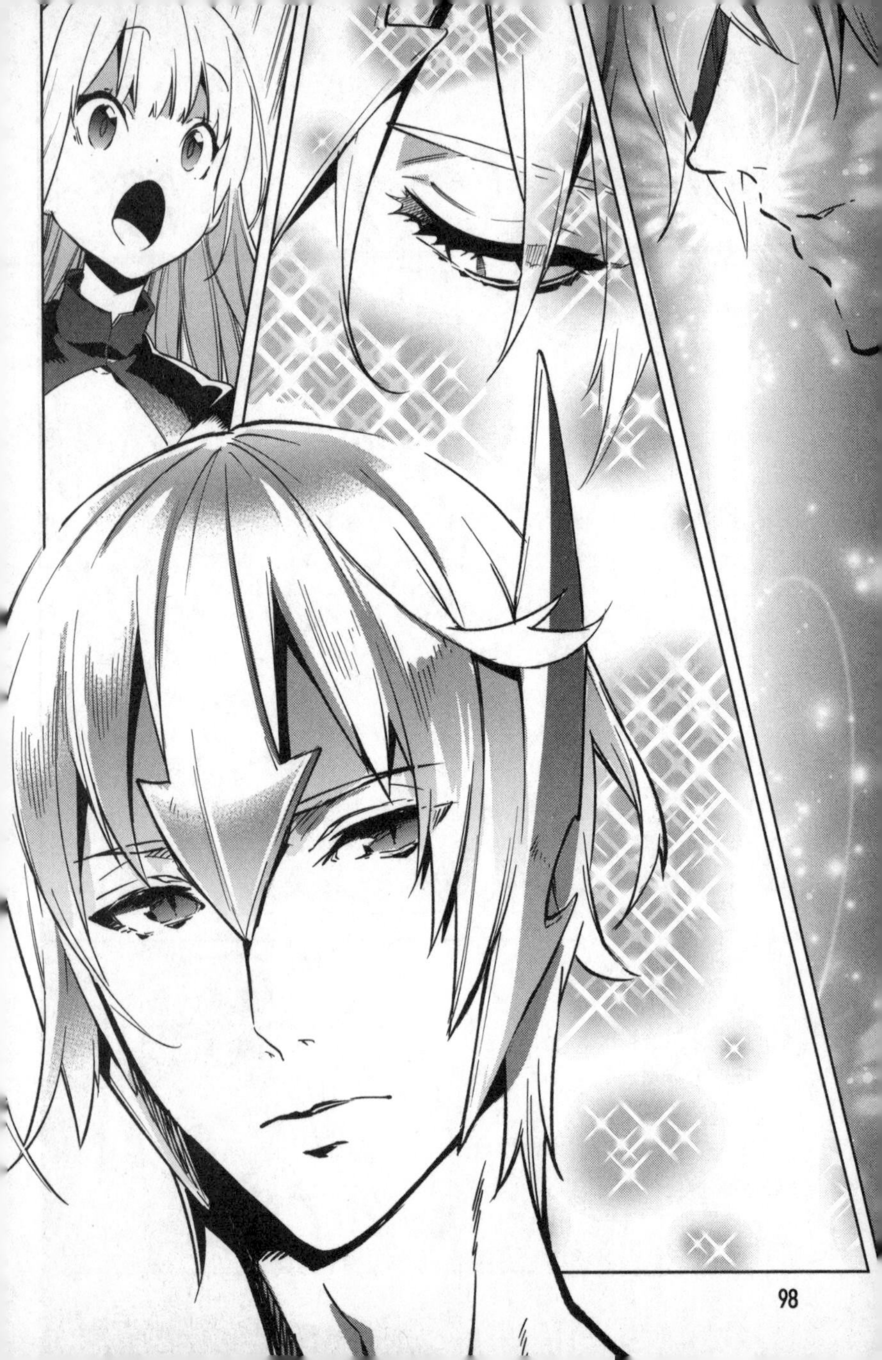

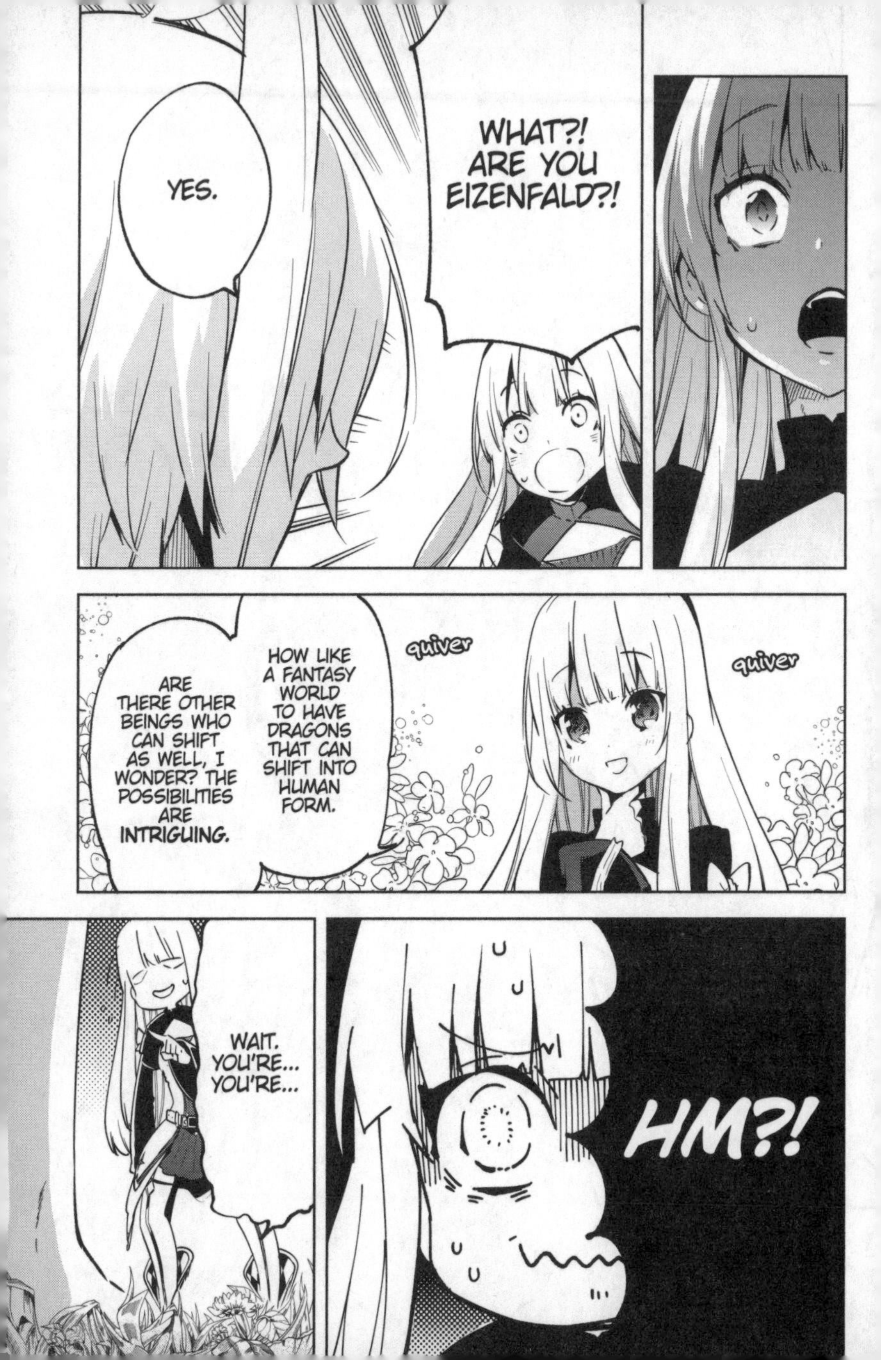
WHAT?! ARE YOU EIZENFALD?!
YES.
quiver
quiver
HOW LIKE A FANTASY WORLD TO HAVE DRAGONS THAT CAN SHIFT INTO HUMAN FORM.
ARE THERE OTHER BEINGS WHO CAN SHIFT AS WELL, I WONDER? THE POSSIBILITIES ARE INTRIGUING.
HM?!
WAIT. YOU'RE... YOU'RE...

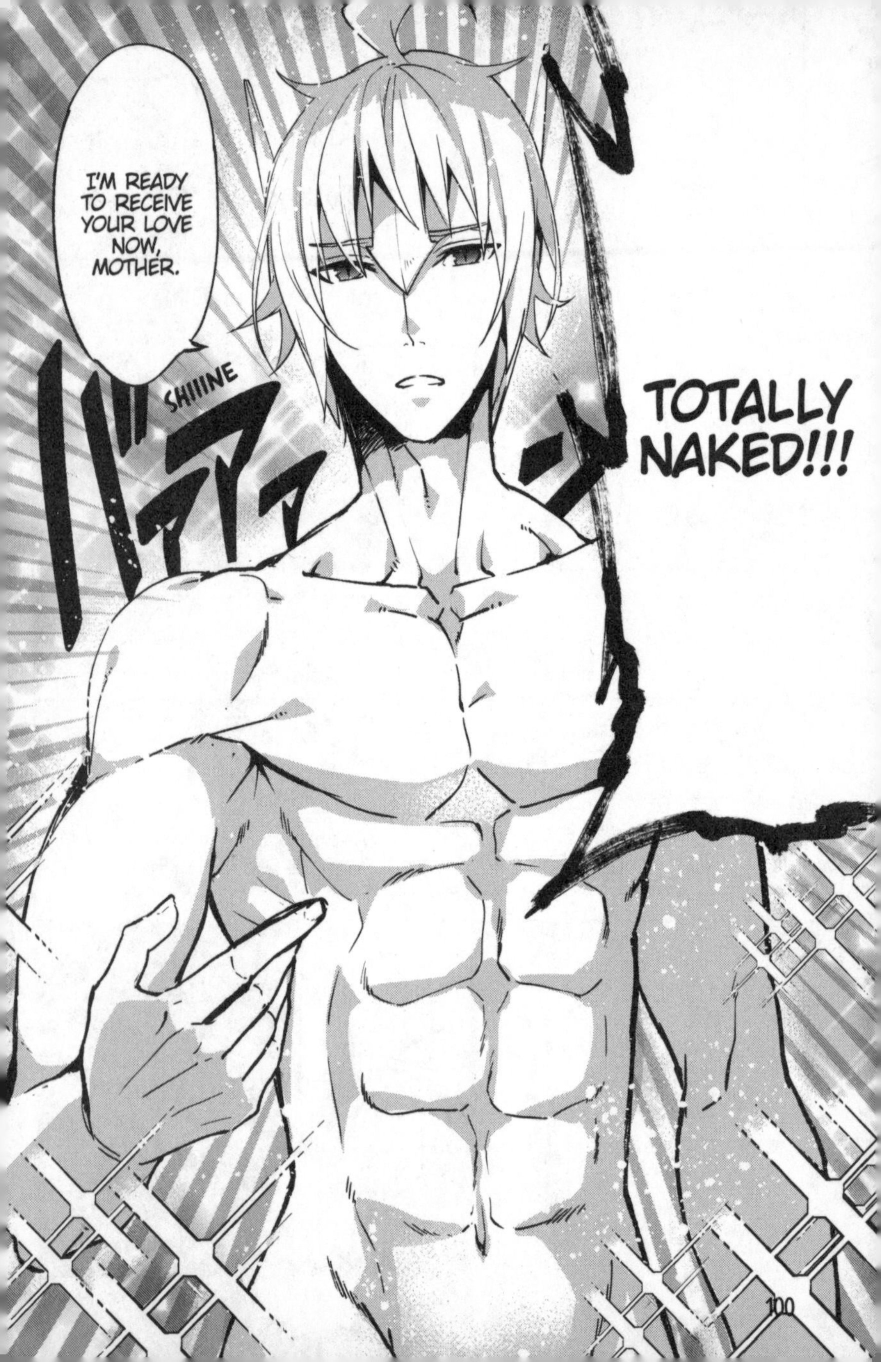
I'M READY TO RECEIVE YOUR LOVE NOW, MOTHER.
TOTALLY NAKED!!!
SHIIINE

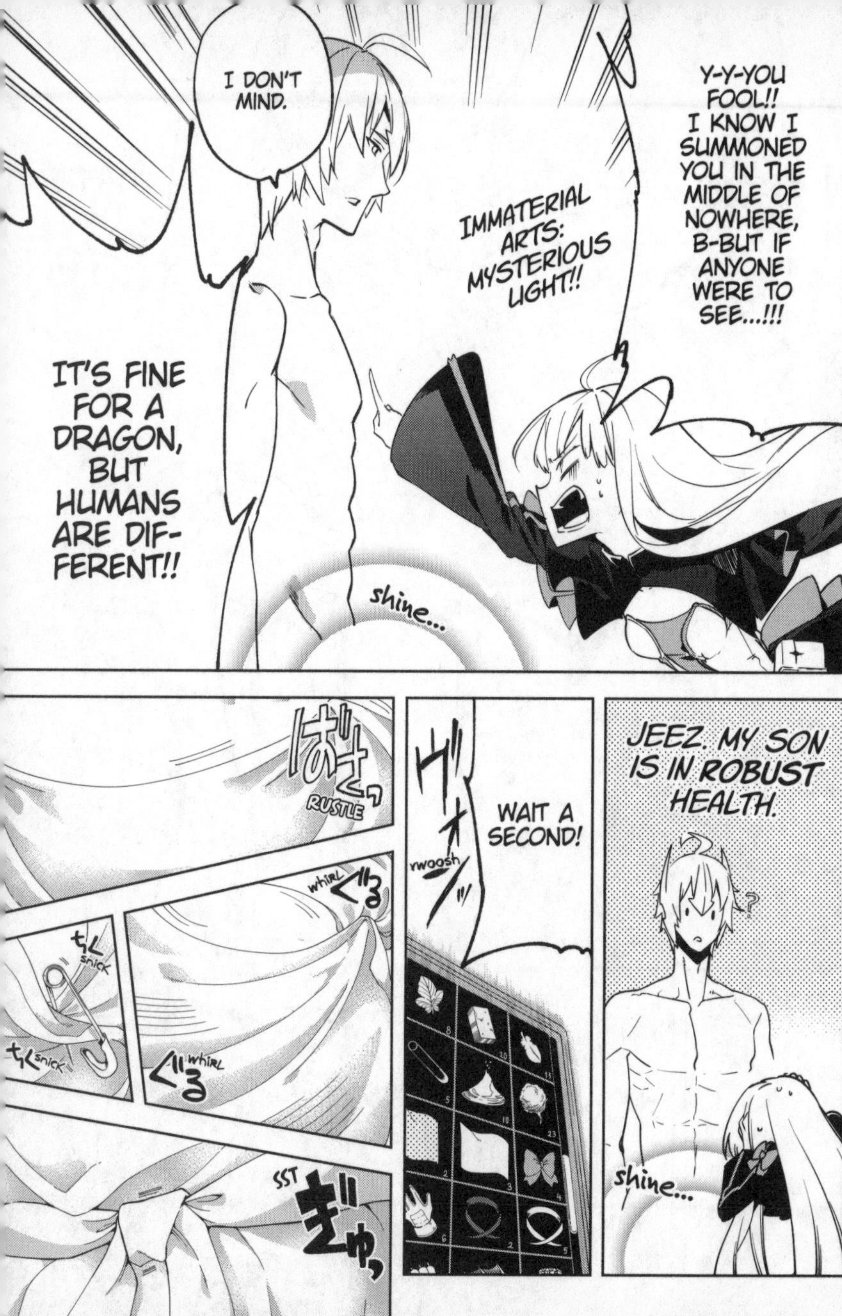
Y-Y-YOU FOOL!! I KNOW I SUMMONED YOU IN THE MIDDLE OF NOWHERE, B-BUT IF ANYONE WERE TO SEE...!!!
I DON'T MIND.
IMMATERIAL ARTS: MYSTERIOUS LIGHT!!
IT'S FINE FOR A DRAGON, BUT HUMANS ARE DIF-FERENT!!
shine...
JEEZ. MY SON IS IN ROBUST HEALTH.
?
shine...
WAIT A SECOND!
rwoosh
RUSTLE
whirl
snick
snick
whirl
SST

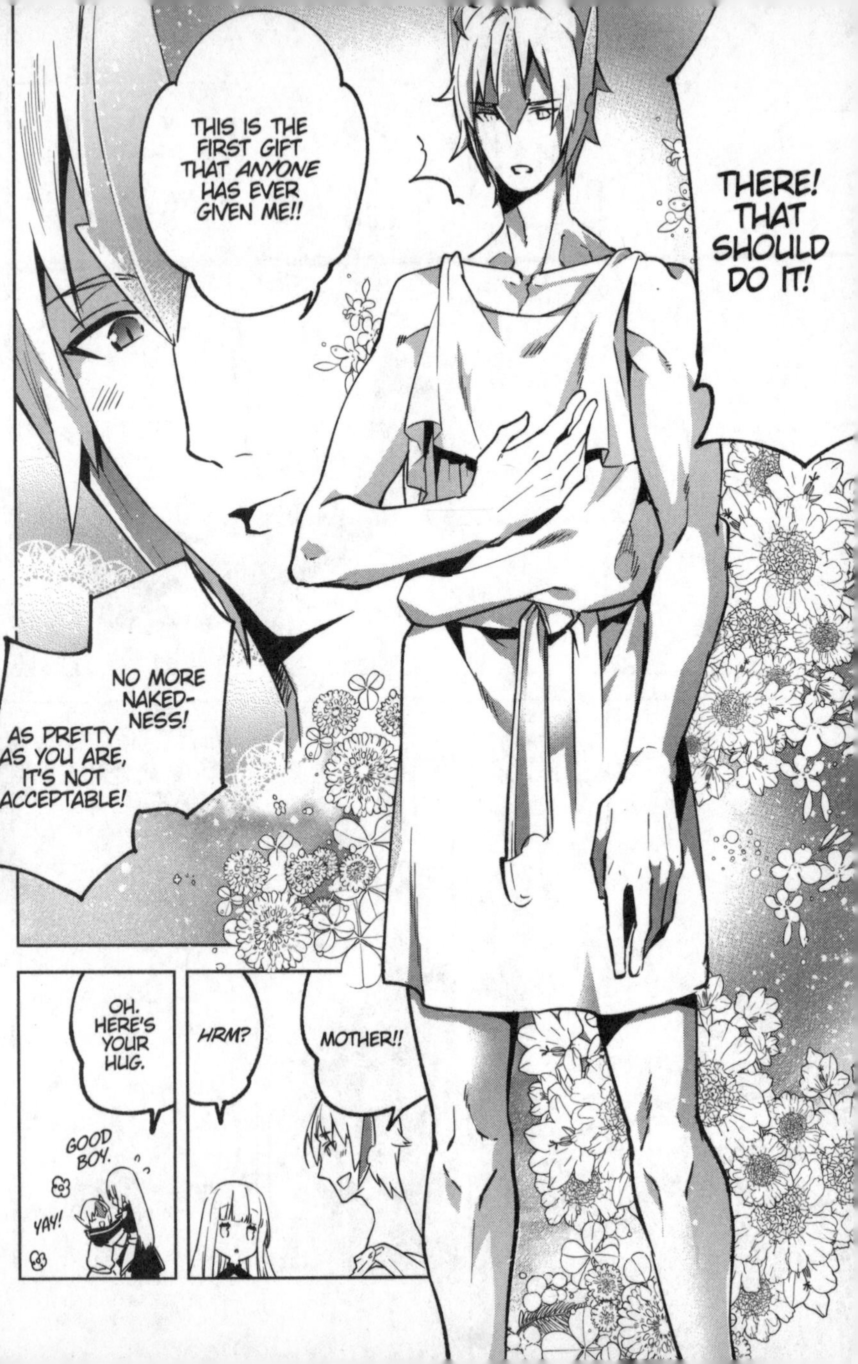
THERE! THAT SHOULD DO IT!
THIS IS THE FIRST GIFT THAT ANYONE HAS EVER GIVEN ME!!
NO MORE NAKED-NESS!
AS PRETTY AS YOU ARE, IT'S NOT ACCEPTABLE!
MOTHER!!
HRM?
OH. HERE'S YOUR HUG.
GOOD BOY.
YAY!

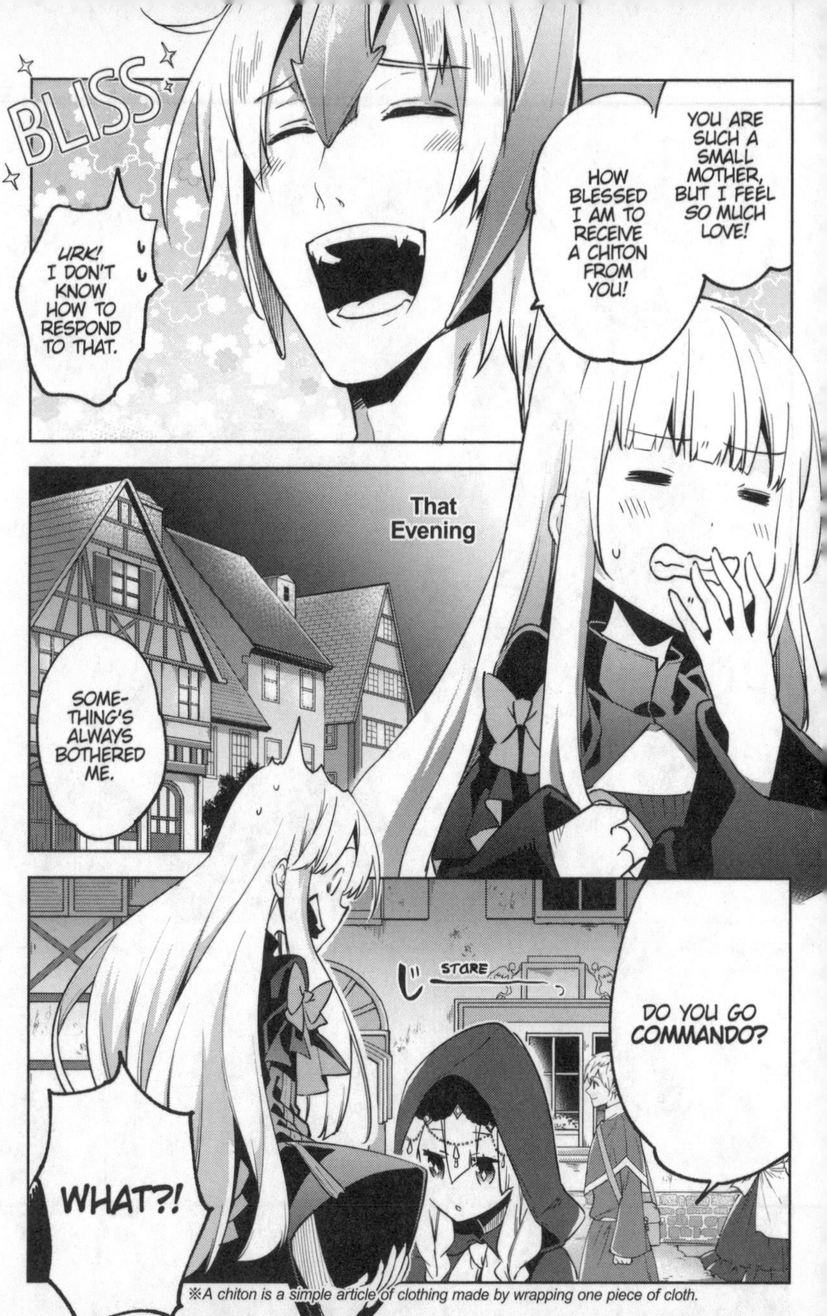
YOU ARE SUCH A SMALL MOTHER, BUT I FEEL SO MUCH LOVE!
HOW BLESSED I AM TO RECEIVE A CHITON FROM YOU!
BLISS
URK! I DON'T KNOW HOW TO RESPOND TO THAT.
That Evening
SOME-THING'S ALWAYS BOTHERED ME.
DO YOU GO COMMANDO?
STARE
WHAT?!

※A chiton is a simple article of clothing made by wrapping one piece of cloth.

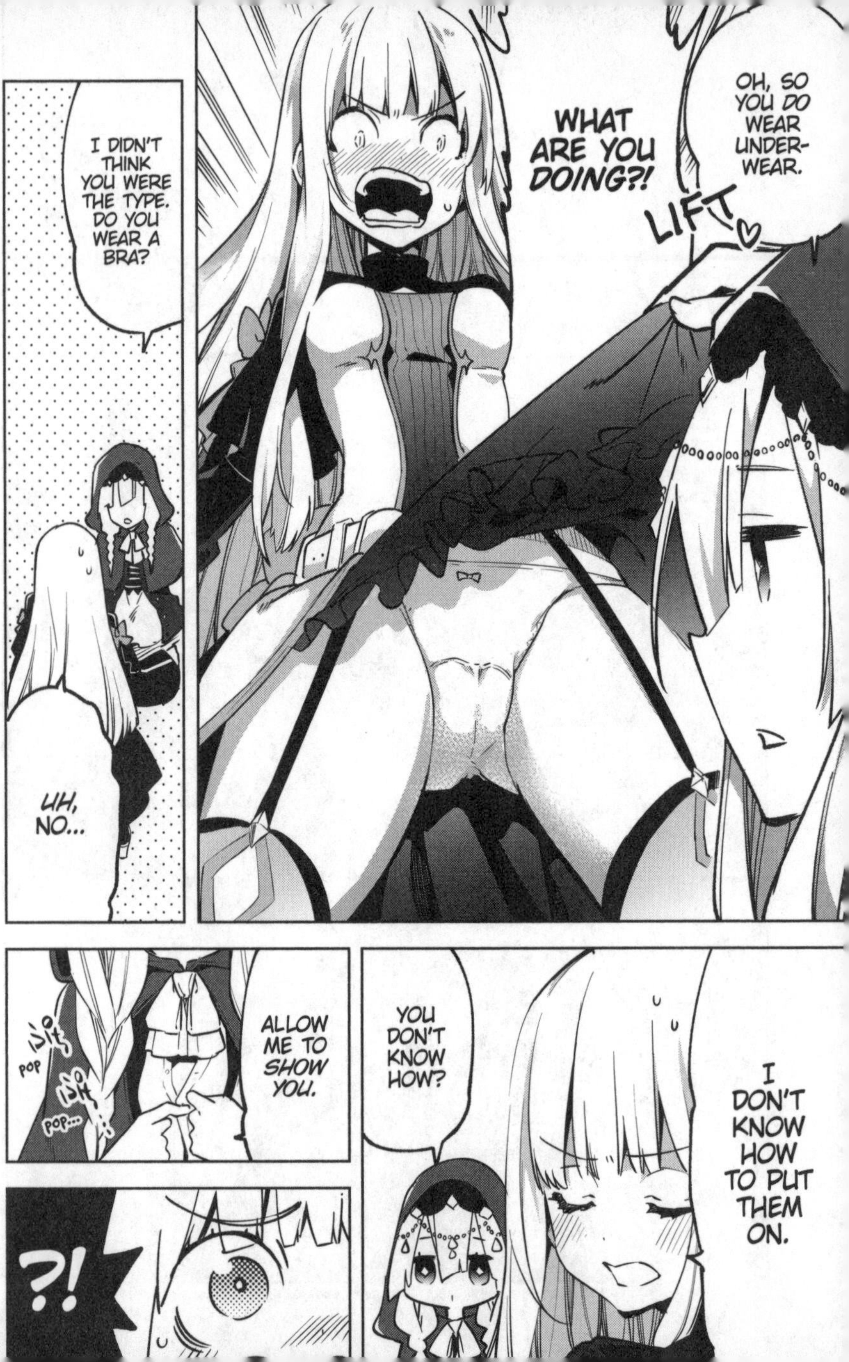

OH, SO YOU DO WEAR UNDER-WEAR.
LIFT ♥
WHAT ARE YOU DOING?!
I DIDN'T THINK YOU WERE THE TYPE. DO YOU WEAR A BRA?
UH, NO...
I DON'T KNOW HOW TO PUT THEM ON.
YOU DON'T KNOW HOW?
ALLOW ME TO SHOW YOU.
pop
pop...
?!

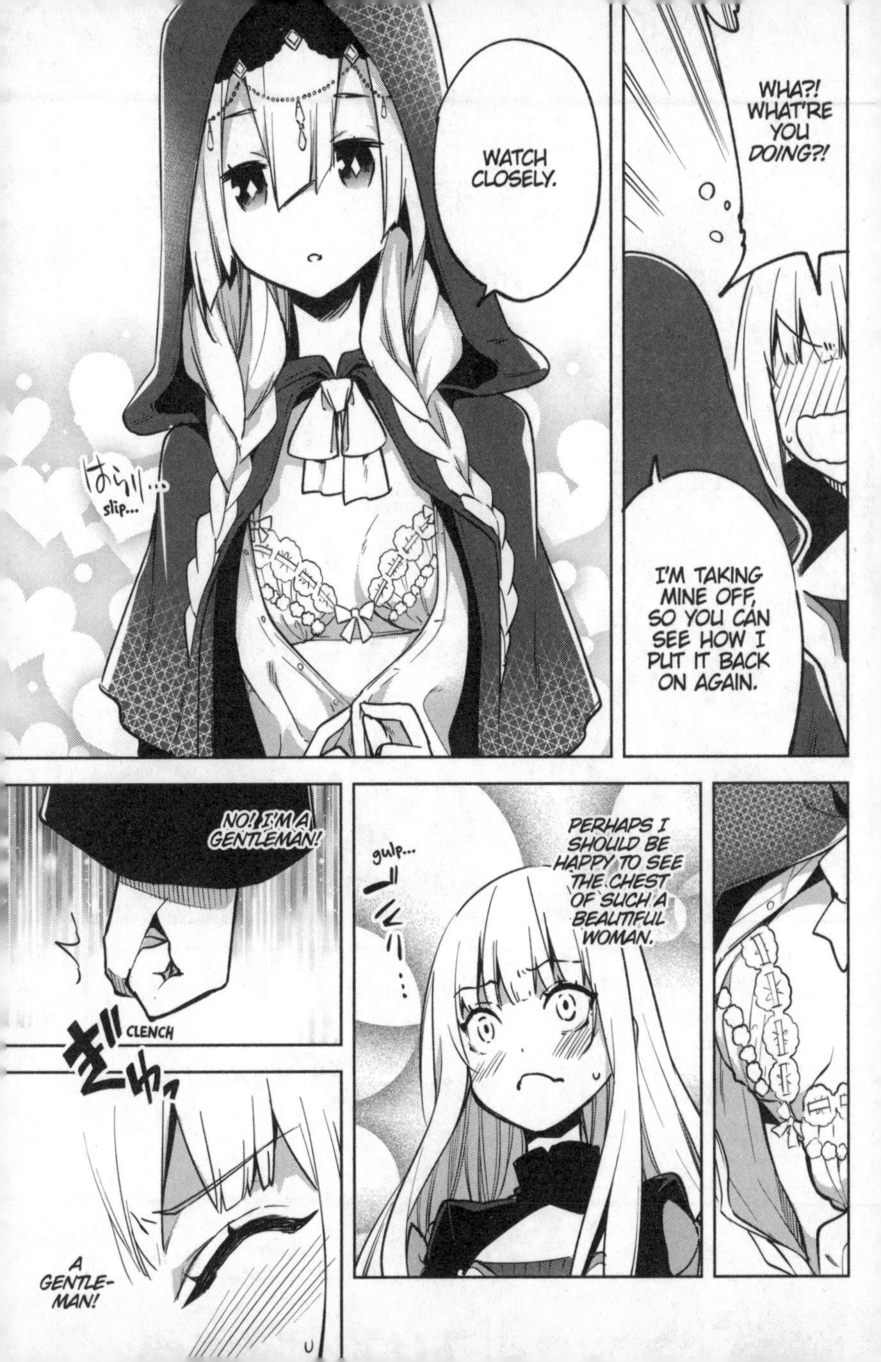
WHA?! WHAT'RE YOU DOING?!
I'M TAKING MINE OFF, SO YOU CAN SEE HOW I PUT IT BACK ON AGAIN.
WATCH CLOSELY.
はらり…
slip...
PERHAPS I SHOULD BE HAPPY TO SEE THE CHEST OF SUCH A BEAUTIFUL WOMAN.
gulp...
NO! I'M A GENTLEMAN!
ぎゅっ
CLENCH
A GENTLE-MAN!

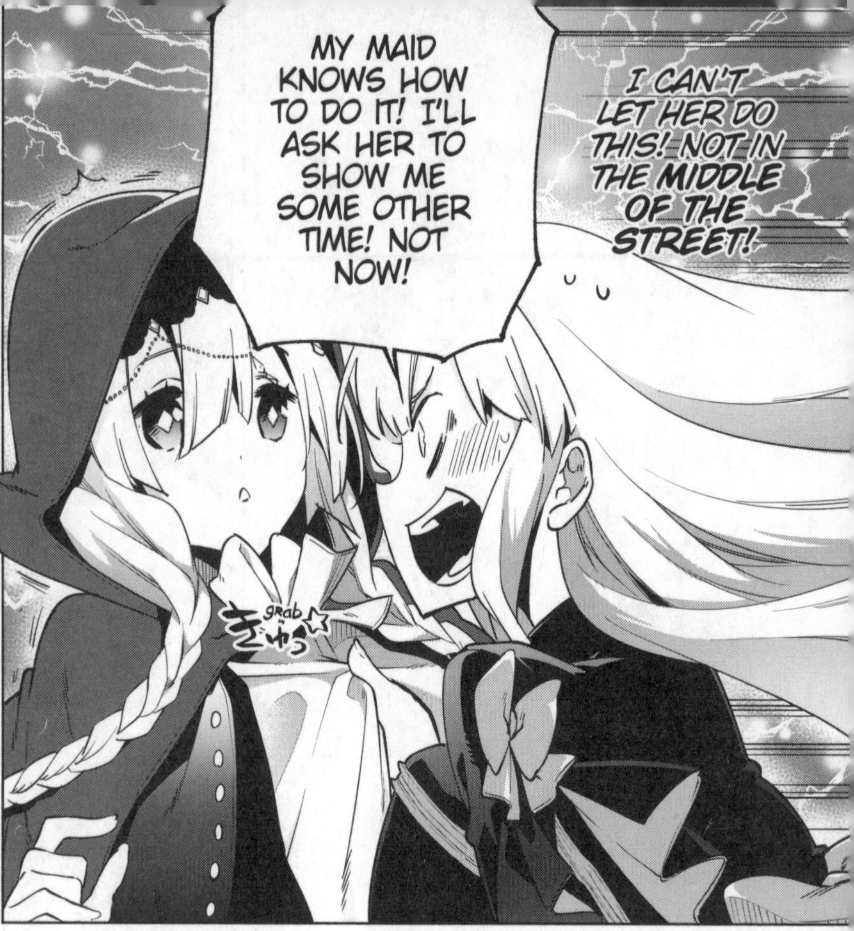
I CAN'T LET HER DO THIS! NOT IN THE MIDDLE OF THE STREET!
MY MAID KNOWS HOW TO DO IT! I'LL ASK HER TO SHOW ME SOME OTHER TIME! NOT NOW!
grab
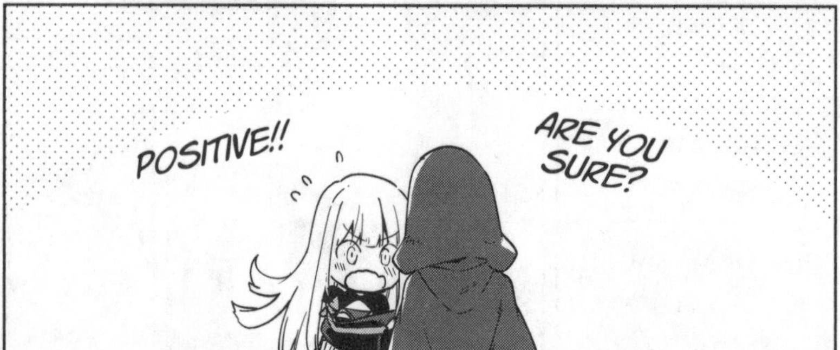
ARE YOU SURE?
POSITIVE!!

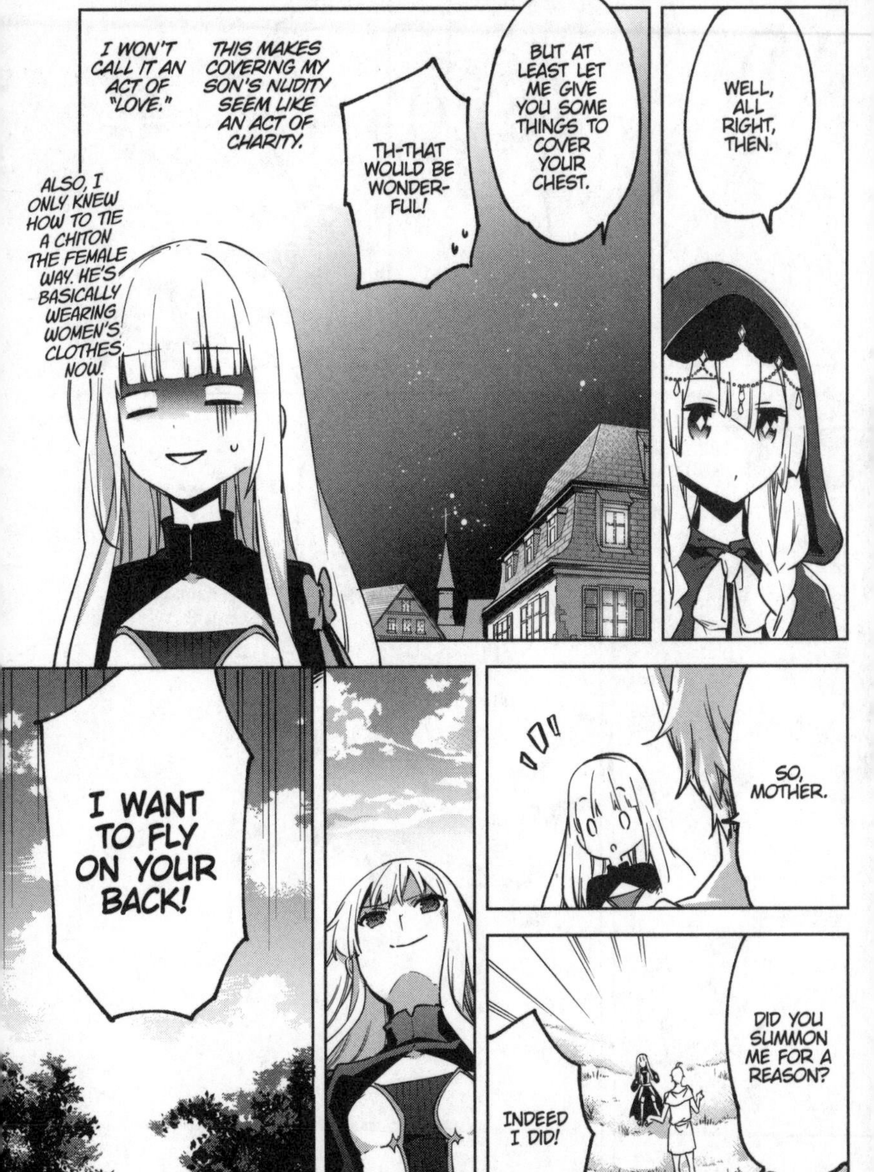

WELL, ALL RIGHT, THEN.
BUT AT LEAST LET ME GIVE YOU SOME THINGS TO COVER YOUR CHEST.
TH-THAT WOULD BE WONDER-FUL!
THIS MAKES COVERING MY SON'S NUDITY SEEM LIKE AN ACT OF CHARITY.
I WON'T CALL IT AN ACT OF "LOVE."
ALSO, I ONLY KNEW HOW TO TIE A CHITON THE FEMALE WAY. HE'S BASICALLY WEARING WOMEN'S CLOTHES NOW.
SO, MOTHER.
DID YOU SUMMON ME FOR A REASON?
INDEED I DID!
I WANT TO FLY ON YOUR BACK!

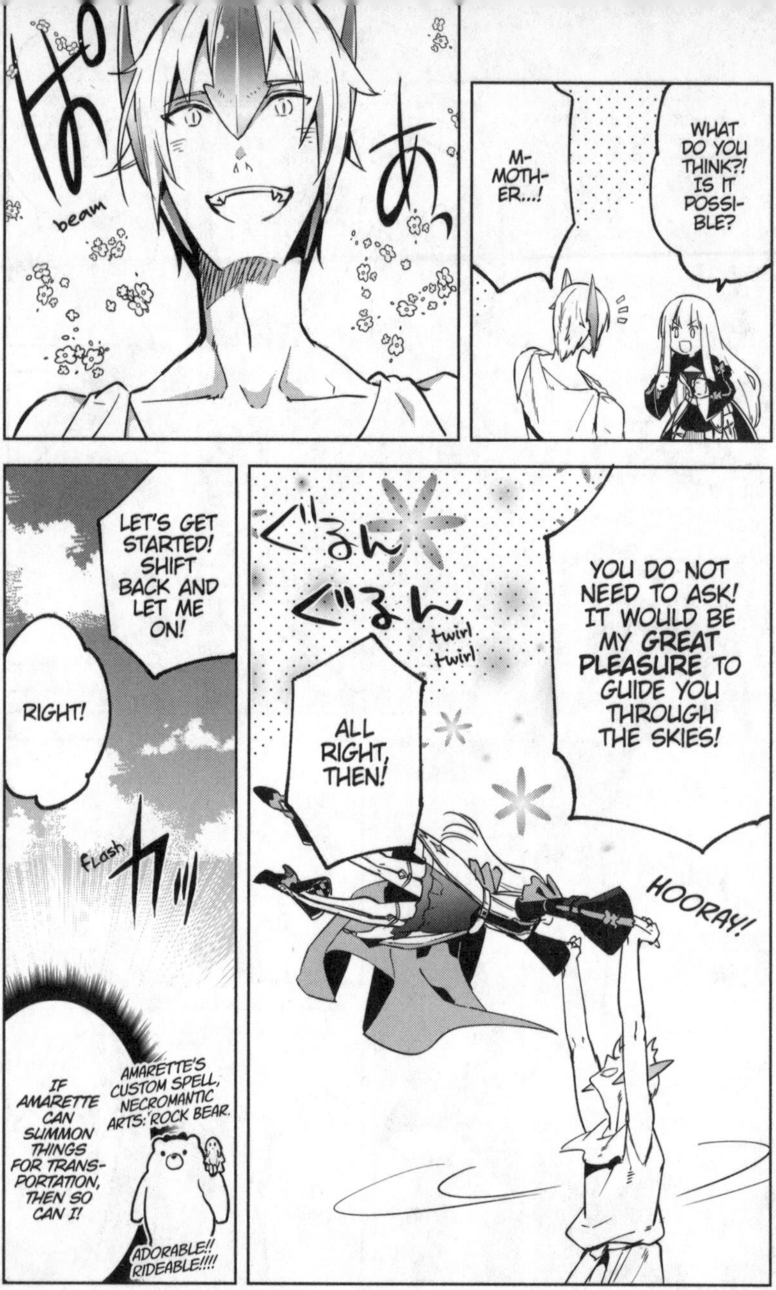
WHAT DO YOU THINK?! IS IT POSSIBLE?
M-MOTHER...!
beam
YOU DO NOT NEED TO ASK! IT WOULD BE MY GREAT PLEASURE TO GUIDE YOU THROUGH THE SKIES!
ぐるん ぐるん
twirl twirl
ALL RIGHT, THEN!
HOORAY!
LET'S GET STARTED! SHIFT BACK AND LET ME ON!
RIGHT!
Flash
AMARETTE'S CUSTOM SPELL, NECROMANTIC ARTS: ROCK BEAR.
IF AMARETTE CAN SUMMON THINGS FOR TRANSPORTATION, THEN SO CAN I!
ADORABLE!! RIDEABLE!!!!

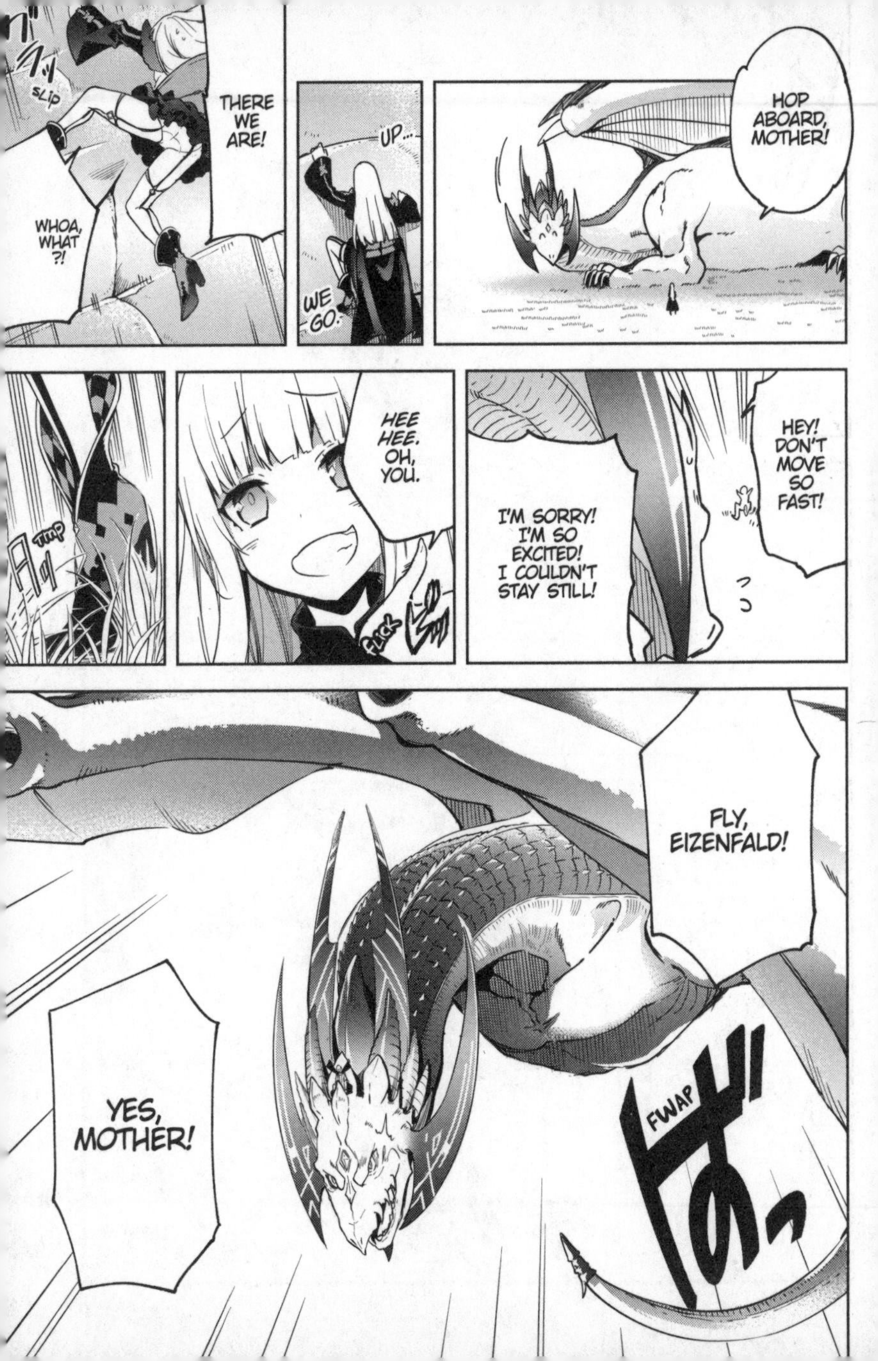
HOP ABOARD, MOTHER!
UP...
WE GO.
THERE WE ARE!
SLIP
WHOA, WHAT ?!
HEY! DON'T MOVE SO FAST!
I'M SORRY! I'M SO EXCITED! I COULDN'T STAY STILL!
HEE HEE. OH, YOU.
FLICK
TMP
FLY, EIZENFALD!
FWAP
YES, MOTHER!

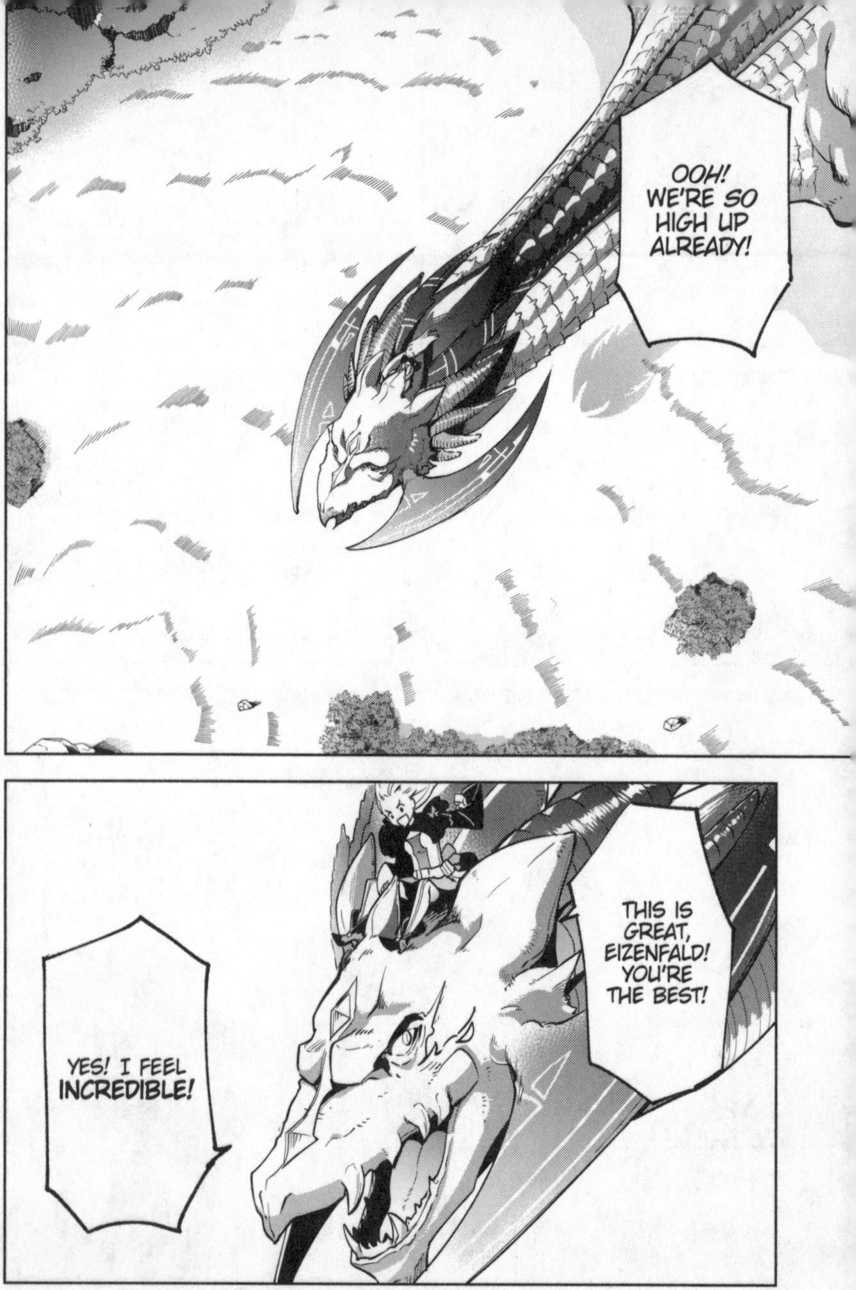
OOH! WE'RE SO HIGH UP ALREADY!
THIS IS GREAT, EIZENFALD! YOU'RE THE BEST!
YES! I FEEL INCREDIBLE!

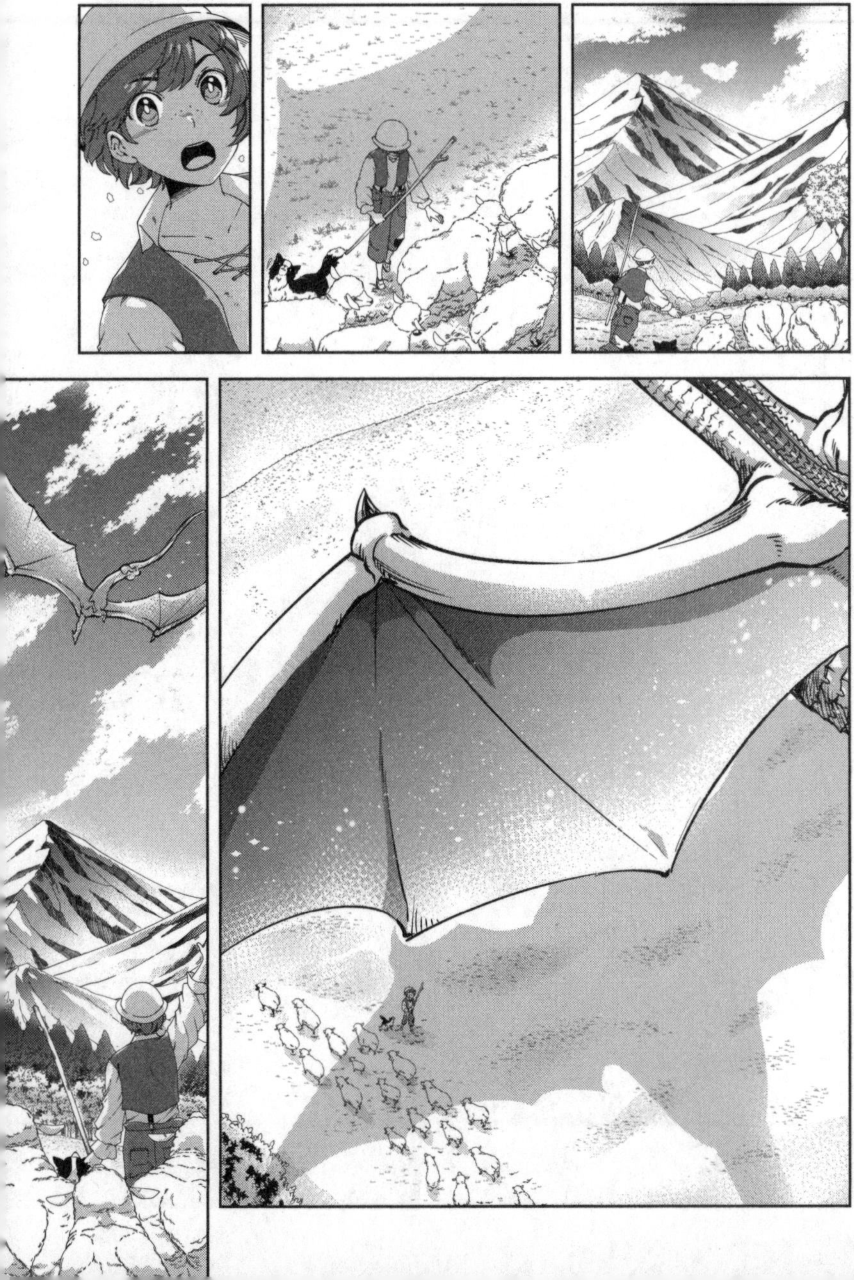

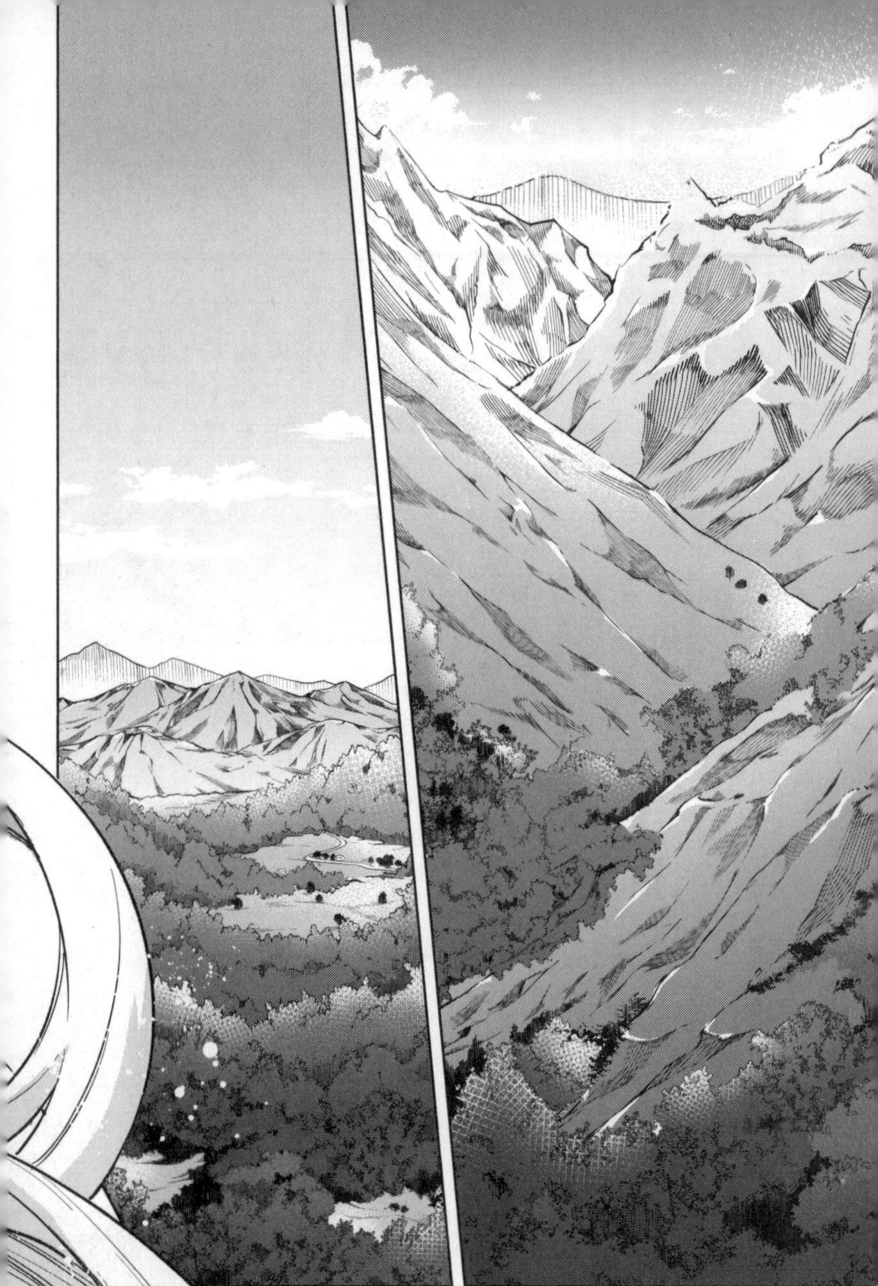

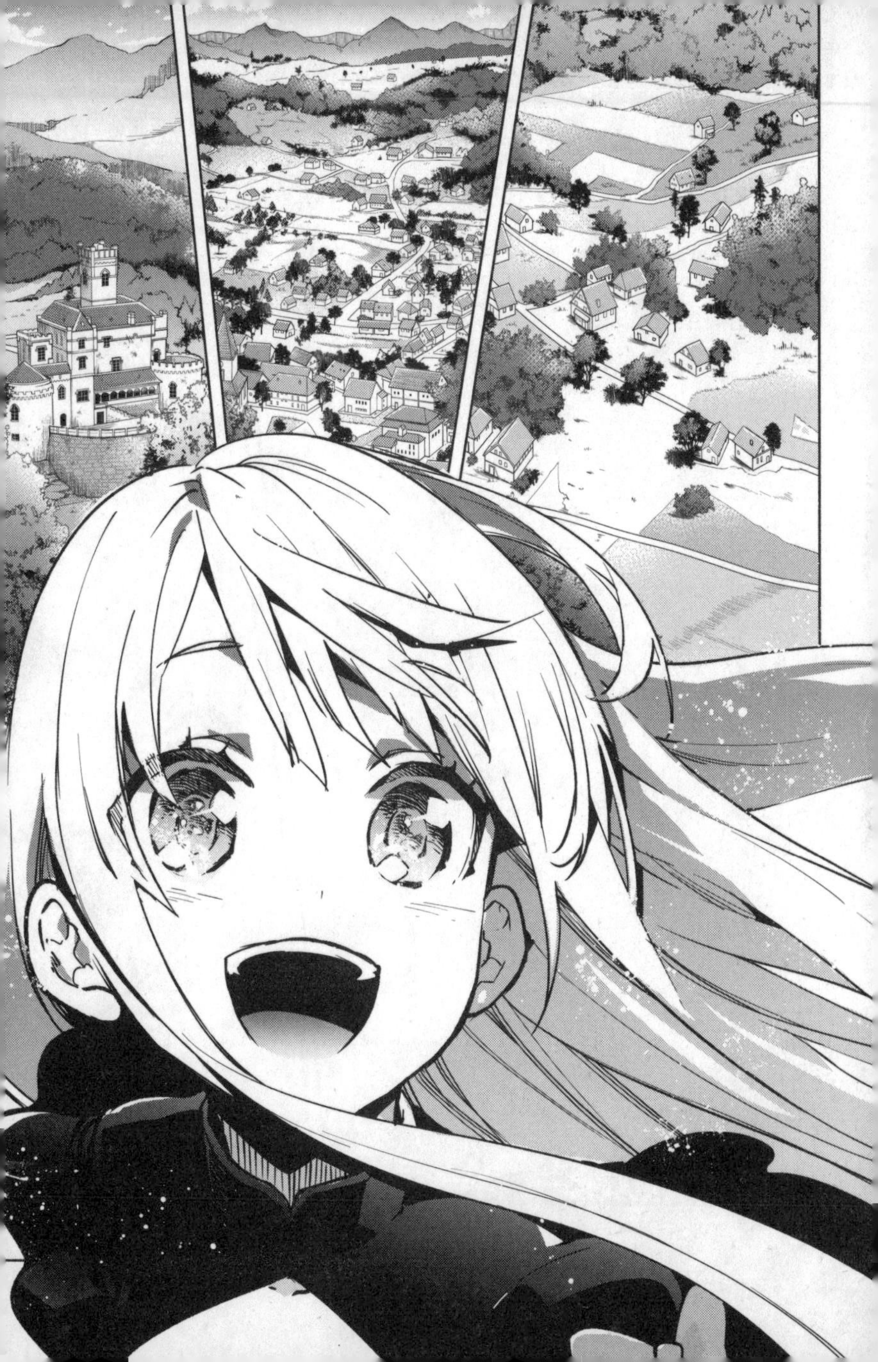

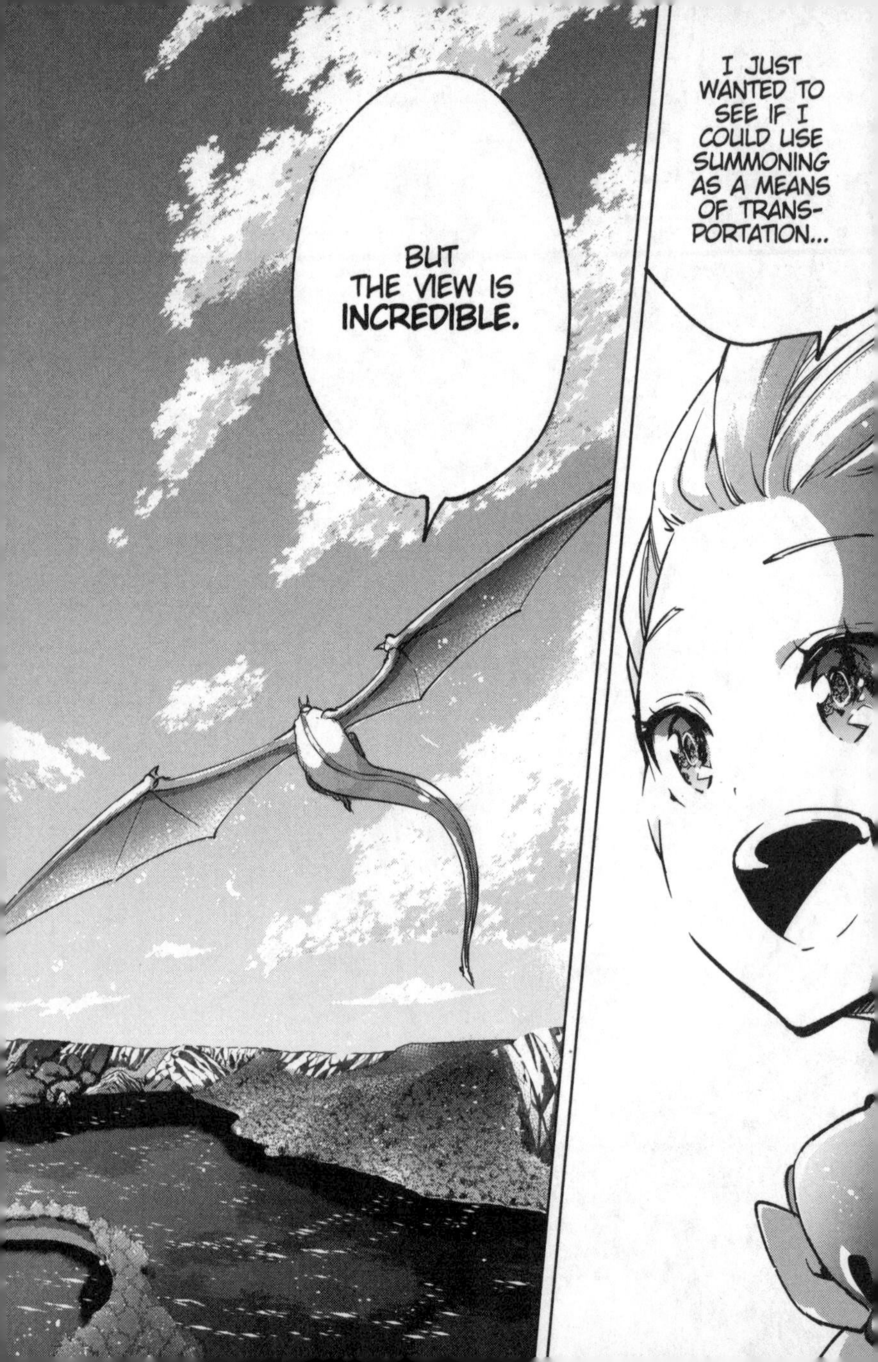
I JUST WANTED TO SEE IF I COULD USE SUMMONING AS A MEANS OF TRANS-PORTATION...
BUT THE VIEW IS INCREDIBLE.

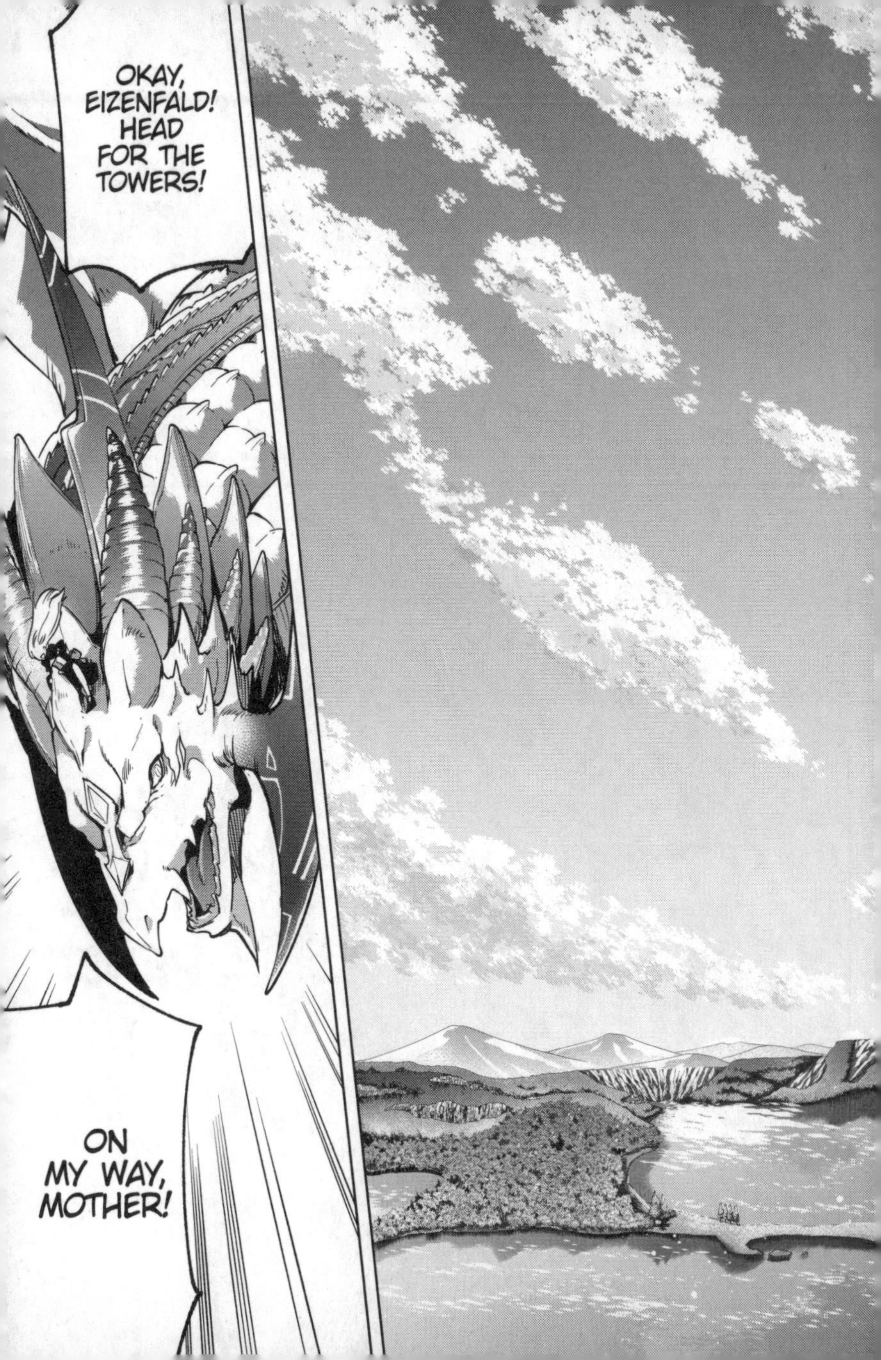
OKAY, EIZENFALD! HEAD FOR THE TOWERS!
ON MY WAY, MOTHER!

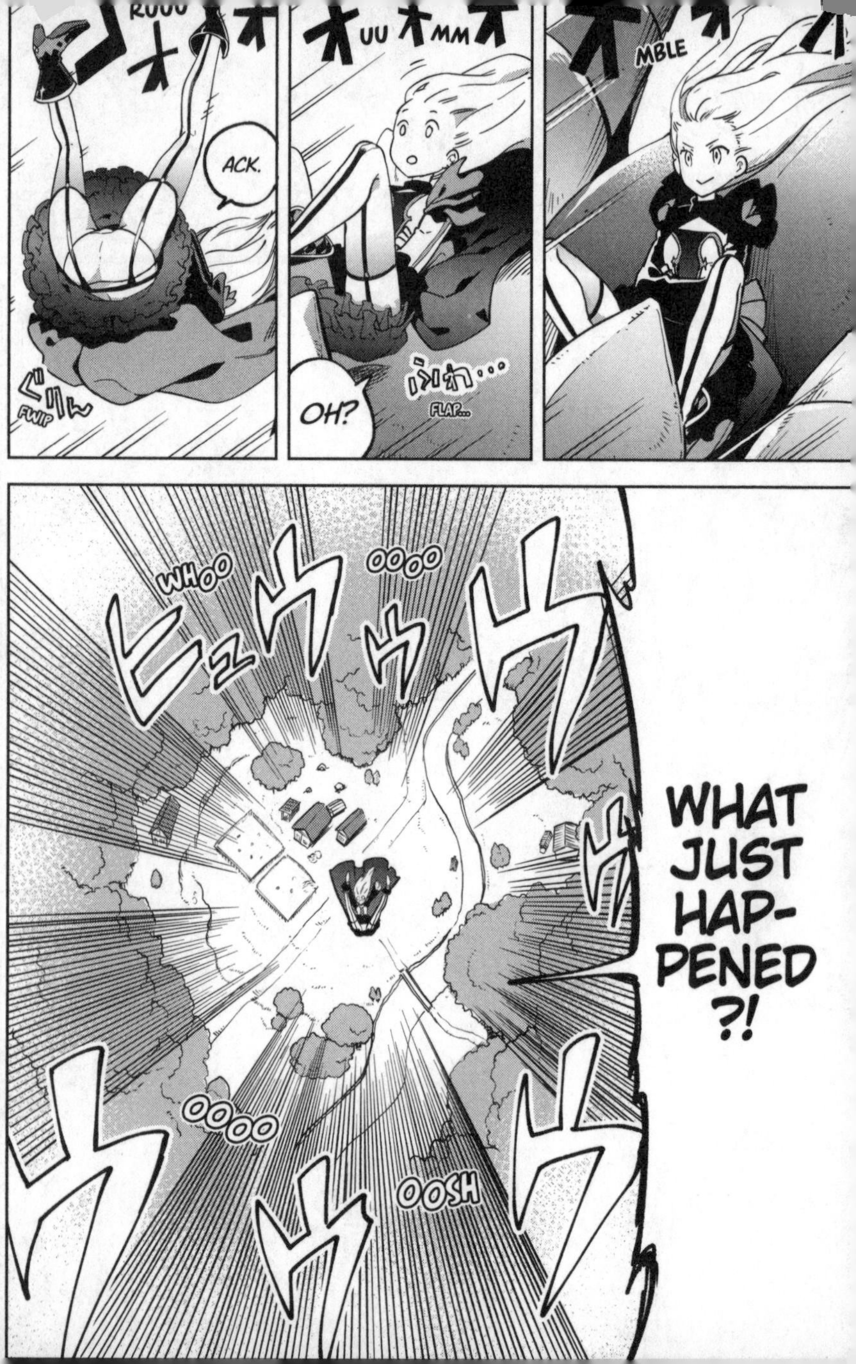
MBLE
UU
MM
ふわ…
FLAP...
OH?
RUUU
ACK.
ぐりん
FWIP
WHOO
OOOO
WHAT JUST HAP-PENED?!
OOOO
OOSH

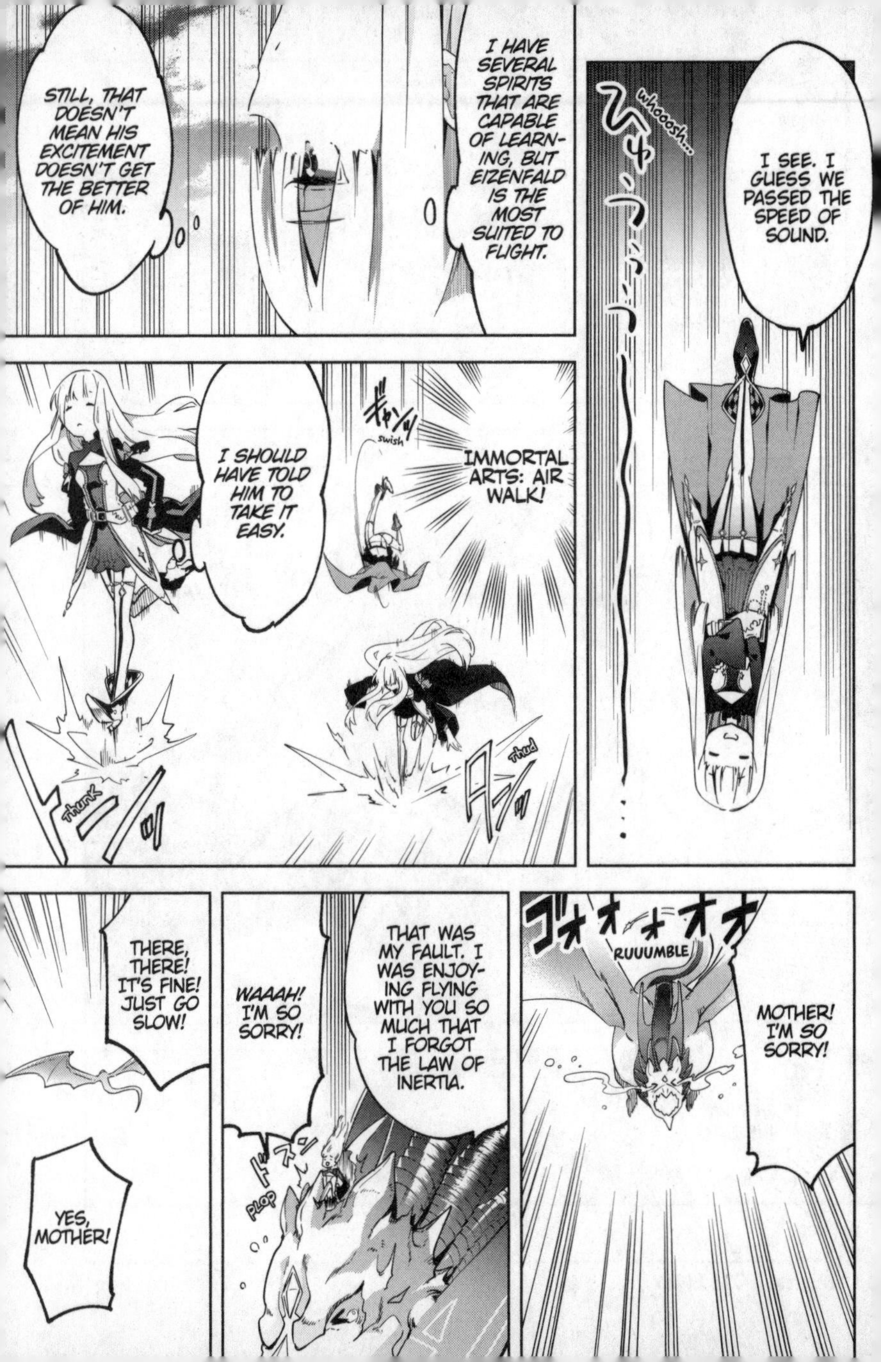
whoooosh...
I SEE. I GUESS WE PASSED THE SPEED OF SOUND.
I HAVE SEVERAL SPIRITS THAT ARE CAPABLE OF LEARNING, BUT EIZENFALD IS THE MOST SUITED TO FLIGHT.
STILL, THAT DOESN'T MEAN HIS EXCITEMENT DOESN'T GET THE BETTER OF HIM.
swish
IMMORTAL ARTS: AIR WALK!
I SHOULD HAVE TOLD HIM TO TAKE IT EASY.
thud
thunk
RUUUMBLE
MOTHER! I'M SO SORRY!
THAT WAS MY FAULT. I WAS ENJOYING FLYING WITH YOU SO MUCH THAT I FORGOT THE LAW OF INERTIA.
WAAAH! I'M SO SORRY!
PLOP
THERE, THERE! IT'S FINE! JUST GO SLOW!
YES, MOTHER!

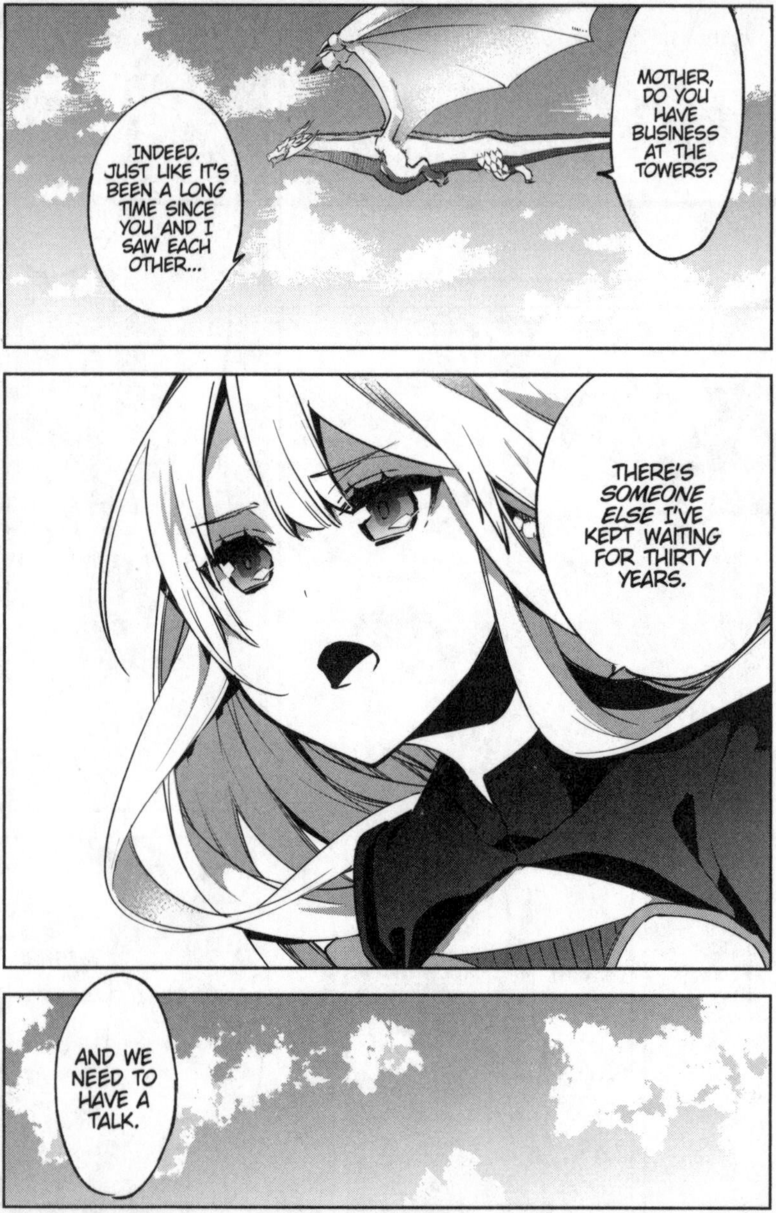
MOTHER, DO YOU HAVE BUSINESS AT THE TOWERS?
INDEED. JUST LIKE IT'S BEEN A LONG TIME SINCE YOU AND I SAW EACH OTHER...
THERE'S *SOMEONE ELSE* I'VE KEPT WAITING FOR THIRTY YEARS.
AND WE NEED TO HAVE A TALK.

Summon 28: END

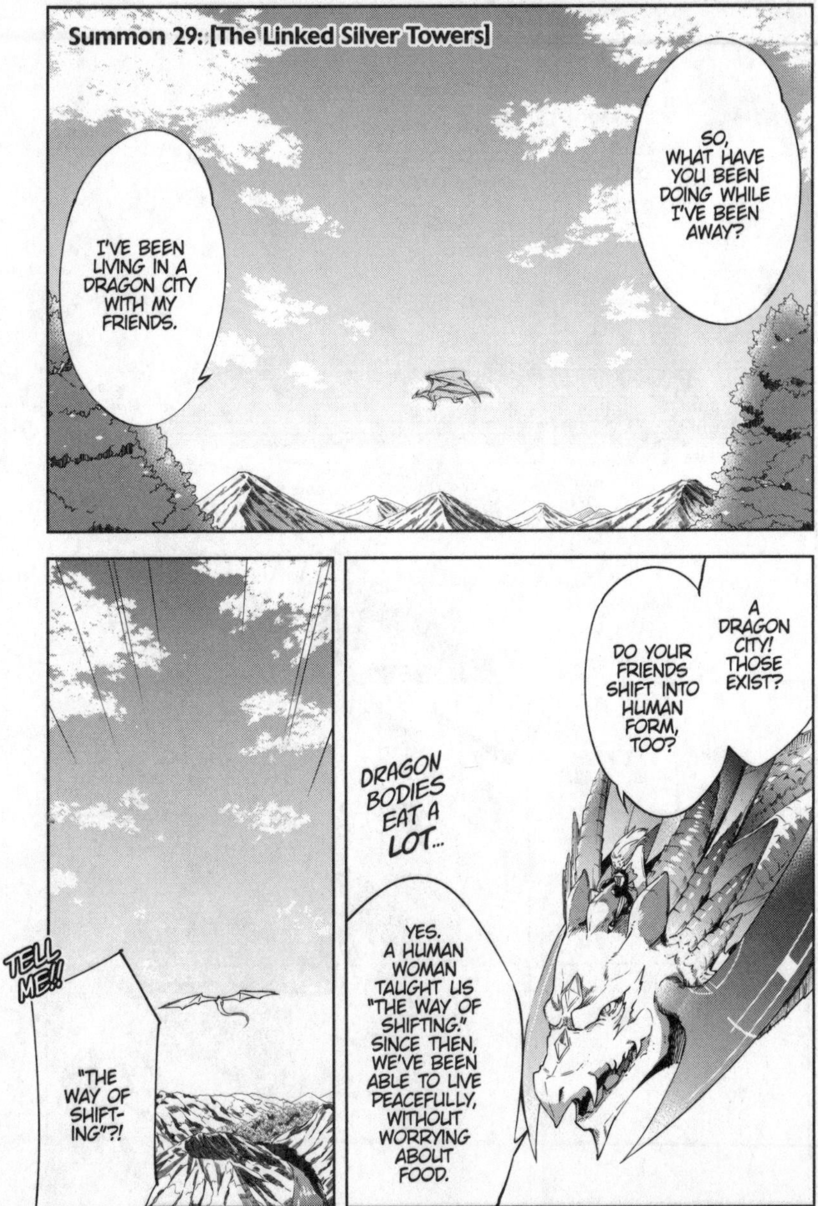
Summon 29: [The Linked Silver Towers]
SO, WHAT HAVE YOU BEEN DOING WHILE I'VE BEEN AWAY?
I'VE BEEN LIVING IN A DRAGON CITY WITH MY FRIENDS.
A DRAGON CITY! THOSE EXIST?
DO YOUR FRIENDS SHIFT INTO HUMAN FORM, TOO?
DRAGON BODIES EAT A LOT...
YES. A HUMAN WOMAN TAUGHT US "THE WAY OF SHIFTING." SINCE THEN, WE'VE BEEN ABLE TO LIVE PEACEFULLY, WITHOUT WORRYING ABOUT FOOD.
"THE WAY OF SHIFT-ING"?!
TELL ME!!

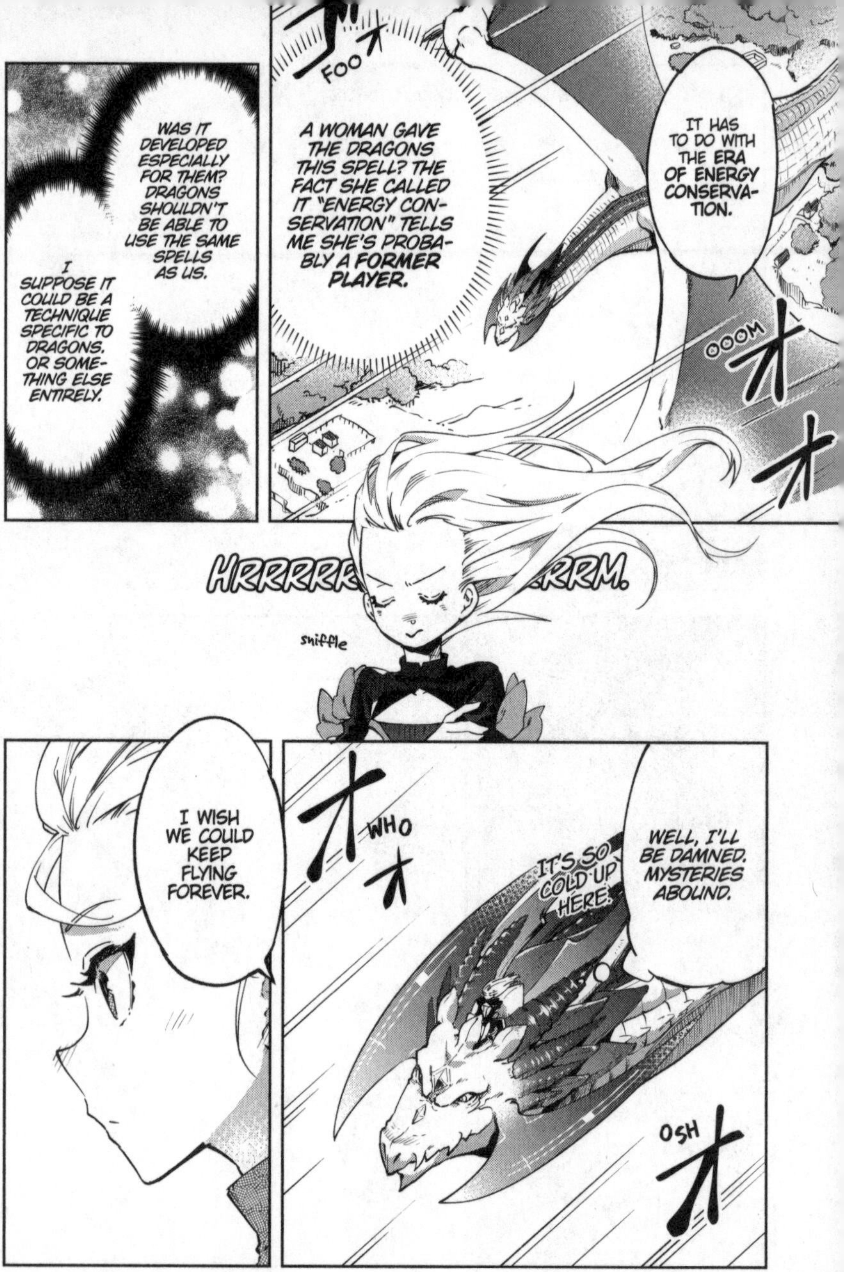
FOO
IT HAS TO DO WITH THE ERA OF ENERGY CONSERVATION.
A WOMAN GAVE THE DRAGONS THIS SPELL? THE FACT SHE CALLED IT "ENERGY CONSERVATION" TELLS ME SHE'S PROBABLY A FORMER PLAYER.
OOOM
WAS IT DEVELOPED ESPECIALLY FOR THEM? DRAGONS SHOULDN'T BE ABLE TO USE THE SAME SPELLS AS US.
I SUPPOSE IT COULD BE A TECHNIQUE SPECIFIC TO DRAGONS. OR SOMETHING ELSE ENTIRELY.
HRRRRR
RRRM.
sniffle
WELL, I'LL BE DAMNED. MYSTERIES ABOUND.
IT'S SO COLD UP HERE!
WHO
OSH
I WISH WE COULD KEEP FLYING FOREVER.

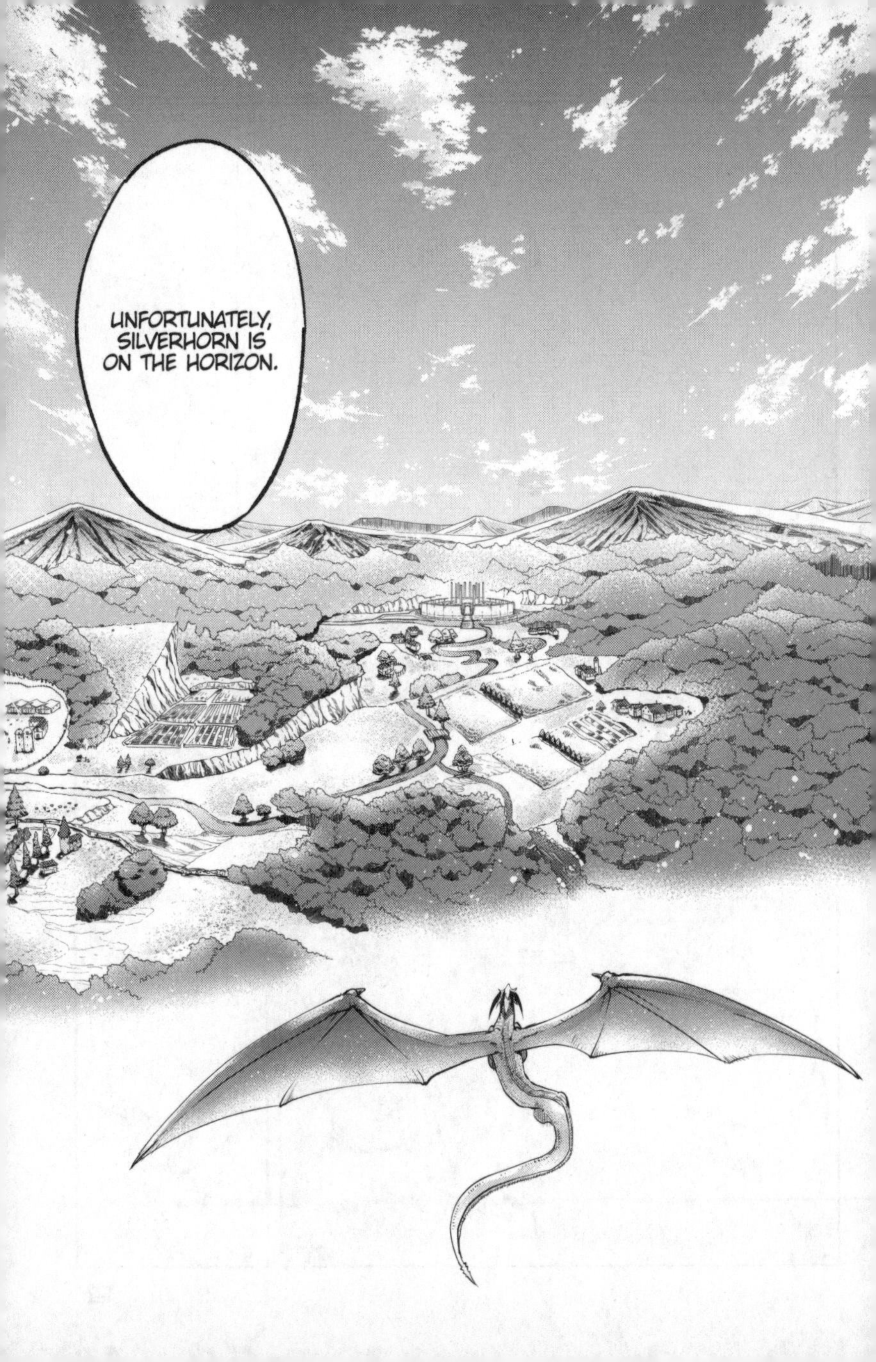
UNFORTUNATELY, SILVERHORN IS ON THE HORIZON.

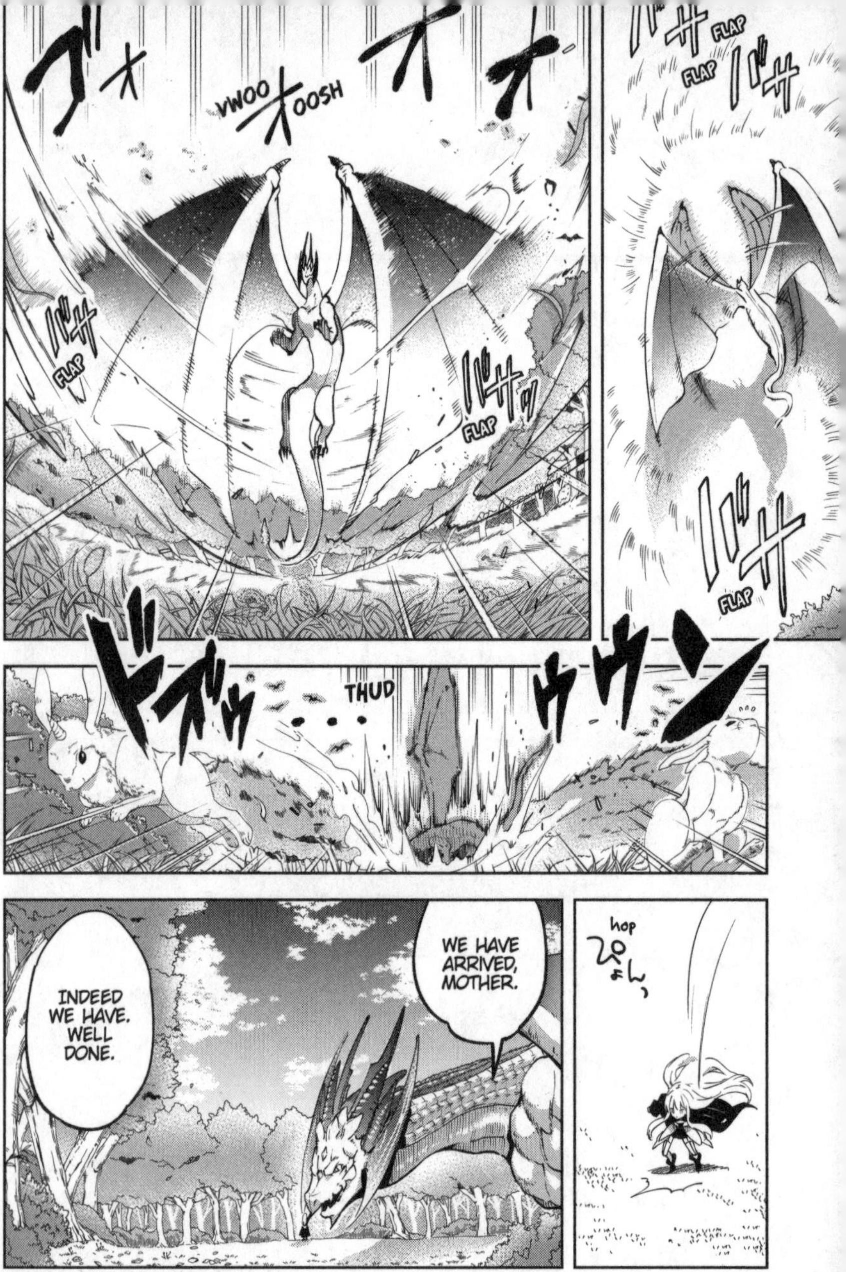
バサ FLAP
FLAP バサ
バサ FLAP
ゴォォォ VWOOOOSH
バサ FLAP
バサッ FLAP
ドォゥウン THUD
hop ぴょん
WE HAVE ARRIVED, MOTHER.
INDEED WE HAVE. WELL DONE.

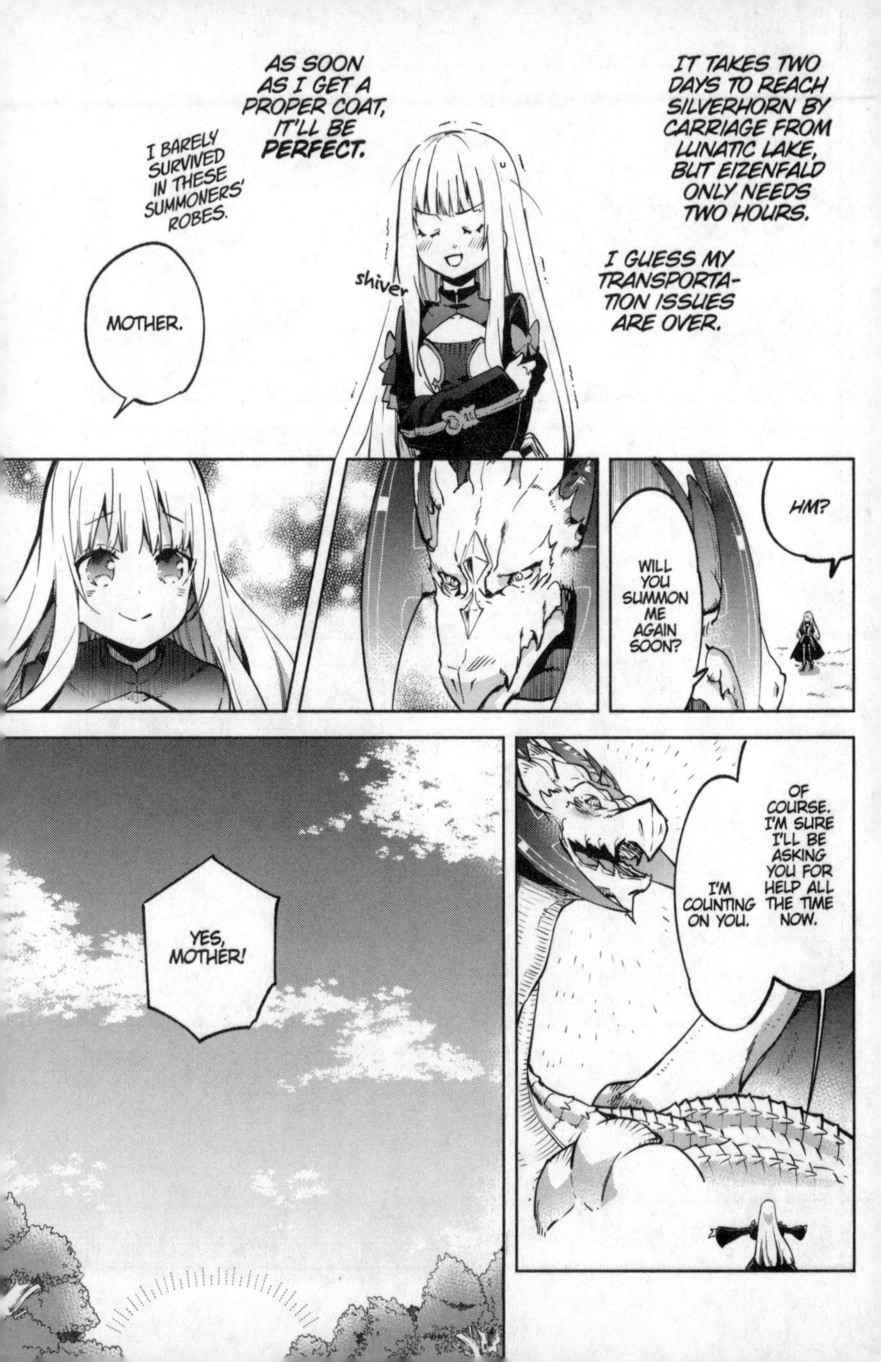
IT TAKES TWO DAYS TO REACH SILVERHORN BY CARRIAGE FROM LUNATIC LAKE, BUT EIZENFALD ONLY NEEDS TWO HOURS.
I GUESS MY TRANSPORTATION ISSUES ARE OVER.
I BARELY SURVIVED IN THESE SUMMONERS' ROBES.
AS SOON AS I GET A PROPER COAT, IT'LL BE PERFECT.
shiver
MOTHER.
HM?
WILL YOU SUMMON ME AGAIN SOON?
OF COURSE. I'M SURE I'LL BE ASKING YOU FOR HELP ALL THE TIME NOW.
I'M COUNTING ON YOU.
YES, MOTHER!

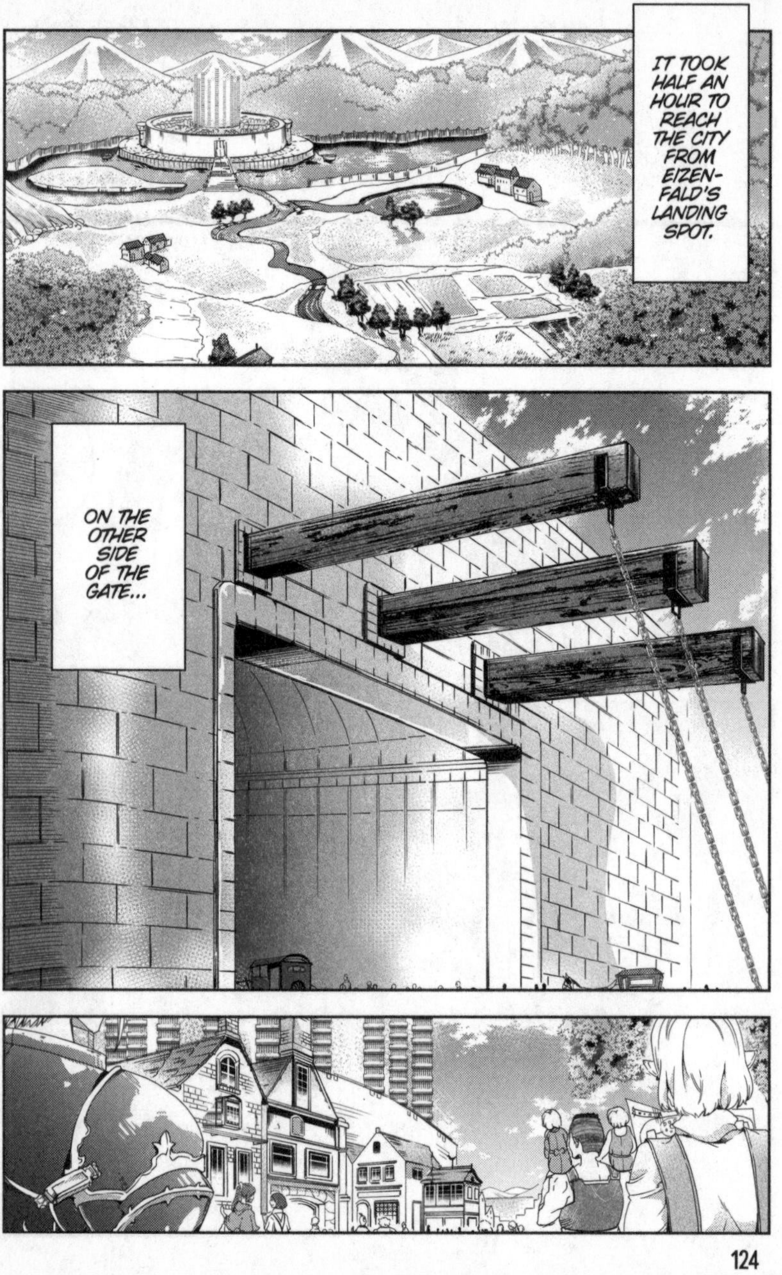
IT TOOK HALF AN HOUR TO REACH THE CITY FROM EIZEN-FALD'S LANDING SPOT.
ON THE OTHER SIDE OF THE GATE...

LAY SILVERHORN'S MAIN ROAD. BUSY ENOUGH TO RIVAL LUNATIC LAKE.

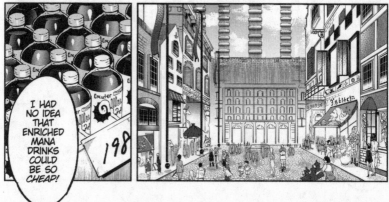

I HAD NO IDEA THAT ENRICHED MANA DRINKS COULD BE SO CHEAP!

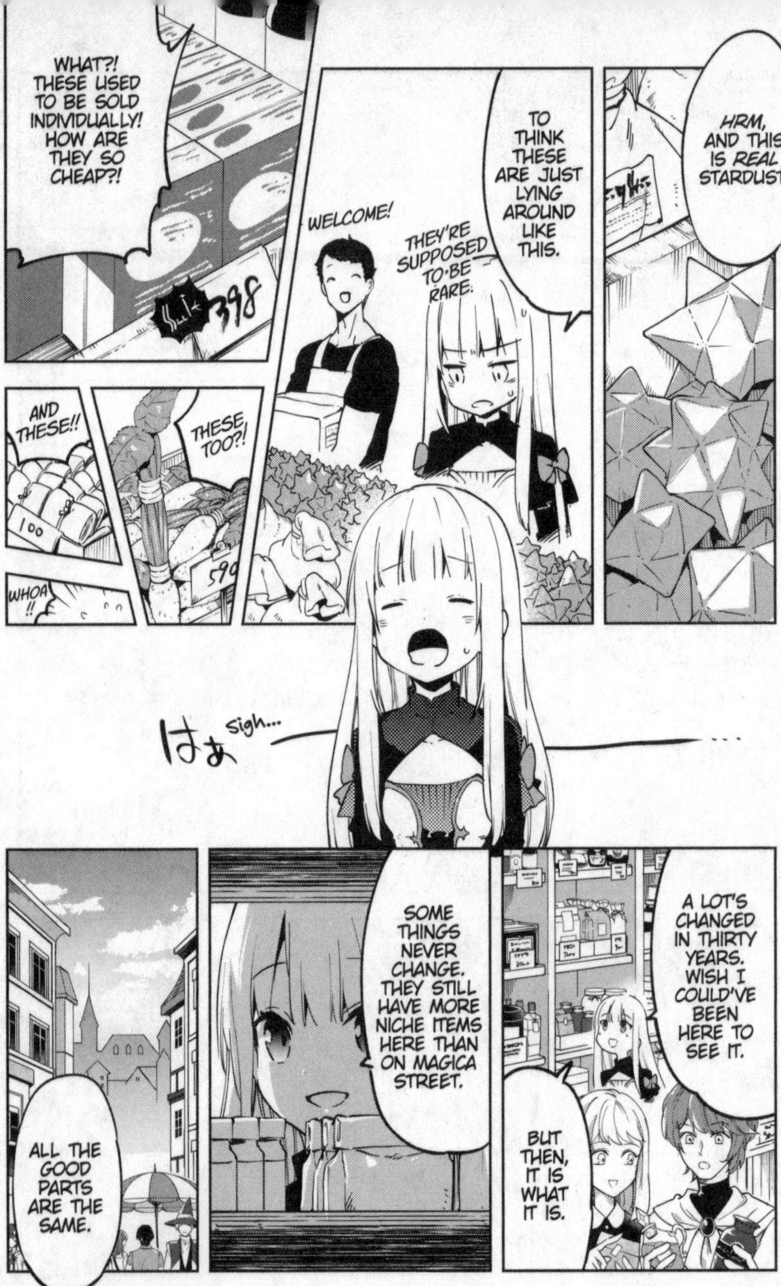
HRM, AND THIS IS REAL STARDUST.
TO THINK THESE ARE JUST LYING AROUND LIKE THIS.
THEY'RE SUPPOSED TO BE RARE.
WELCOME!
WHAT?! THESE USED TO BE SOLD INDIVIDUALLY! HOW ARE THEY SO CHEAP?!
398
THESE TOO?!
AND THESE!!
100
WHOA!!
はぁ Sigh...
A LOT'S CHANGED IN THIRTY YEARS. WISH I COULD'VE BEEN HERE TO SEE IT.
BUT THEN, IT IS WHAT IT IS.
SOME THINGS NEVER CHANGE. THEY STILL HAVE MORE NICHE ITEMS HERE THAN ON MAGICA STREET.
ALL THE GOOD PARTS ARE THE SAME.

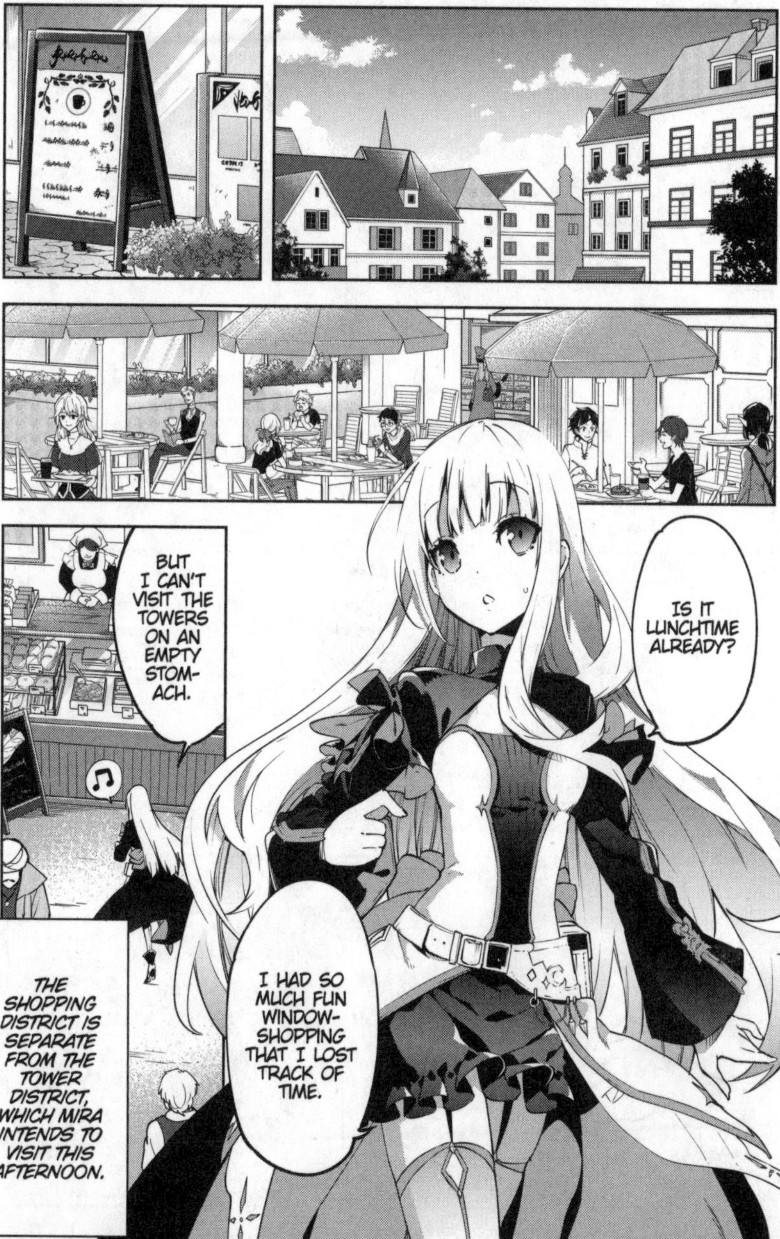
IS IT LUNCHTIME ALREADY?
I HAD SO MUCH FUN WINDOW-SHOPPING THAT I LOST TRACK OF TIME.
BUT I CAN'T VISIT THE TOWERS ON AN EMPTY STOM-ACH.
THE SHOPPING DISTRICT IS SEPARATE FROM THE TOWER DISTRICT, WHICH MIRA INTENDS TO VISIT THIS AFTERNOON.

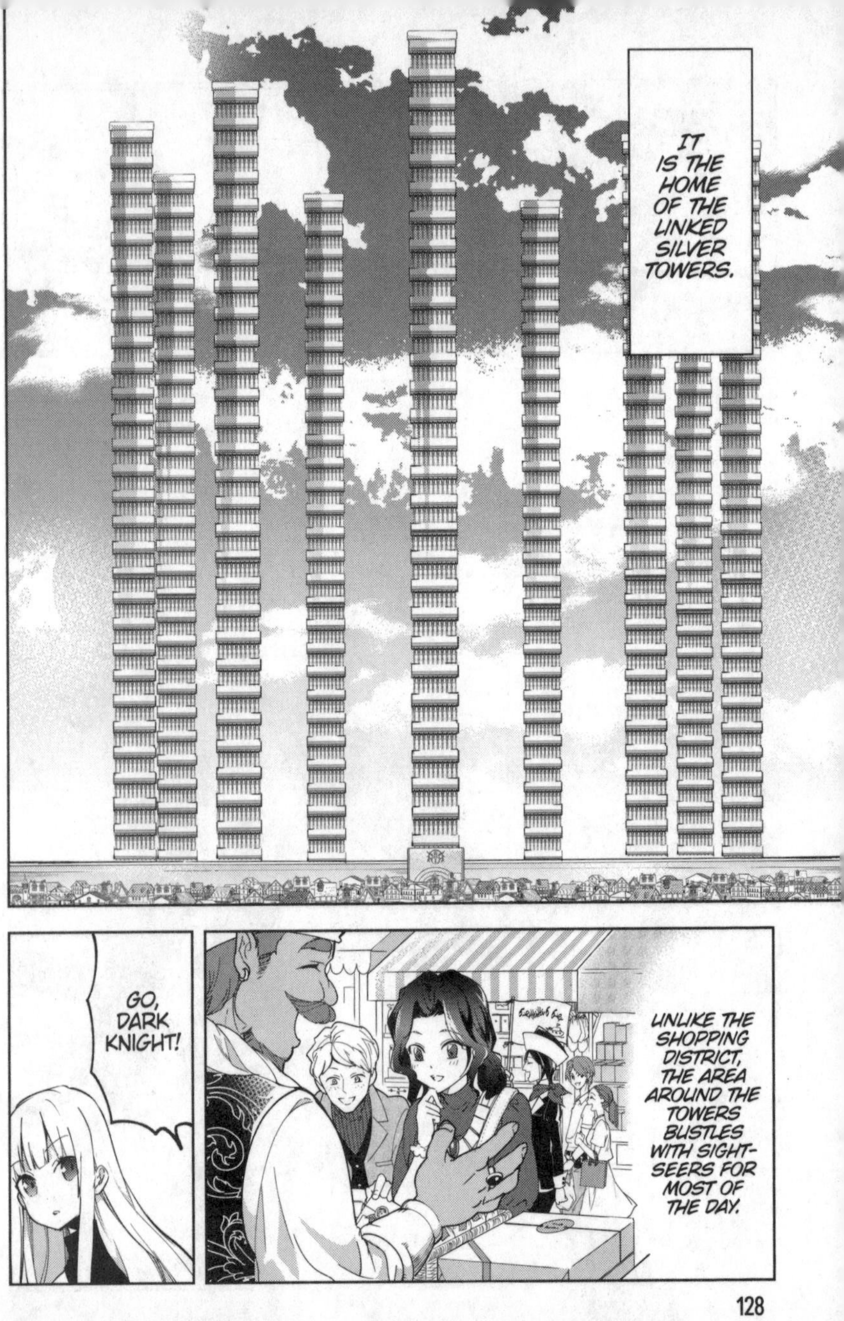
IT IS THE HOME OF THE LINKED SILVER TOWERS.
UNLIKE THE SHOPPING DISTRICT, THE AREA AROUND THE TOWERS BUSTLES WITH SIGHT-SEERS FOR MOST OF THE DAY.
GO, DARK KNIGHT!

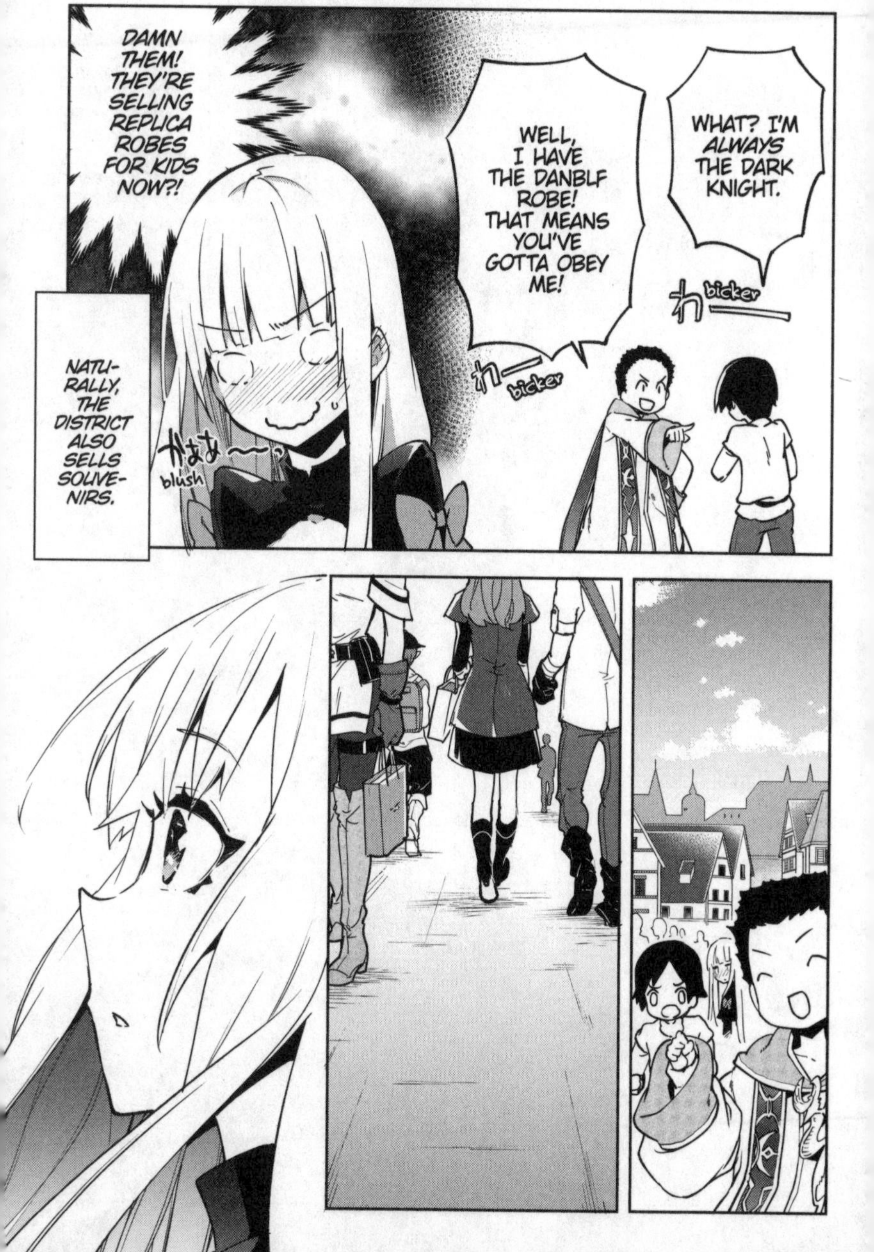
WHAT? I'M ALWAYS THE DARK KNIGHT.
わ bicker
WELL, I HAVE THE DANBLF ROBE! THAT MEANS YOU'VE GOTTA OBEY ME!
わー bicker
DAMN THEM! THEY'RE SELLING REPLICA ROBES FOR KIDS NOW?!
blush
NATU-RALLY, THE DISTRICT ALSO SELLS SOUVE-NIRS.

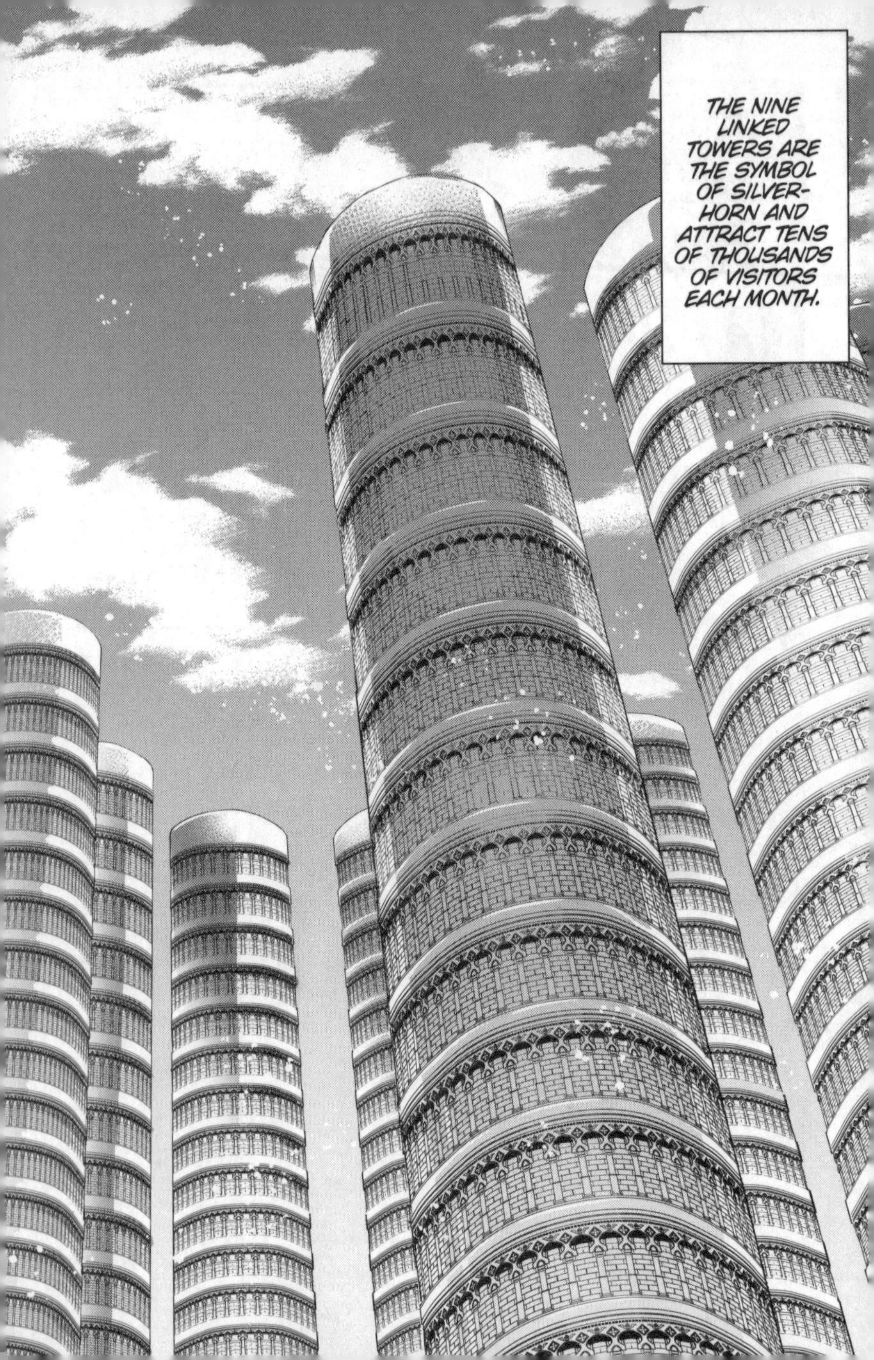
THE NINE LINKED TOWERS ARE THE SYMBOL OF SILVER-HORN AND ATTRACT TENS OF THOUSANDS OF VISITORS EACH MONTH.

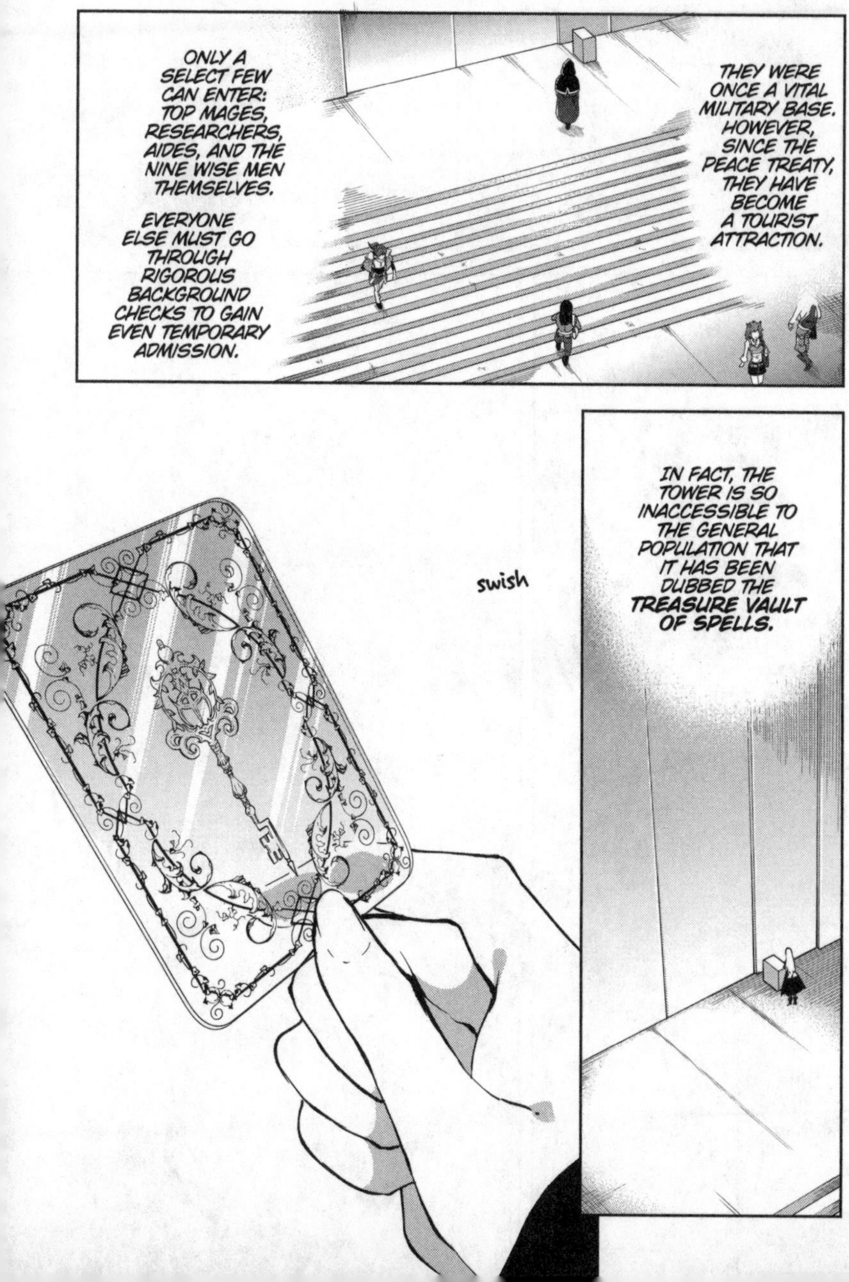
THEY WERE ONCE A VITAL MILITARY BASE. HOWEVER, SINCE THE PEACE TREATY, THEY HAVE BECOME A TOURIST ATTRACTION.
ONLY A SELECT FEW CAN ENTER: TOP MAGES, RESEARCHERS, AIDES, AND THE NINE WISE MEN THEMSELVES.
EVERYONE ELSE MUST GO THROUGH RIGOROUS BACKGROUND CHECKS TO GAIN EVEN TEMPORARY ADMISSION.
IN FACT, THE TOWER IS SO INACCESSIBLE TO THE GENERAL POPULATION THAT IT HAS BEEN DUBBED THE **TREASURE VAULT OF SPELLS.**
swish

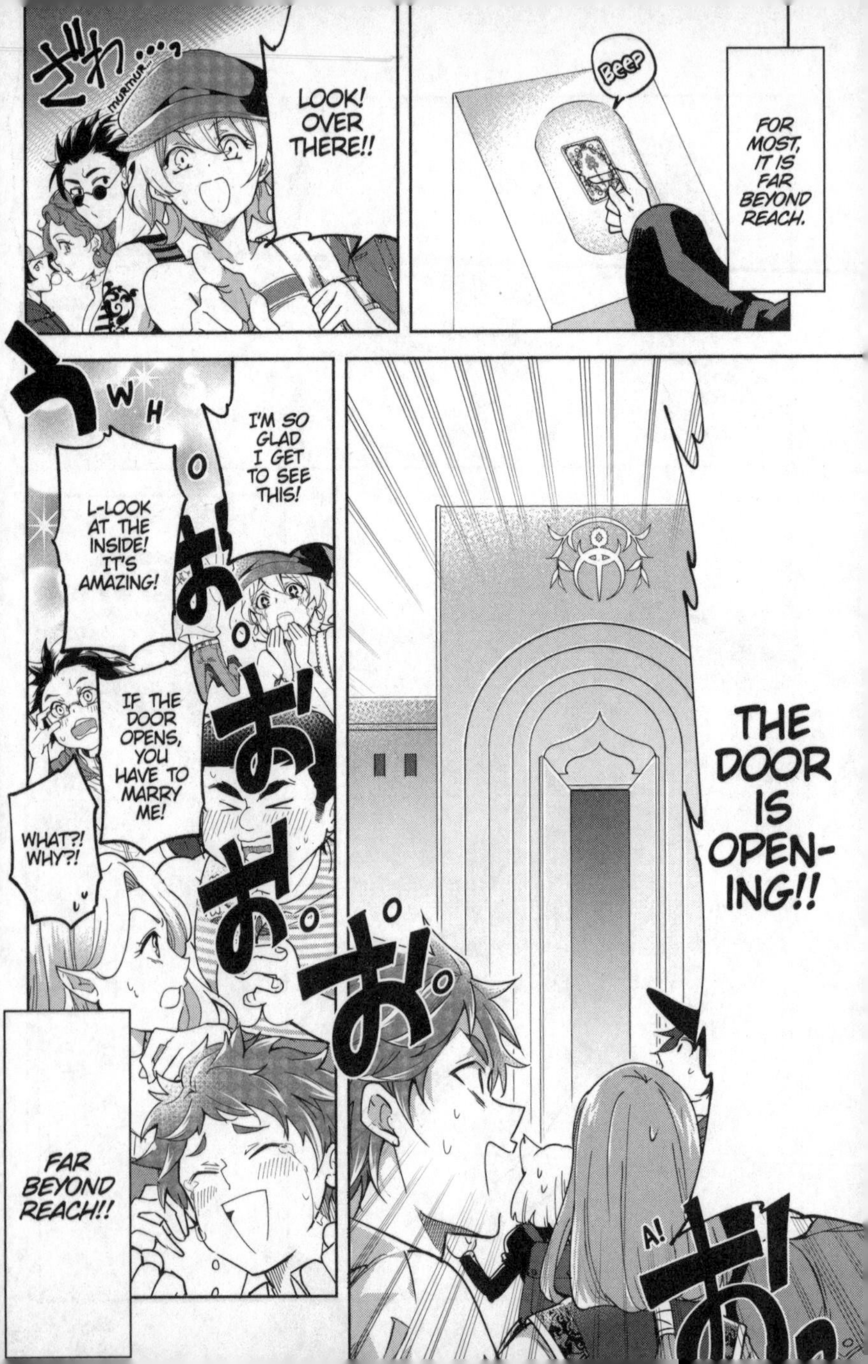
BEEP
FOR MOST, IT IS FAR BEYOND REACH.
ざわ…
MURMUR...
LOOK! OVER THERE!!
THE DOOR IS OPEN-ING!!
A!
W H O
I'M SO GLAD I GET TO SEE THIS!
L-LOOK AT THE INSIDE! IT'S AMAZING!
IF THE DOOR OPENS, YOU HAVE TO MARRY ME!
WHAT?! WHY?!
FAR BEYOND REACH!!

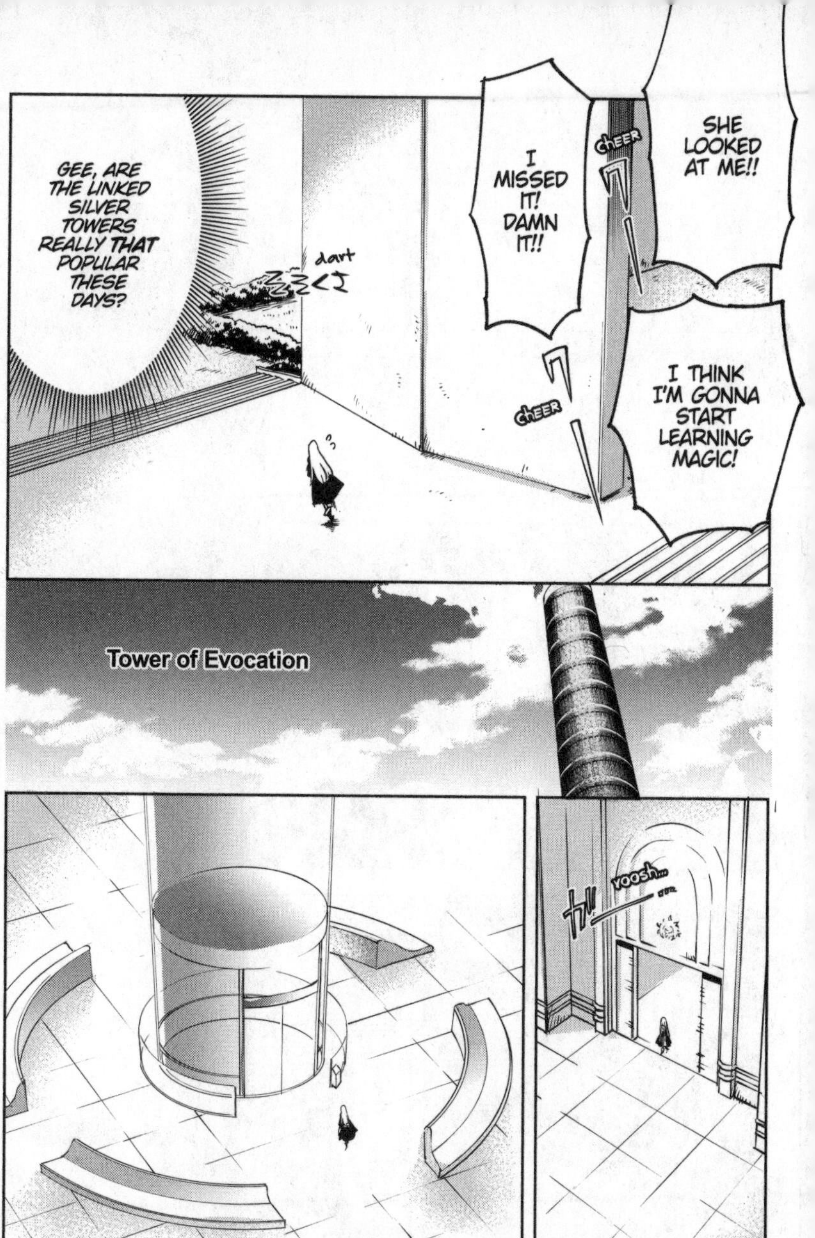
SHE LOOKED AT ME!!
I THINK I'M GONNA START LEARNING MAGIC!
cheer
cheer
I MISSED IT! DAMN IT!!
dart
GEE, ARE THE LINKED SILVER TOWERS REALLY THAT POPULAR THESE DAYS?
Tower of Evocation
yoosh...

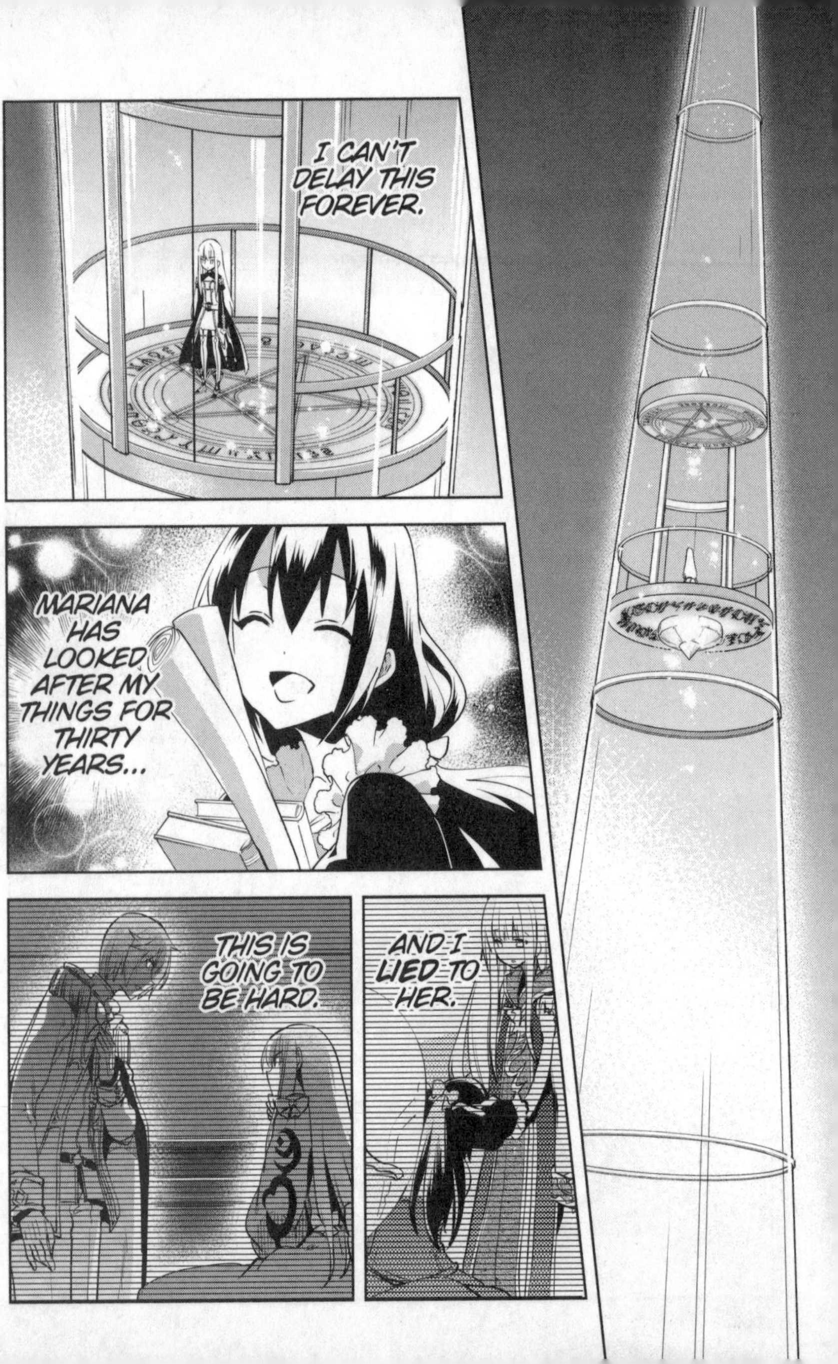
I CAN'T DELAY THIS FOREVER.
MARIANA HAS LOOKED AFTER MY THINGS FOR THIRTY YEARS...
AND I LIED TO HER.
THIS IS GOING TO BE HARD.

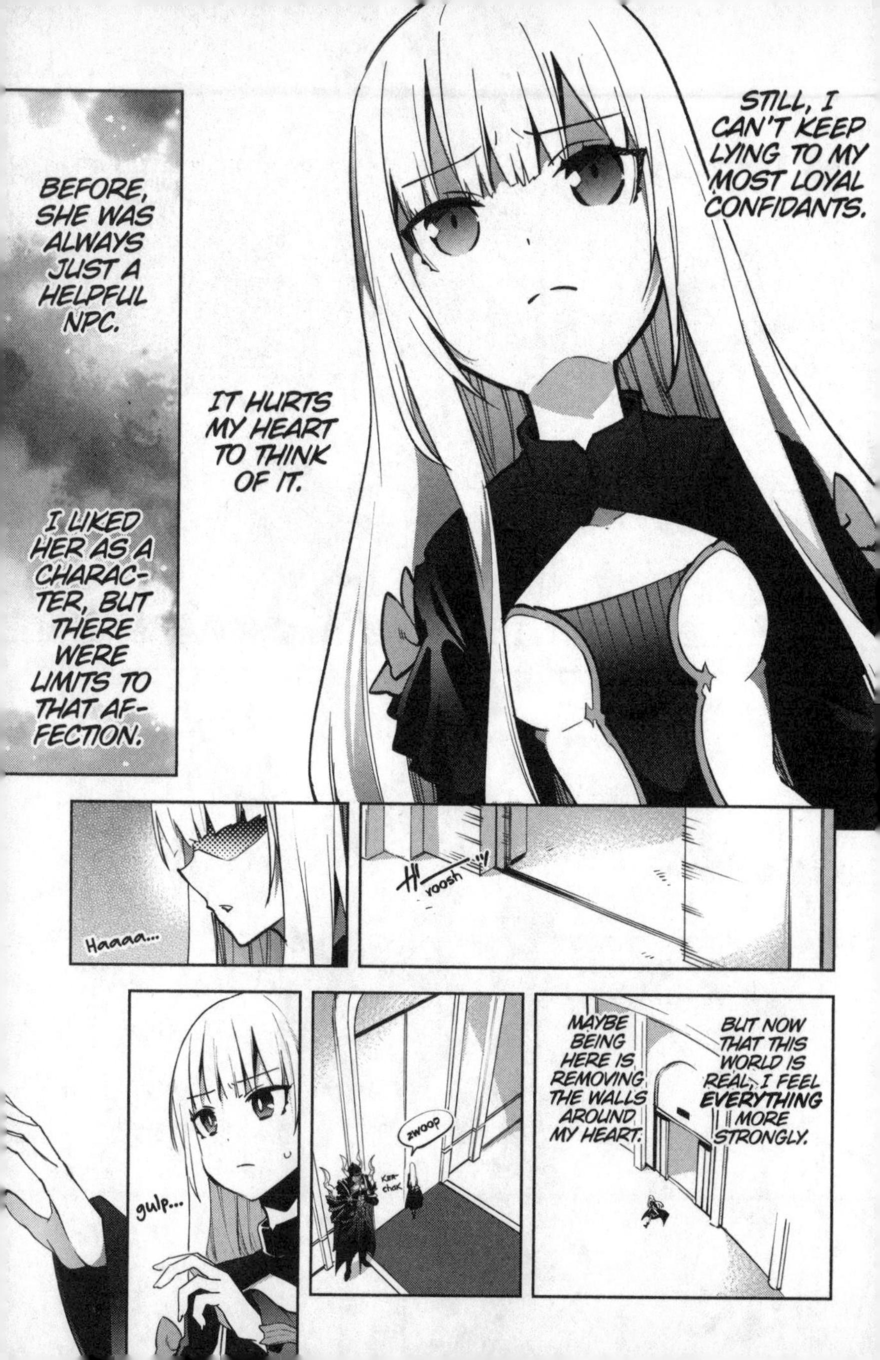
STILL, I CAN'T KEEP LYING TO MY MOST LOYAL CONFIDANTS.
IT HURTS MY HEART TO THINK OF IT.
BEFORE, SHE WAS ALWAYS JUST A HELPFUL NPC.
I LIKED HER AS A CHARAC-TER, BUT THERE WERE LIMITS TO THAT AF-FECTION.
yoosh
Haaaa...
BUT NOW THAT THIS WORLD IS REAL, I FEEL EVERYTHING MORE STRONGLY.
MAYBE BEING HERE IS REMOVING THE WALLS AROUND MY HEART.
zwoop
Ker-chak
gulp...

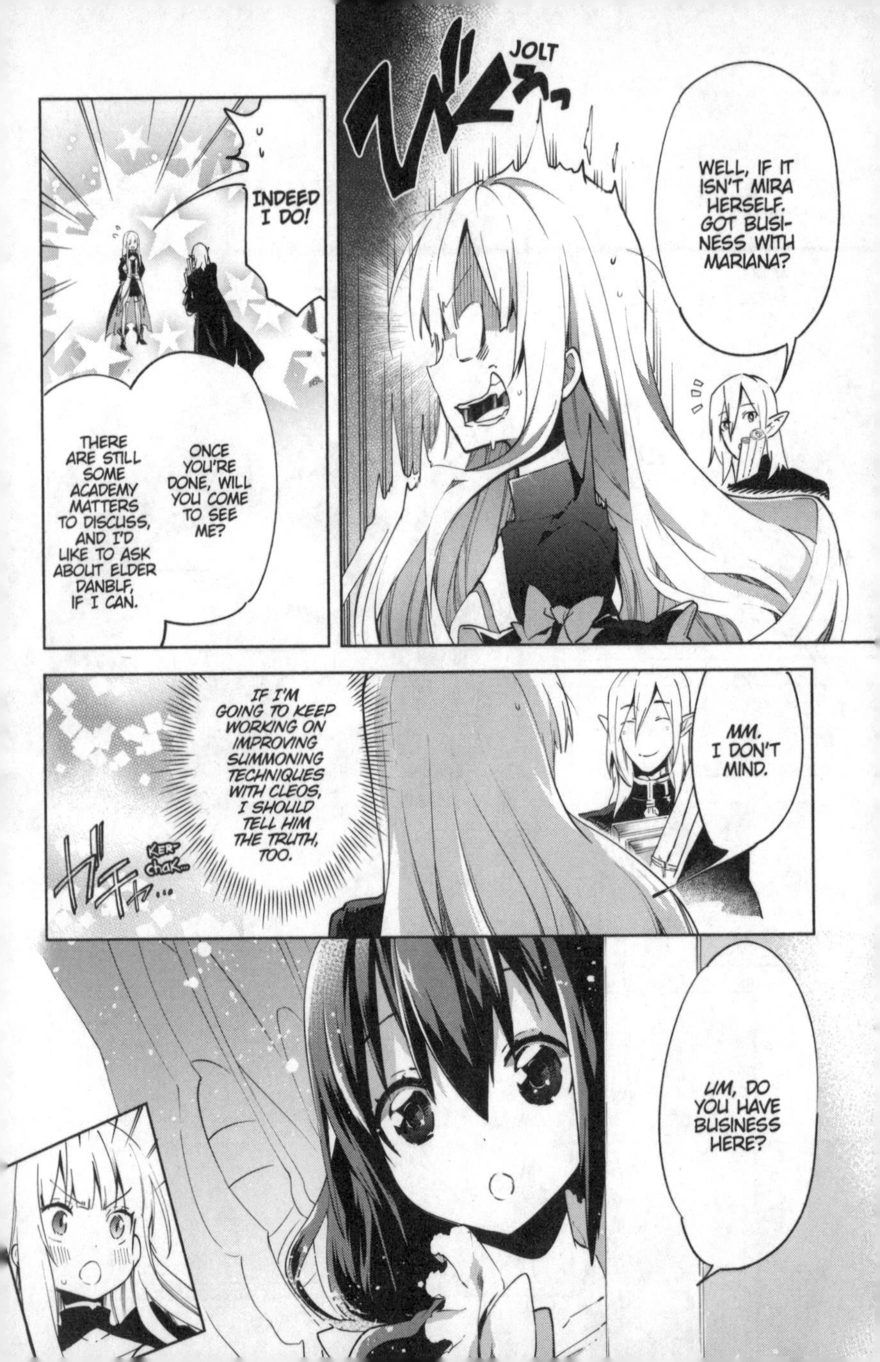
JOLT
WELL, IF IT ISN'T MIRA HERSELF. GOT BUSINESS WITH MARIANA?
INDEED I DO!
ONCE YOU'RE DONE, WILL YOU COME TO SEE ME?
THERE ARE STILL SOME ACADEMY MATTERS TO DISCUSS, AND I'D LIKE TO ASK ABOUT ELDER DANBLF, IF I CAN.
MM. I DON'T MIND.
IF I'M GOING TO KEEP WORKING ON IMPROVING SUMMONING TECHNIQUES WITH CLEOS, I SHOULD TELL HIM THE TRUTH, TOO.
KER-chak...
UM, DO YOU HAVE BUSINESS HERE?

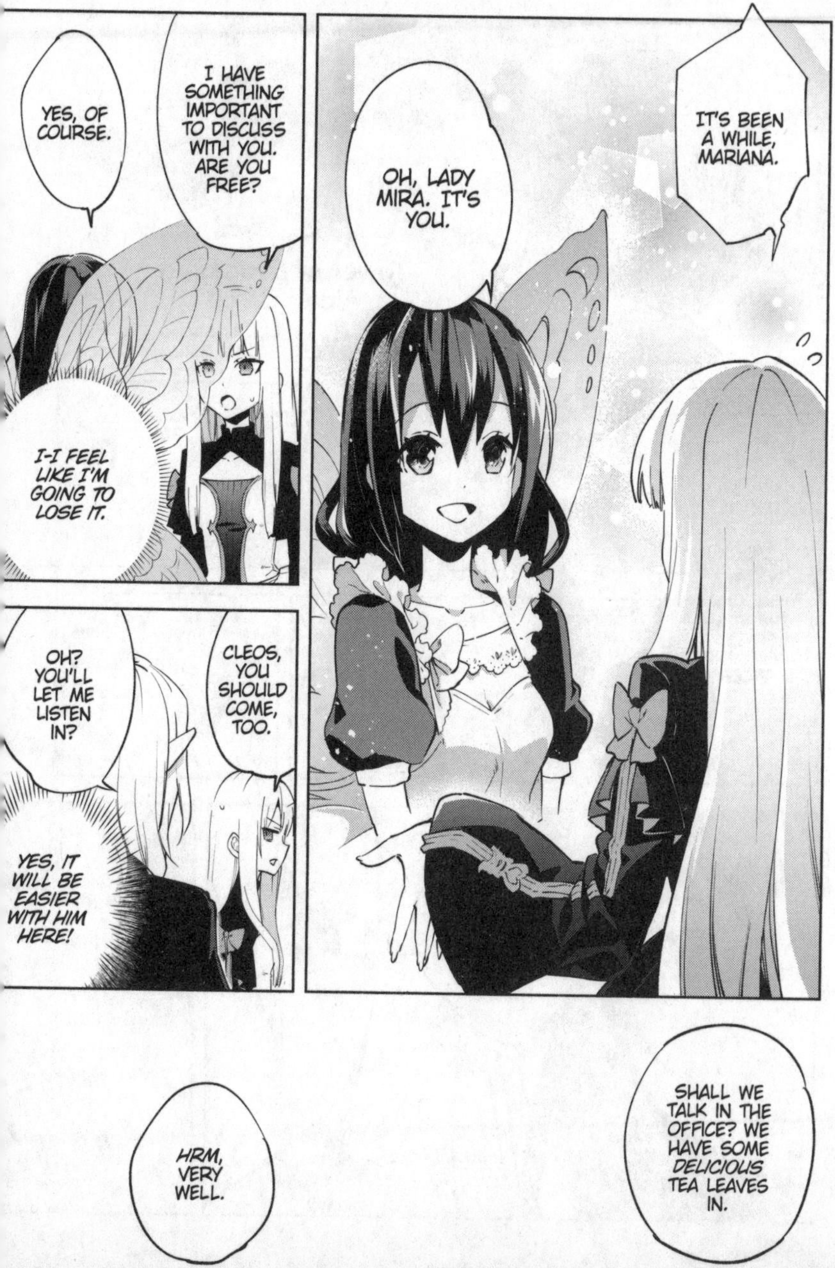
IT'S BEEN A WHILE, MARIANA.
OH, LADY MIRA. IT'S YOU.
I HAVE SOMETHING IMPORTANT TO DISCUSS WITH YOU. ARE YOU FREE?
YES, OF COURSE.
I-I FEEL LIKE I'M GOING TO LOSE IT.
CLEOS, YOU SHOULD COME, TOO.
OH? YOU'LL LET ME LISTEN IN?
YES, IT WILL BE EASIER WITH HIM HERE!
SHALL WE TALK IN THE OFFICE? WE HAVE SOME *DELICIOUS* TEA LEAVES IN.
HRM, VERY WELL.

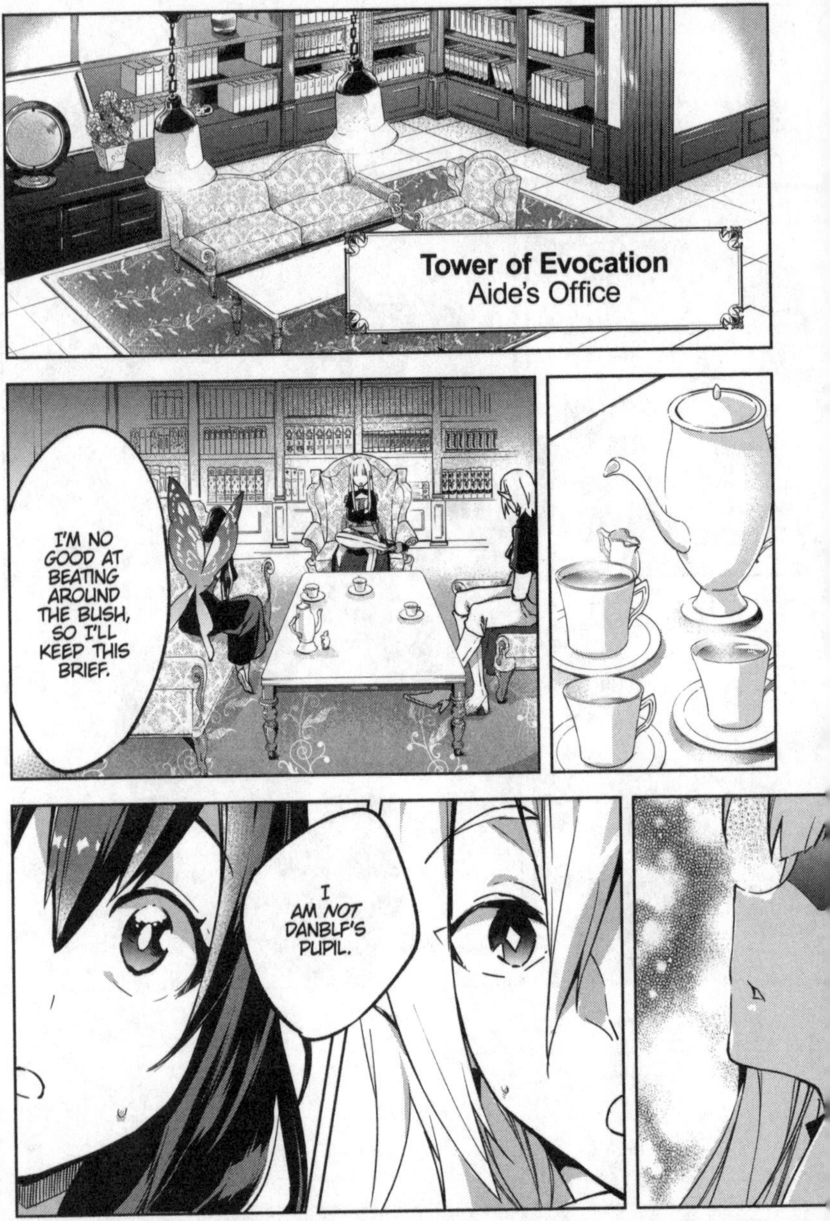
Tower of Evocation
Aide's Office
I'M NO GOOD AT BEATING AROUND THE BUSH, SO I'LL KEEP THIS BRIEF.
I AM *NOT* DANBLF'S PUPIL.

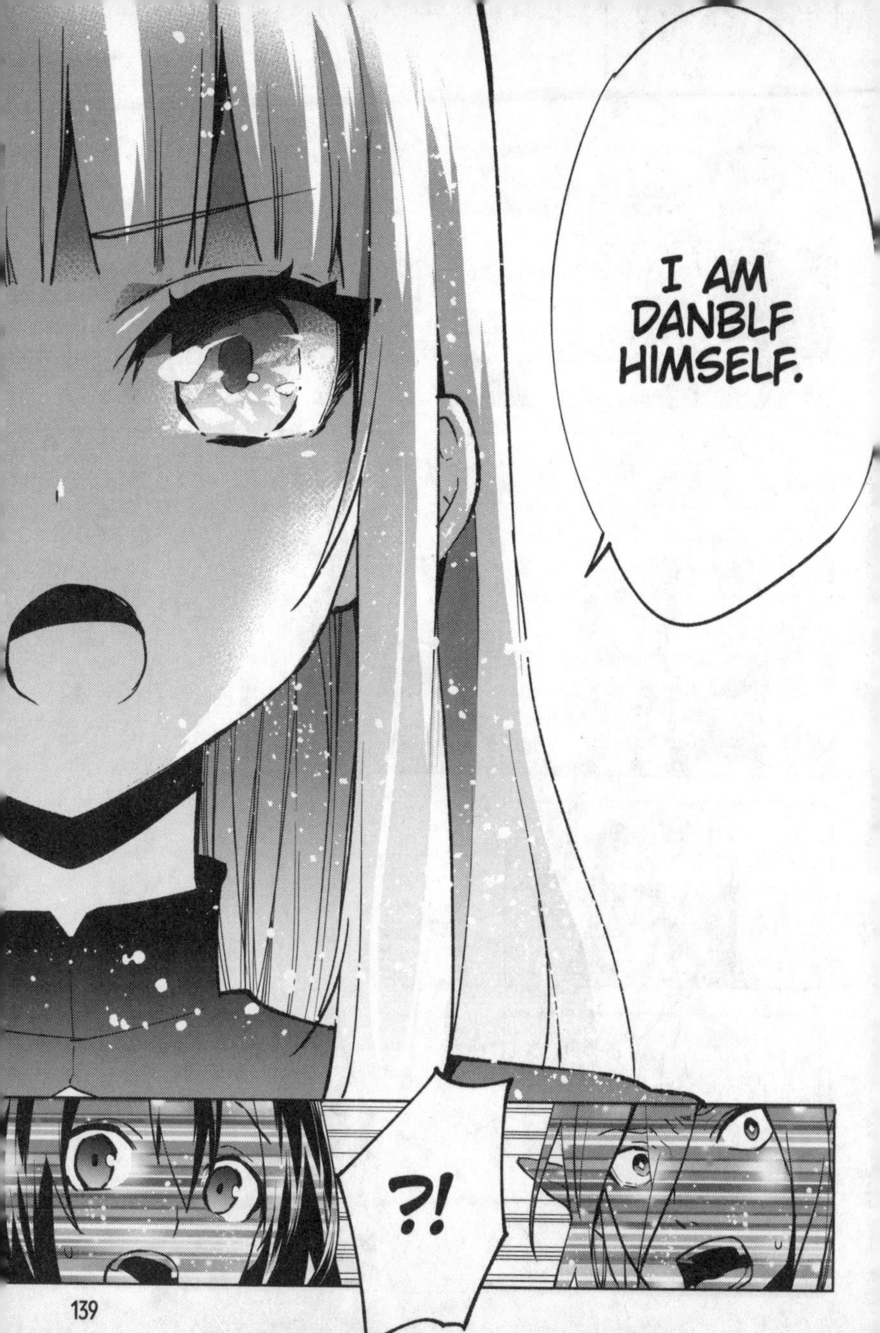
I AM DANBLF HIMSELF.
?!

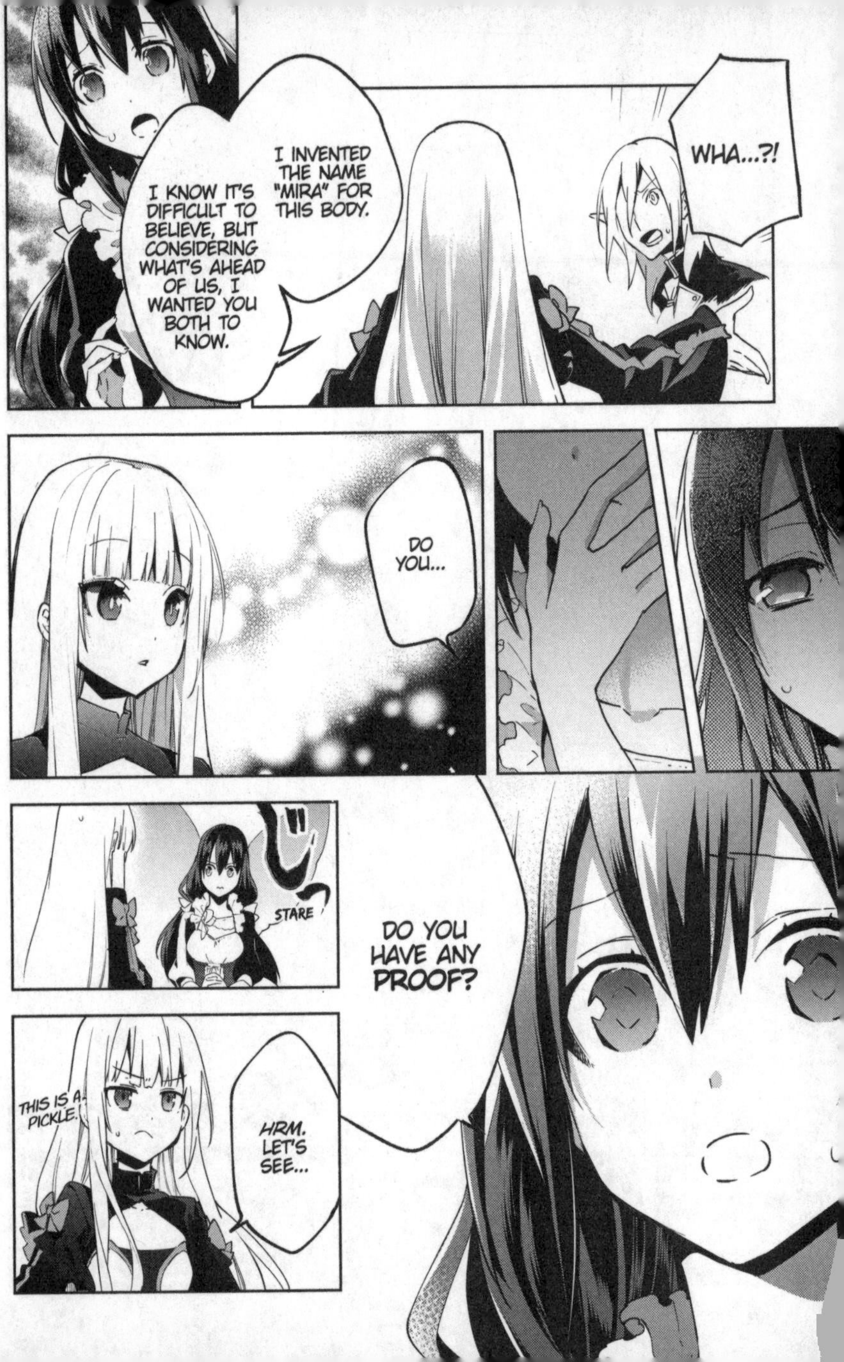
WHA...?!
I INVENTED THE NAME "MIRA" FOR THIS BODY.
I KNOW IT'S DIFFICULT TO BELIEVE, BUT CONSIDERING WHAT'S AHEAD OF US, I WANTED YOU BOTH TO KNOW.
DO YOU...
DO YOU HAVE ANY PROOF?
STARE
HRM. LET'S SEE...
THIS IS A PICKLE.

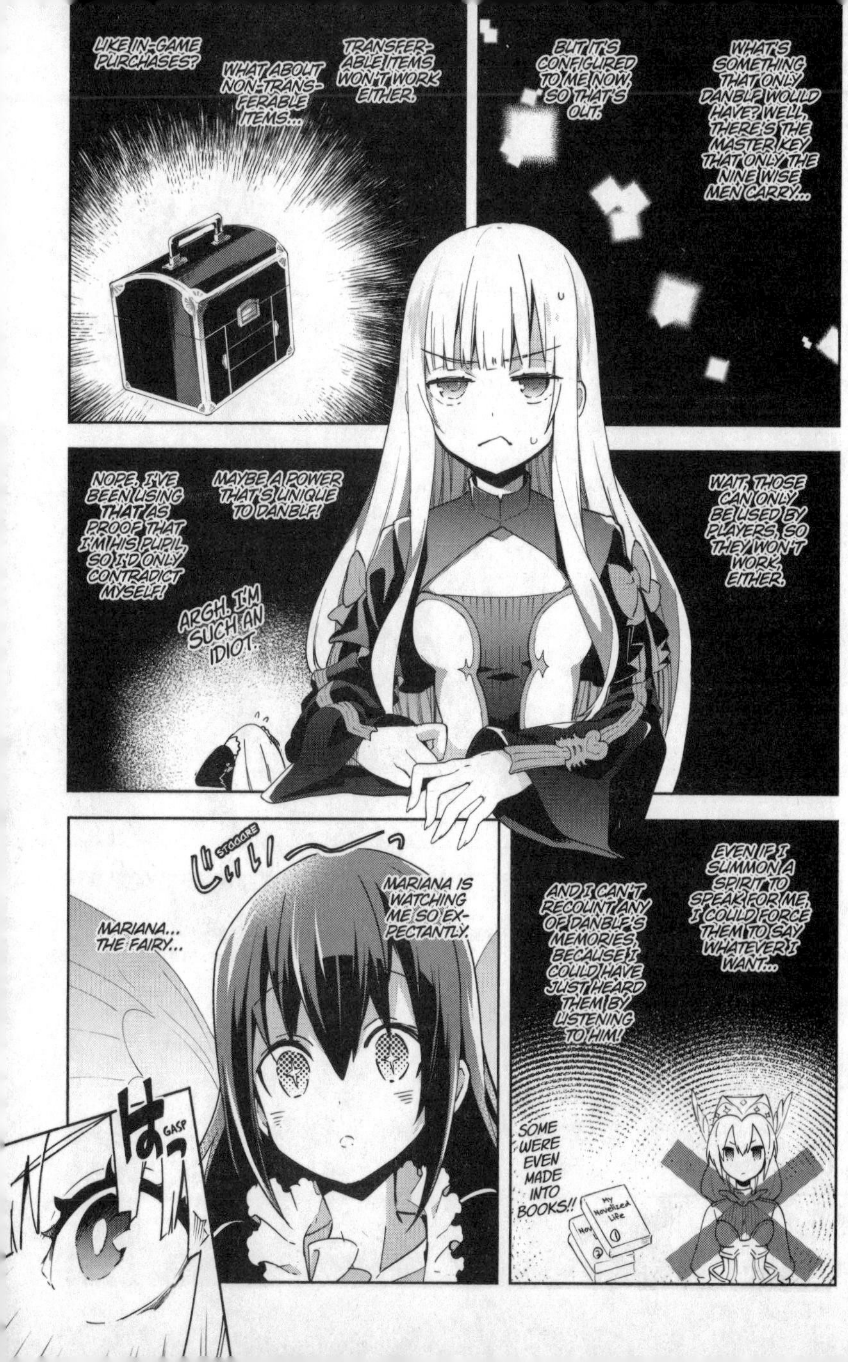
WHAT'S SOMETHING THAT ONLY DANBLF WOULD HAVE? WELL, THERE'S THE MASTER KEY THAT ONLY THE NINE WISE MEN CARRY...
BUT IT'S CONFIGURED TO ME NOW, SO THAT'S OUT.
TRANSFERABLE ITEMS WON'T WORK EITHER.
WHAT ABOUT NON-TRANSFERABLE ITEMS...
LIKE IN-GAME PURCHASES?
WAIT, THOSE CAN ONLY BE USED BY PLAYERS, SO THEY WON'T WORK EITHER.
MAYBE A POWER THAT'S UNIQUE TO DANBLF!
NOPE, I'VE BEEN USING THAT AS PROOF THAT I'M HIS PUPIL, SO I'D ONLY CONTRADICT MYSELF!
ARGH. I'M SUCH AN IDIOT.
EVEN IF I SUMMON A SPIRIT TO SPEAK FOR ME, I COULD FORCE THEM TO SAY WHATEVER I WANT...
AND I CAN'T RECOUNT ANY OF DANBLF'S MEMORIES, BECAUSE I COULD HAVE JUST HEARD THEM BY LISTENING TO HIM!
SOME WERE EVEN MADE INTO BOOKS!!
My Novelized Life
STAAARE
MARIANA IS WATCHING ME SO EXPECTANTLY.
MARIANA... THE FAIRY...
GASP

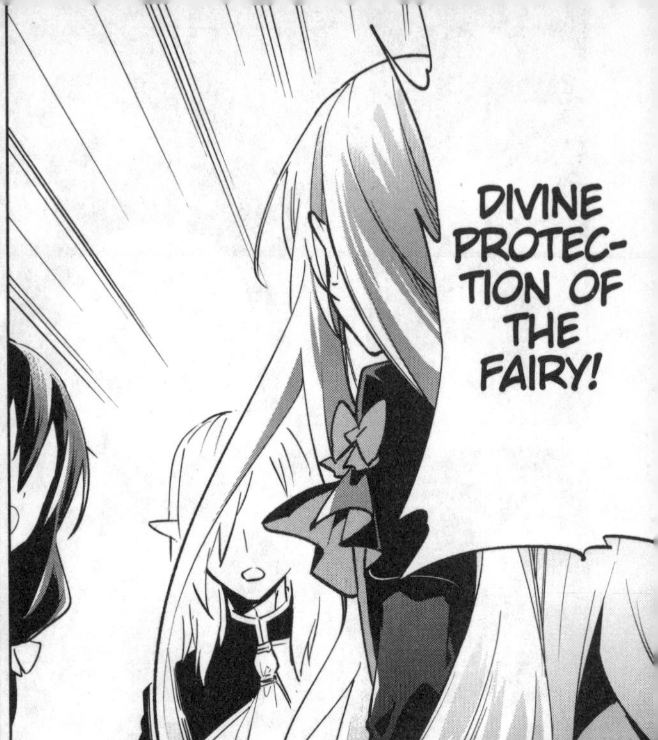
DIVINE PROTECTION OF THE FAIRY!

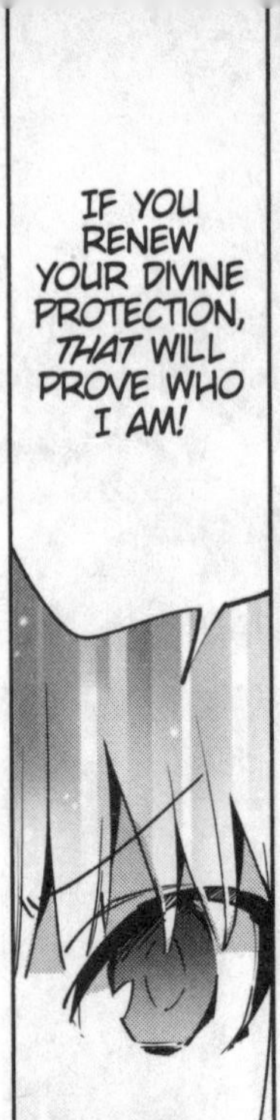
IF YOU RENEW YOUR DIVINE PROTECTION, *THAT* WILL PROVE WHO I AM!

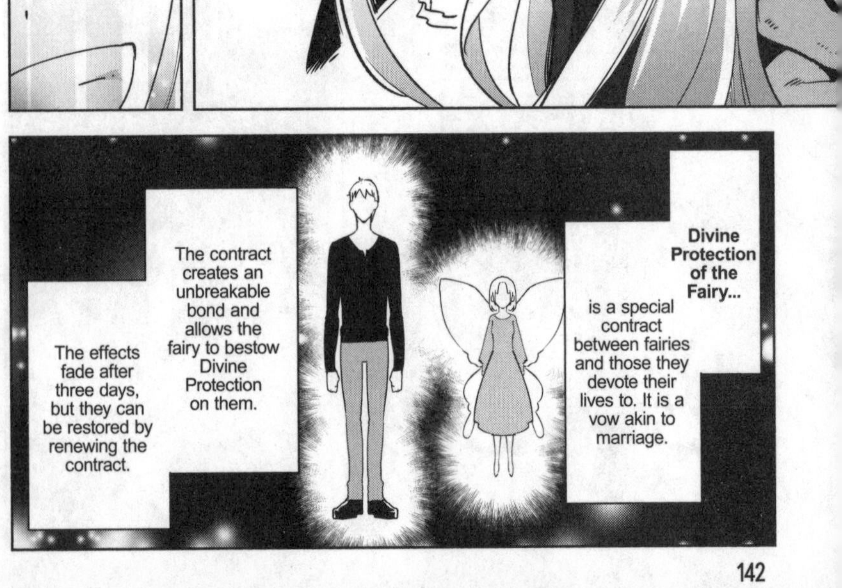
Divine Protection of the Fairy...
is a special contract between fairies and those they devote their lives to. It is a vow akin to marriage.
The contract creates an unbreakable bond and allows the fairy to bestow Divine Protection on them.
The effects fade after three days, but they can be restored by renewing the contract.

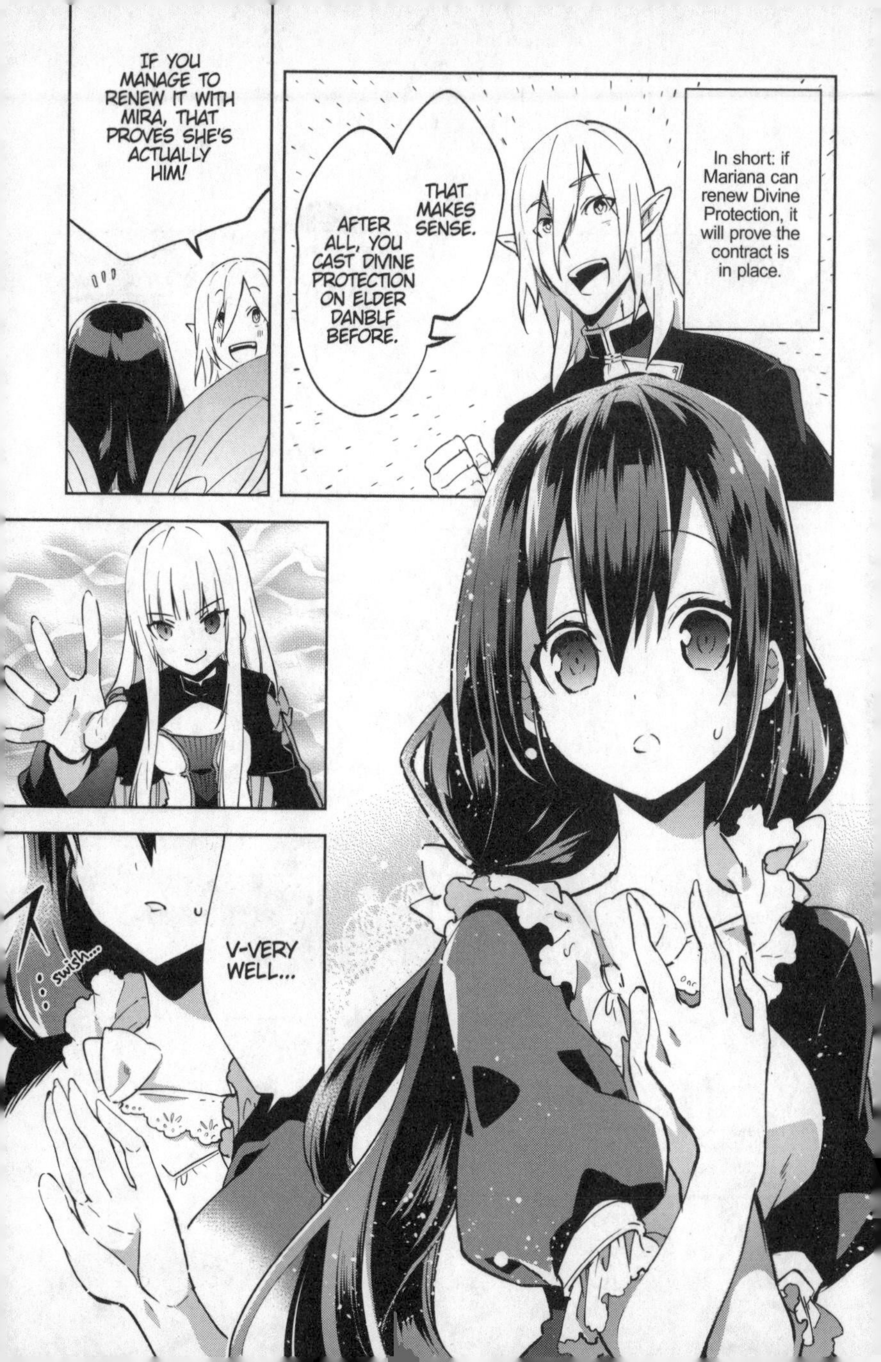
In short: if Mariana can renew Divine Protection, it will prove the contract is in place.
THAT MAKES SENSE. AFTER ALL, YOU CAST DIVINE PROTECTION ON ELDER DANBLF BEFORE.
IF YOU MANAGE TO RENEW IT WITH MIRA, THAT PROVES SHE'S ACTUALLY HIM!
V-VERY WELL...
swish...

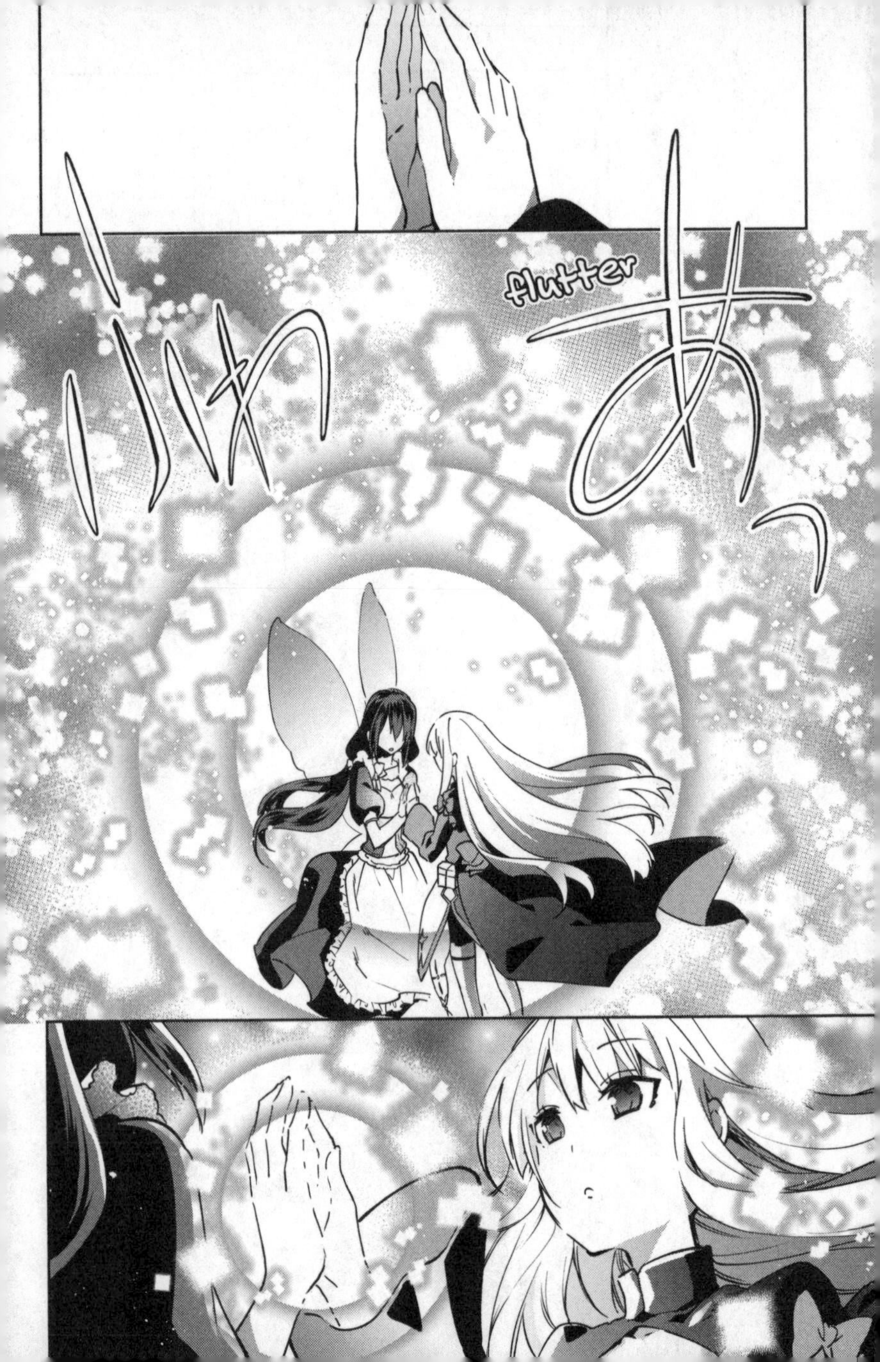
ぱあっ
flutter

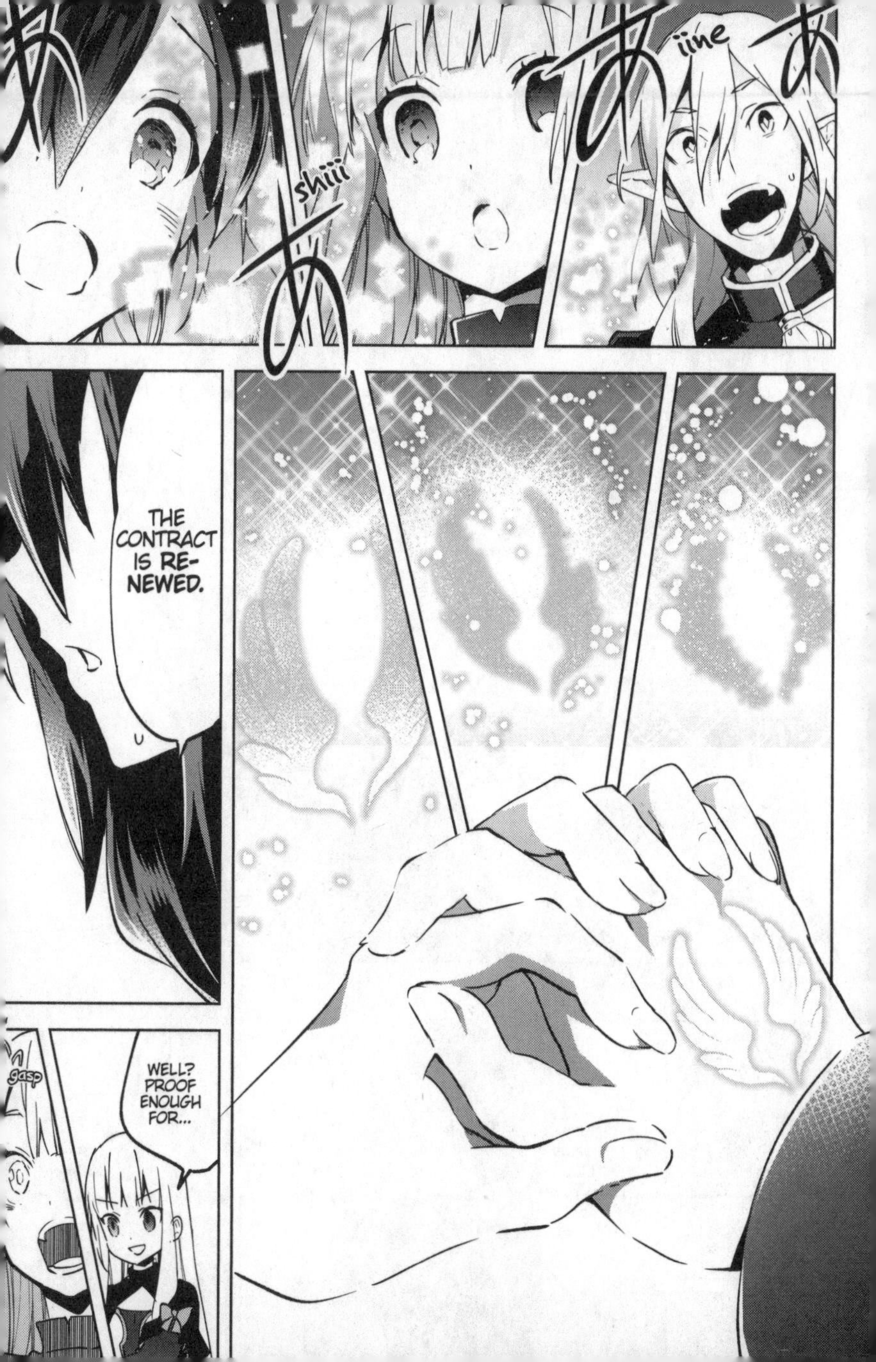
あ
iine
あ
shiii
あ
THE CONTRACT IS RE-NEWED.
WELL? PROOF ENOUGH FOR...
gasp

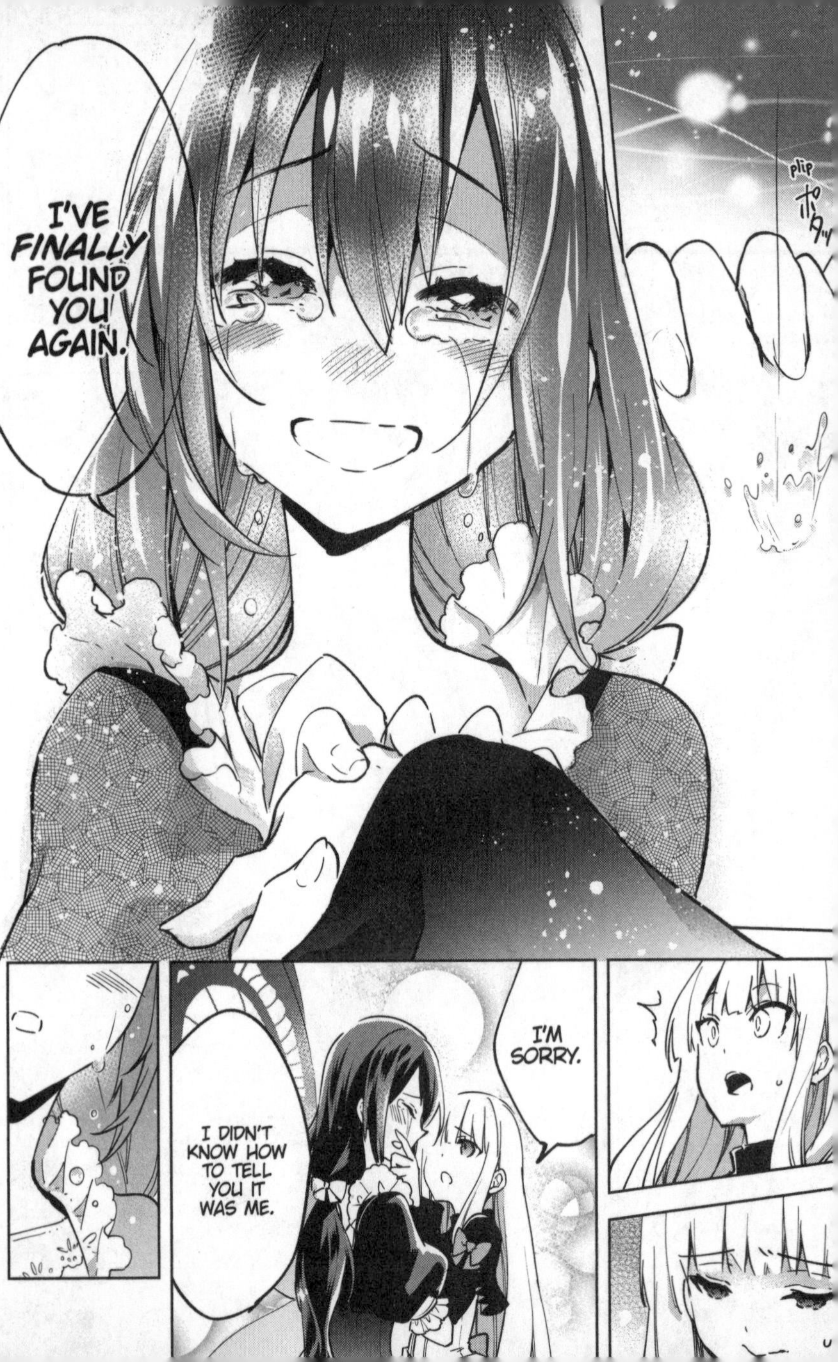
plip
ポタッ
I'VE FINALLY FOUND YOU AGAIN.
I'M SORRY.
I DIDN'T KNOW HOW TO TELL YOU IT WAS ME.

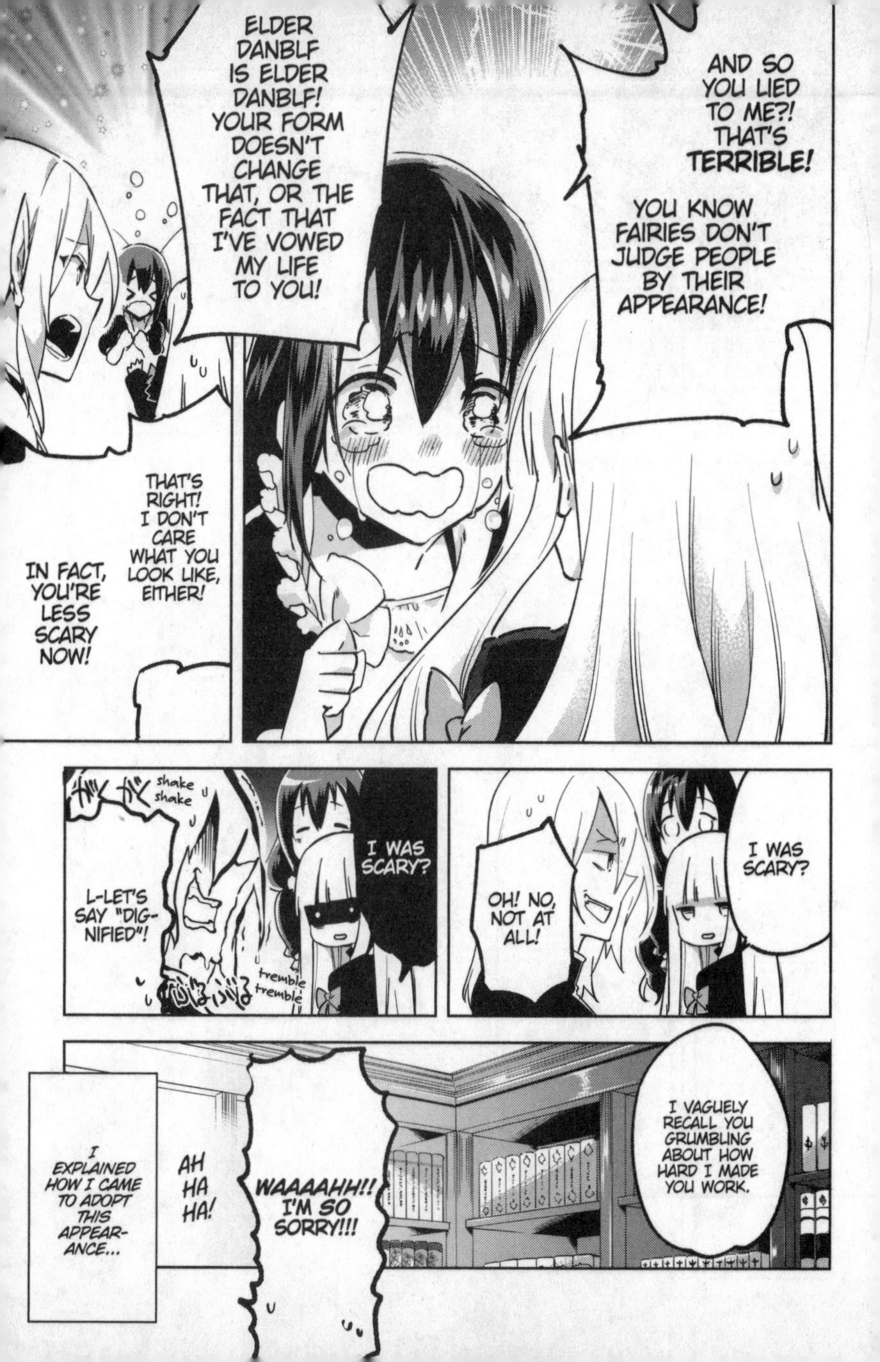
AND SO YOU LIED TO ME?! THAT'S TERRIBLE!
YOU KNOW FAIRIES DON'T JUDGE PEOPLE BY THEIR APPEARANCE!
ELDER DANBLF IS ELDER DANBLF! YOUR FORM DOESN'T CHANGE THAT, OR THE FACT THAT I'VE VOWED MY LIFE TO YOU!
THAT'S RIGHT! I DON'T CARE WHAT YOU LOOK LIKE, EITHER!
IN FACT, YOU'RE LESS SCARY NOW!
I WAS SCARY?
OH! NO, NOT AT ALL!
shake shake
I WAS SCARY?
L-LET'S SAY "DIG-NIFIED"!
tremble tremble
I VAGUELY RECALL YOU GRUMBLING ABOUT HOW HARD I MADE YOU WORK.
WAAAAHH!! I'M SO SORRY!!!
AH HA HA!
I EXPLAINED HOW I CAME TO ADOPT THIS APPEAR-ANCE...

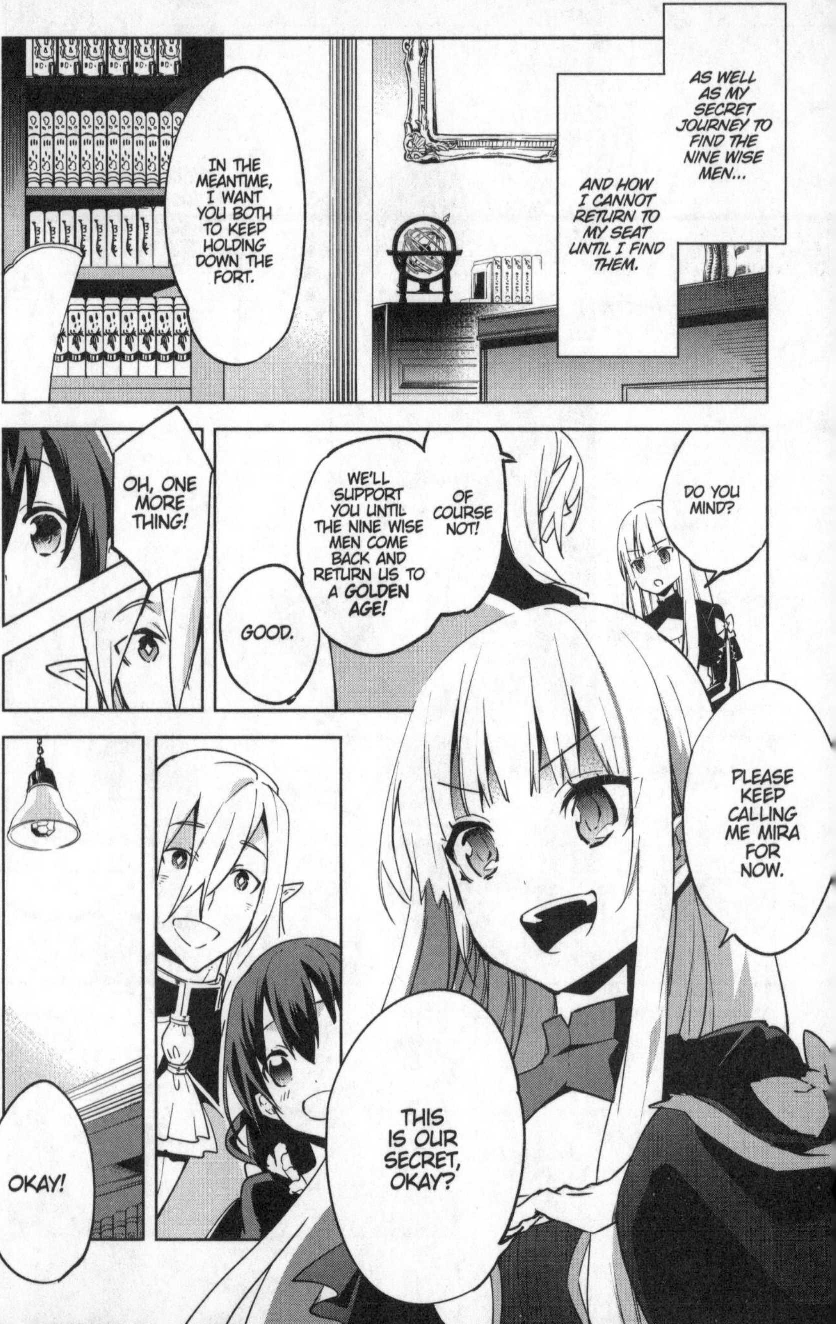
AS WELL AS MY SECRET JOURNEY TO FIND THE NINE WISE MEN...
AND HOW I CANNOT RETURN TO MY SEAT UNTIL I FIND THEM.
IN THE MEANTIME, I WANT YOU BOTH TO KEEP HOLDING DOWN THE FORT.
DO YOU MIND?
OF COURSE NOT!
WE'LL SUPPORT YOU UNTIL THE NINE WISE MEN COME BACK AND RETURN US TO A GOLDEN AGE!
GOOD.
OH, ONE MORE THING!
PLEASE KEEP CALLING ME MIRA FOR NOW.
THIS IS OUR SECRET, OKAY?
OKAY!

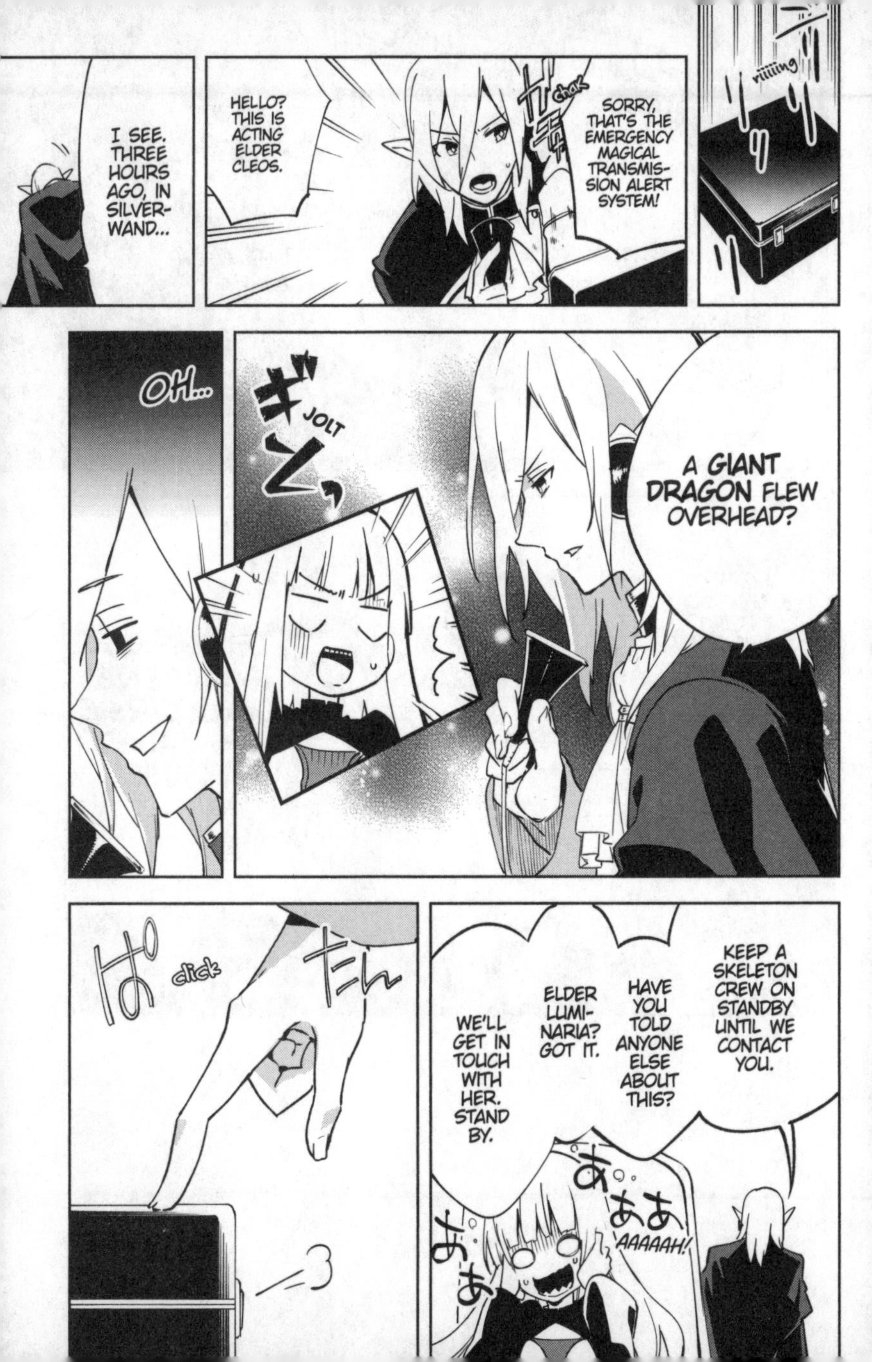
viiiiing
chak
SORRY, THAT'S THE EMERGENCY MAGICAL TRANSMISSION ALERT SYSTEM!
HELLO? THIS IS ACTING ELDER CLEOS.
I SEE. THREE HOURS AGO, IN SILVERWAND...
A GIANT DRAGON FLEW OVERHEAD?
JOLT
OH...
KEEP A SKELETON CREW ON STANDBY UNTIL WE CONTACT YOU.
HAVE YOU TOLD ANYONE ELSE ABOUT THIS?
ELDER LUMINARIA? GOT IT.
WE'LL GET IN TOUCH WITH HER. STAND BY.
AAAAAH!
click

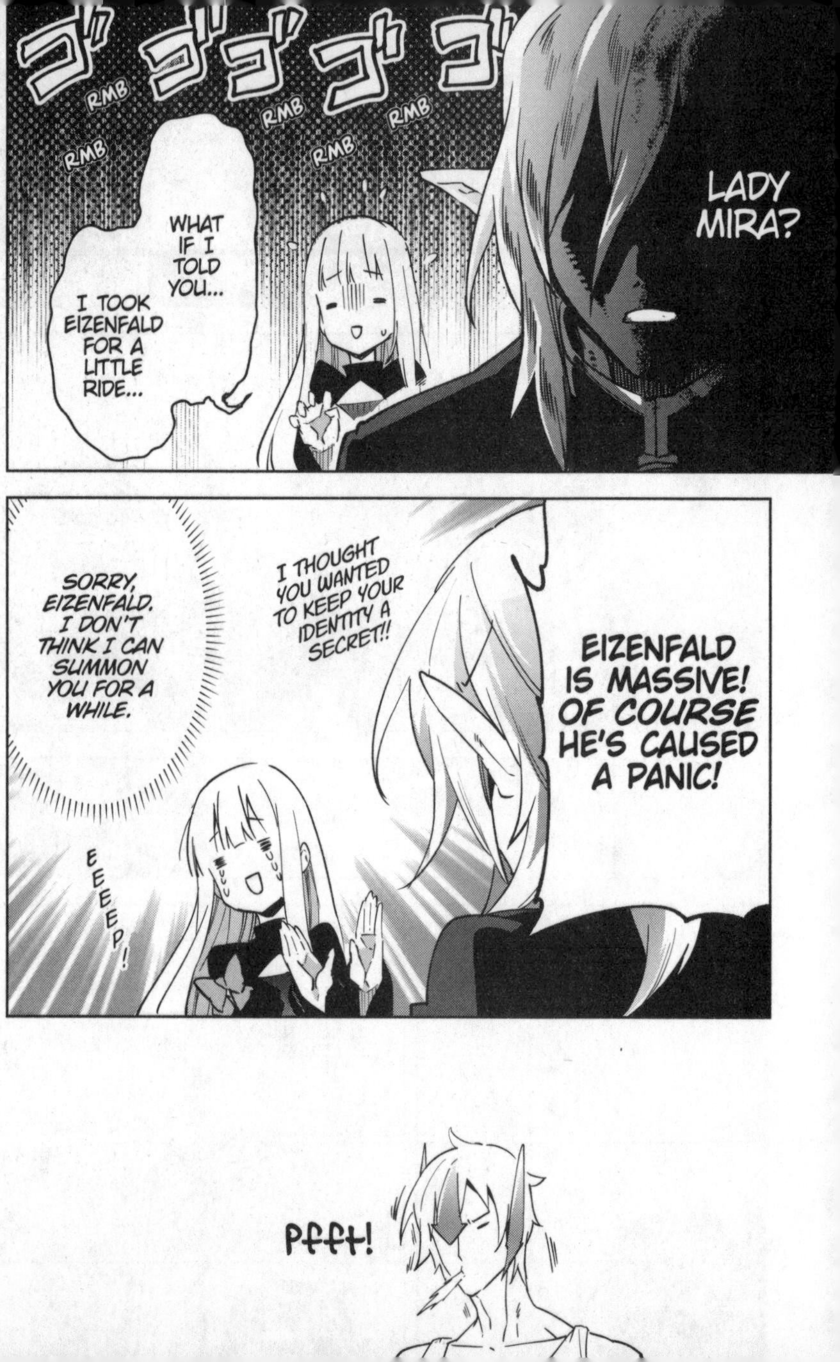
LADY MIRA?
RMB
RMB
RMB
RMB
RMB
WHAT IF I TOLD YOU...
I TOOK EIZENFALD FOR A LITTLE RIDE...
EIZENFALD IS MASSIVE! OF COURSE HE'S CAUSED A PANIC!
I THOUGHT YOU WANTED TO KEEP YOUR IDENTITY A SECRET!!
SORRY, EIZENFALD. I DON'T THINK I CAN SUMMON YOU FOR A WHILE.
EEEEP!
Pfft!

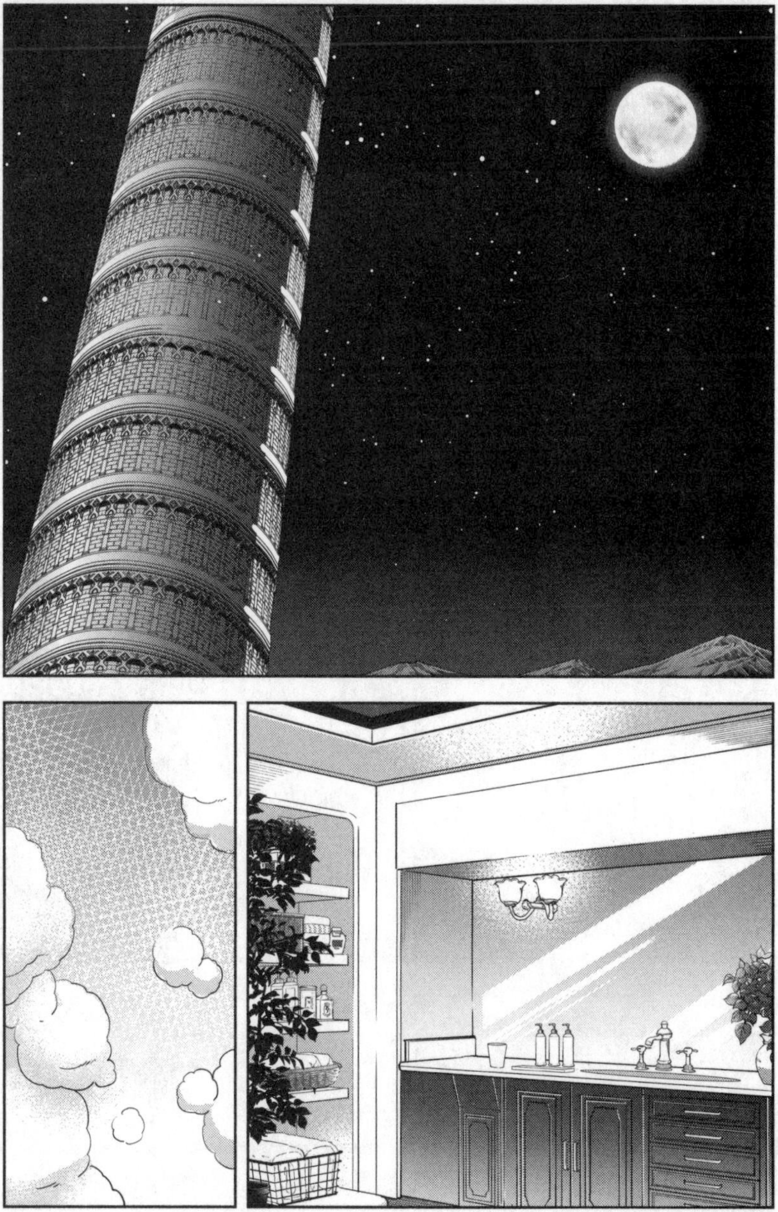

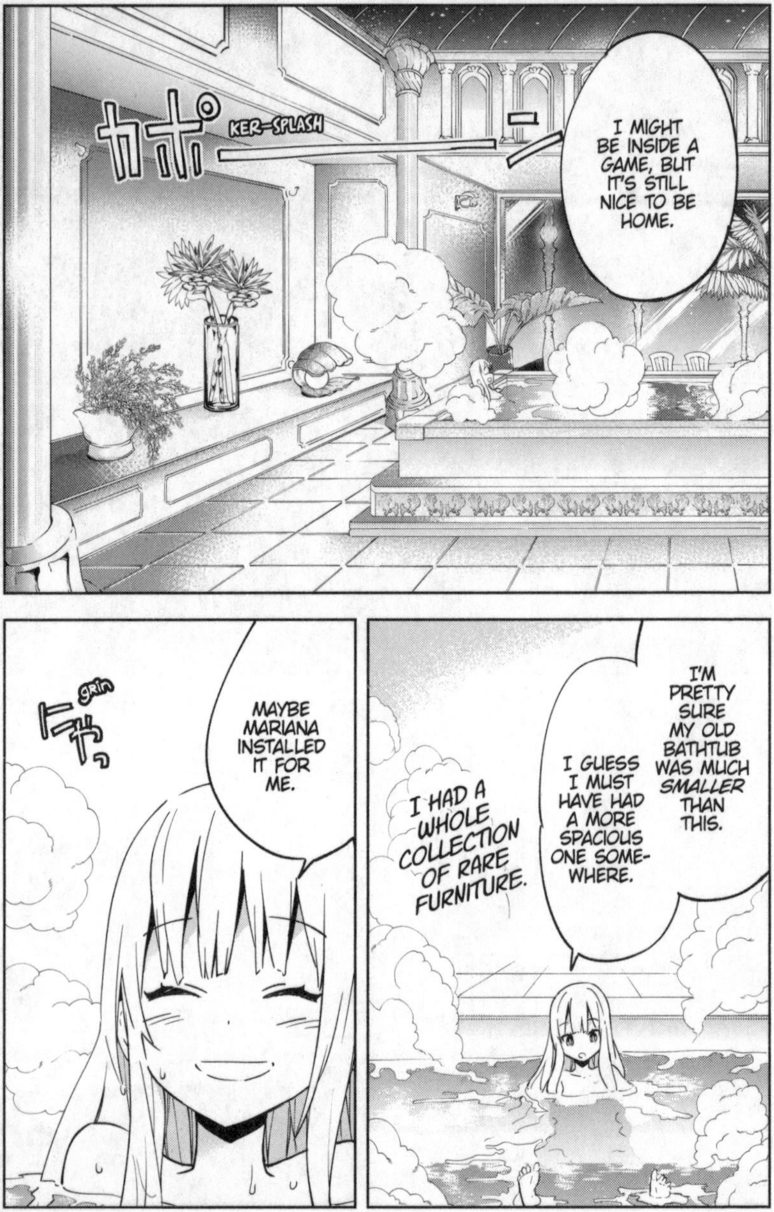

I MIGHT BE INSIDE A GAME, BUT IT'S STILL NICE TO BE HOME.
カポ
KER-SPLASH
I'M PRETTY SURE MY OLD BATHTUB WAS MUCH *SMALLER* THAN THIS.
I GUESS I MUST HAVE HAD A MORE SPACIOUS ONE SOME-WHERE.
I HAD A WHOLE COLLECTION OF RARE FURNITURE.
MAYBE MARIANA INSTALLED IT FOR ME.
ニヤッ
grin

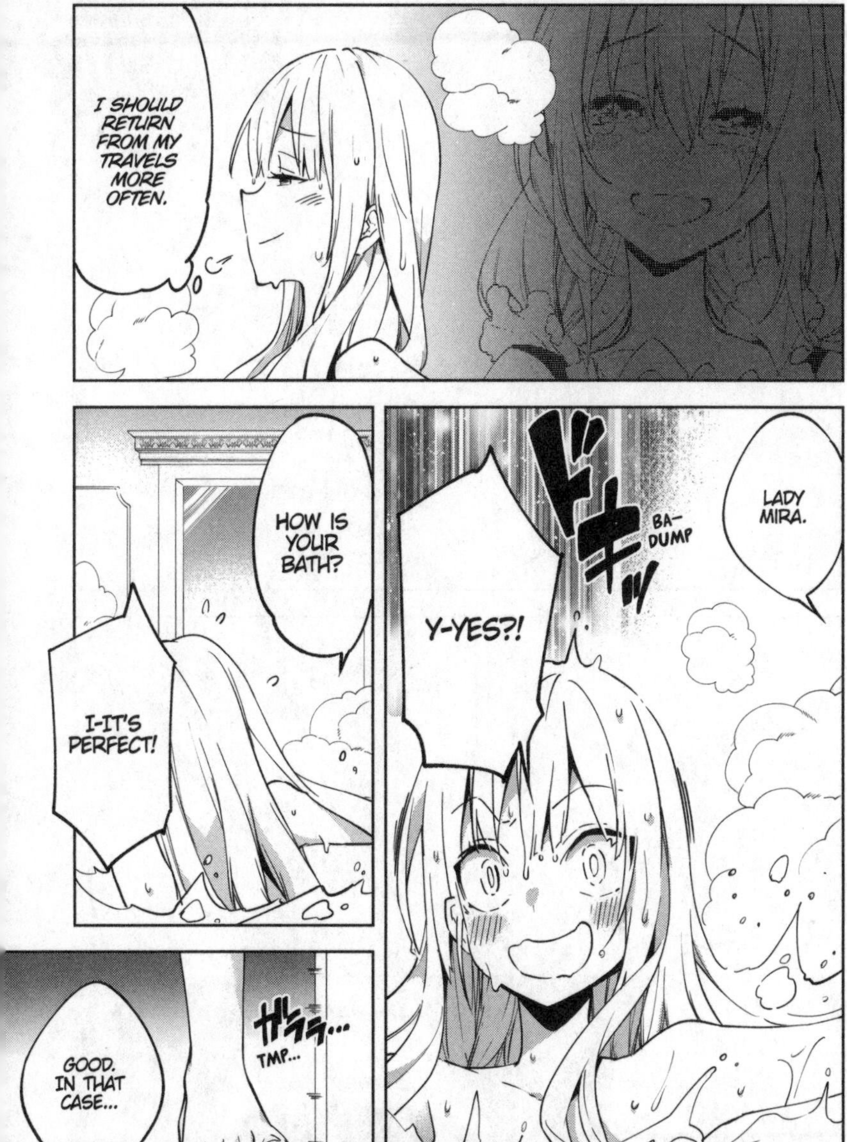
I SHOULD RETURN FROM MY TRAVELS MORE OFTEN.
LADY MIRA.
BA-DUMP
Y-YES?!
HOW IS YOUR BATH?
I-IT'S PERFECT!
TMP...
GOOD. IN THAT CASE...

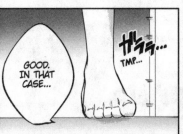

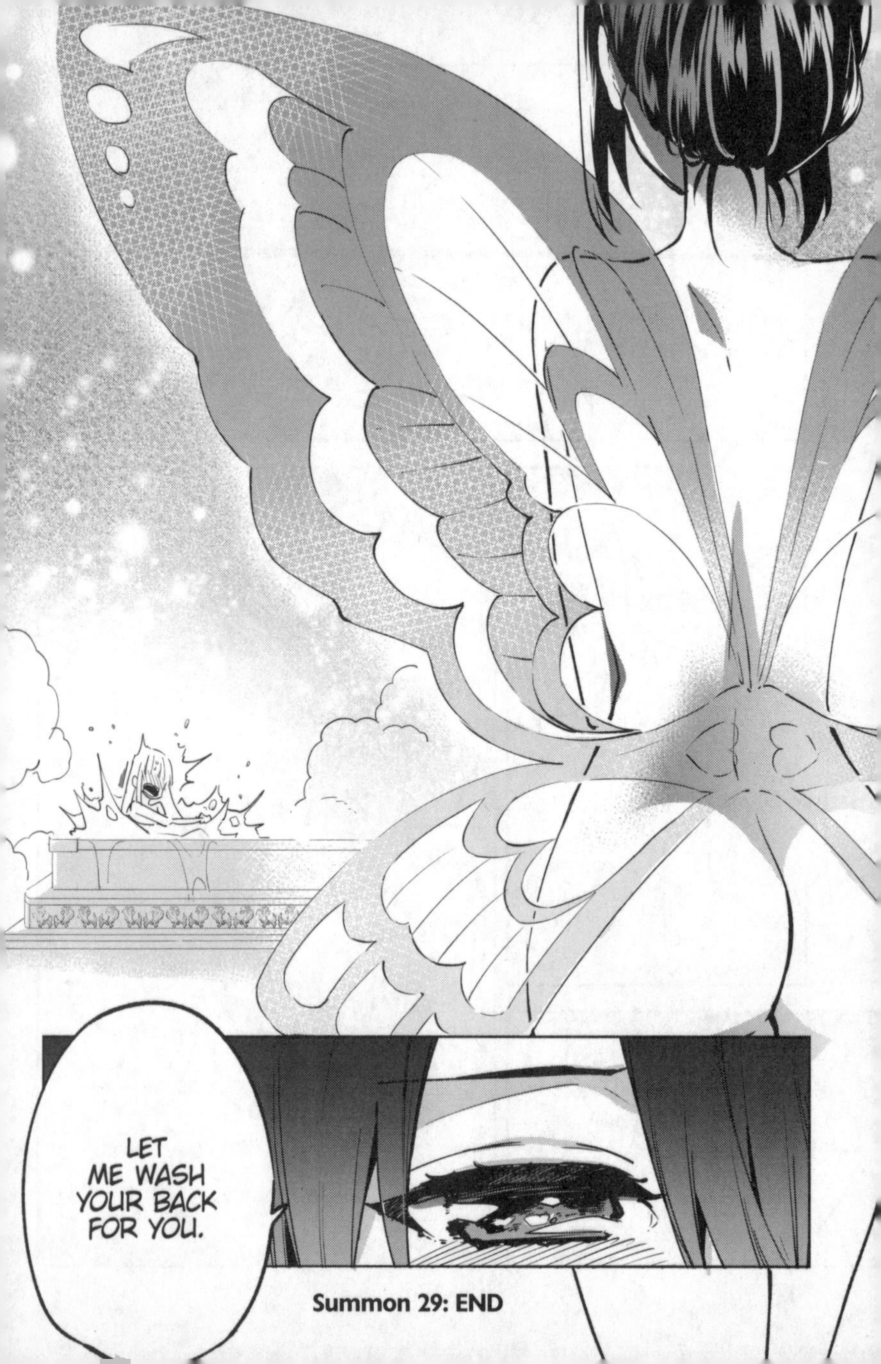
LET ME WASH YOUR BACK FOR YOU.

Summon 29: END

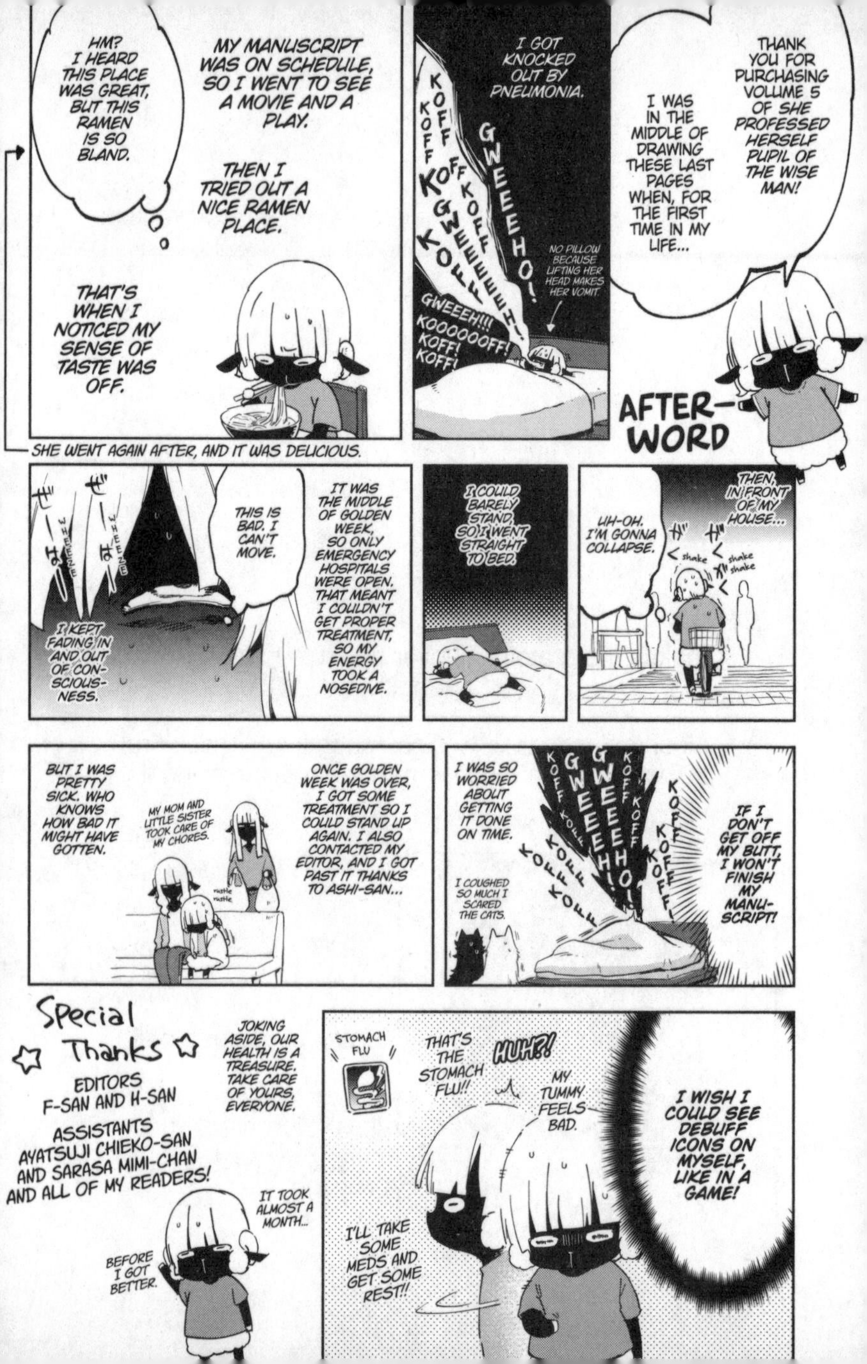
AFTER-WORD
THANK YOU FOR PURCHASING VOLUME 5 OF SHE PROFESSED HERSELF PUPIL OF THE WISE MAN!
I WAS IN THE MIDDLE OF DRAWING THESE LAST PAGES WHEN, FOR THE FIRST TIME IN MY LIFE...
I GOT KNOCKED OUT BY PNEUMONIA.
GWEEEHO!
KOFF KOFF KOFF KOFF KOFF
GWEEEEEEEH!
KOFF KOFF
GWEEEH!!!
KOOOOOOFF!
KOFF!
KOFF!
NO PILLOW BECAUSE LIFTING HER HEAD MAKES HER VOMIT.
MY MANUSCRIPT WAS ON SCHEDULE, SO I WENT TO SEE A MOVIE AND A PLAY.
THEN I TRIED OUT A NICE RAMEN PLACE.
HM? I HEARD THIS PLACE WAS GREAT, BUT THIS RAMEN IS SO BLAND.
THAT'S WHEN I NOTICED MY SENSE OF TASTE WAS OFF.
SHE WENT AGAIN AFTER, AND IT WAS DELICIOUS.
THEN, IN FRONT OF MY HOUSE...
UH-OH. I'M GONNA COLLAPSE.
shake
shake shake
I COULD BARELY STAND, SO I WENT STRAIGHT TO BED.
IT WAS THE MIDDLE OF GOLDEN WEEK, SO ONLY EMERGENCY HOSPITALS WERE OPEN. THAT MEANT I COULDN'T GET PROPER TREATMENT, SO MY ENERGY TOOK A NOSEDIVE.
THIS IS BAD. I CAN'T MOVE.
WHEEZE
WHEEZE
I KEPT FADING IN AND OUT OF CON-SCIOUS-NESS.
IF I DON'T GET OFF MY BUTT, I WON'T FINISH MY MANU-SCRIPT!
KOFF KOFF KOFF KOFF
GWEEEEH!
GWEEEEHO!
I WAS SO WORRIED ABOUT GETTING IT DONE ON TIME.
I COUGHED SO MUCH I SCARED THE CATS.
ONCE GOLDEN WEEK WAS OVER, I GOT SOME TREATMENT SO I COULD STAND UP AGAIN. I ALSO CONTACTED MY EDITOR, AND I GOT PAST IT THANKS TO ASHI-SAN...
MY MOM AND LITTLE SISTER TOOK CARE OF MY CHORES.
rustle rustle
BUT I WAS PRETTY SICK. WHO KNOWS HOW BAD IT MIGHT HAVE GOTTEN.
I WISH I COULD SEE DEBUFF ICONS ON MYSELF, LIKE IN A GAME!
MY TUMMY FEELS BAD.
HUH?!
THAT'S THE STOMACH FLU!!
STOMACH FLU
I'LL TAKE SOME MEDS AND GET SOME REST!!
Special Thanks
EDITORS
F-SAN AND H-SAN
ASSISTANTS
AYATSUJI CHIEKO-SAN AND SARASA MIMI-CHAN
AND ALL OF MY READERS!
JOKING ASIDE, OUR HEALTH IS A TREASURE. TAKE CARE OF YOURS, EVERYONE.
IT TOOK ALMOST A MONTH...
BEFORE I GOT BETTER.

Thank you for purchasing this volume!

This is Ryusen Hirotsugu, the author of the original novel. Allow me to shamelessly express my gratitude once again.

I try to give thanks however I can. Thank you so much, everyone!

Good gracious, we've reached Volume 5. This time, I was allowed to include everything I wanted to—from panty shots to the introduction of Danblf's son, and the reunion with Mariana.

Not to mention the casual introduction of how cute Amarette is. She came out even better in the flesh than I'd imagined her!

It makes me grateful all over again to have this manga adaptation.

All of that is thanks to dicca*suemitsu-sensei. Truly, thank you so much. I'm thoroughly enjoying it.

Right now, my life is all over the place. I'm in the process of moving, but things should be settled by the time this volume is released.

I'm looking forward to reading Volume 5 in my new home.

This has been Ryusen Hirotsugu, signing off!

We should meet again in the next volume. That's a promise, right? I swear that if you break it...

Ryusen Hirotsugu

She
Professed
Herself
Pupil of the
Wise Man

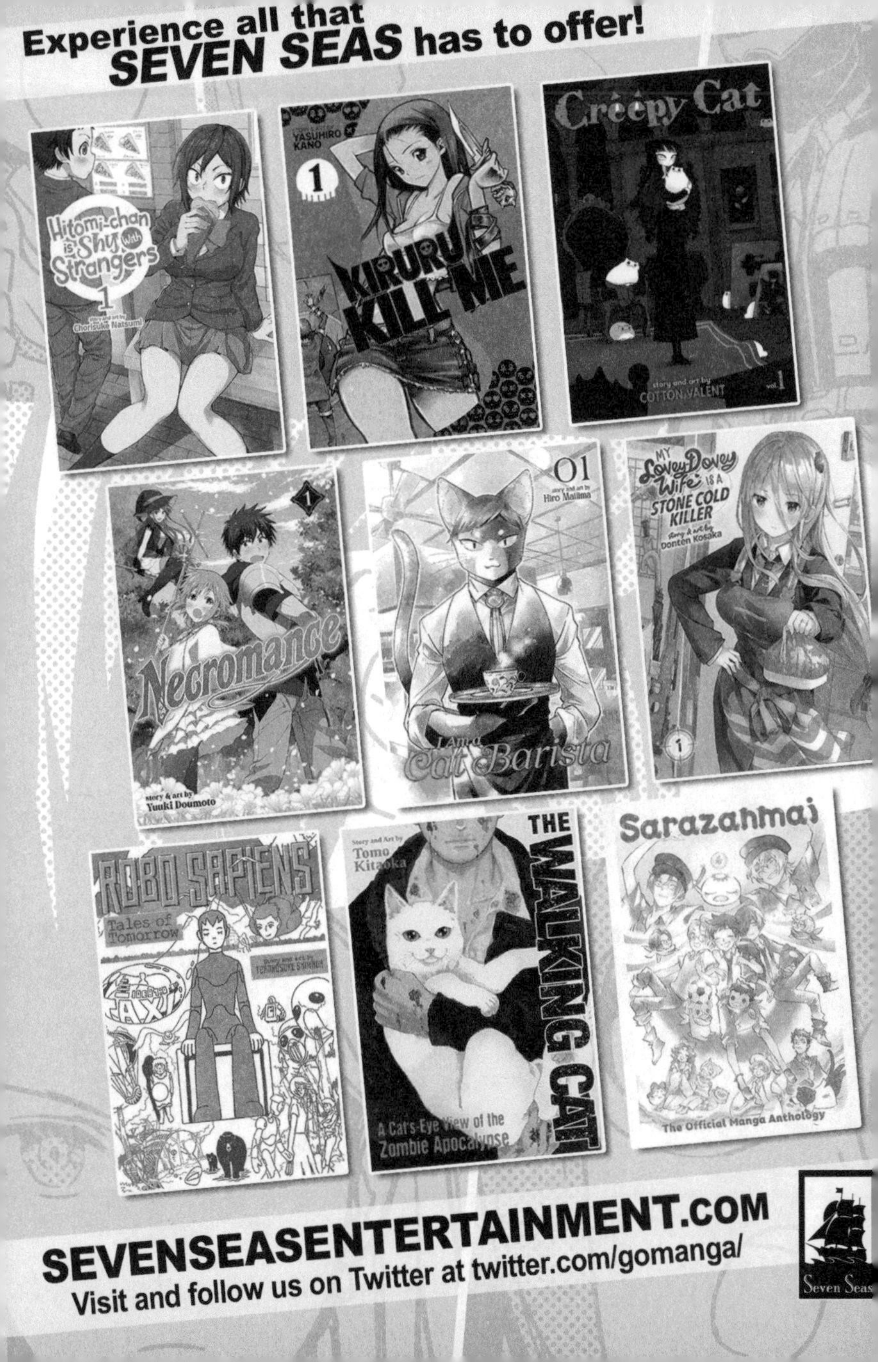
Experience all that
SEVEN SEAS has to offer!
Hitomi-chan is Shy With Strangers
1
story and art by Chorisuke Natsumi
YASUHIRO KANO
1
KIRURU KILL ME
Creepy Cat
story and art by COTTON VALENT
vol.1
1
Necromance
story & art by Yuuki Doumoto
01
story and art by Hiro Majima
I Am a Cat Barista
MY Lovey-Dovey Wife IS A STONE COLD KILLER
story & art by Donten Kosaka
1
ROBO SAPIENS
Tales of Tomorrow
THE WALKING CAT
Story and Art by Tomo Kitaoka
A Cat's-Eye View of the Zombie Apocalypse
Sarazanmai
The Official Manga Anthology
SEVENSEASENTERTAINMENT.COM
Visit and follow us on Twitter at twitter.com/gomanga/
Seven Seas

SEVEN SEAS ENTERTAINMENT PRESENTS

She Professed Herself Pupil of the Wise Man

Vol. 5

story by RYUSEN HIROTSUGU

art by DICCA*SUEMITSU

character design by FUZICHOCO

TRANSLATION
Morgan Watchorn

ADAPTATION
C.A Hawksmoor

LETTERING
Carl Vanstiphout

COVER DESIGN
Nicky Lim

LOGO DESIGN
George Panella

PROOFREADER
Danielle King
B. Lillian Martin

SENIOR COPY EDITOR
Dawn Davis

SENIOR EDITOR
Peter Adrian Behravesh

PRODUCTION DESIGNER
Christa Miesner

PRODUCTION MANAGER
Lissa Pattillo

PREPRESS TECHNICIAN
Melanie Ujimori

PRINT MANAGER
Rhiannon Rasmussen-Silverstein

EDITOR-IN-CHIEF
Julie Davis

ASSOCIATE PUBLISHER
Adam Arnold

PUBLISHER
Jason DeAngelis

Kenja no deshi wo nanoru kenja THE COMIC Vol. 5

This edition originally published in Japan in 2019 by
MICRO MAGAZINE, INC., Tokyo.
English translation rights arranged with MICRO MAGAZINE, INC., Tokyo.

Seven Seas press and purchase enquiries can be sent to Marketing Manager Lianne Sentar at press@gomanga.com. Information regarding the distribution and purchase of digital editions is available from Digital Manager CK Russell at digital@gomanga.com.

ISBN:978-1-63858-236-6
Printed in Canada
First Printing: July 2022
10 9 8 7 6 5 4 3 2 1

READING DIRECTIONS

This book reads from ***right to left***, Japanese style. If this is your first time reading manga, you start reading from the top right panel on each page and take it from there. If you get lost, just follow the numbered diagram here. It may seem backwards at first, but you'll get the hang of it! Have fun!!

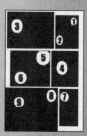

1
2
3
4
5
6
7
8
9